AMONG NATIONS

Readings in International Relations

Compiled by:

Professor Barry N. Stein
Failed States; National Interest; Counterinsurgency
ISS325 War and Revolution
Michigan State University
Spring 2008

Director of Database Publishing: Michael Payne
Senior Sponsoring Editor: Robin Lazrus
Development Editor: Catherine O'Keefe
Assistant Editor: Ana Díaz-Caneja
Marketing Manager: Kathleen Kourian
Operations Manager: Eric Kenney
Production Manager: Jennifer Berry
Rights Editor: Francesca Marcantonio
Cover Designer: Renée Sartell

Cover Art: "Needle"/EyeWire, "Barbed Wire"/Corbis, "Dove"/Comstock. All other photographs courtesy of Getty Images.

Printed in the United States of America

Please visit our website at *www.pearsoncustom.com*
Attention Bookstores: For permission to return any unsold stock, contact Pearson Custom Publishing at 1-800- 777-6842

ISBN-10: 0536371733
ISBN-13: 9780536371737

Package ISBN-10: N/A
Package ISBN-13: N/A

PEARSON CUSTOM PUBLISHING
75 Arlington Street, Suite 300, Boston, MA 02116
A Pearson Education Company

GENERAL EDITORS

GIDEON ROSE, managing editor of *Foreign Affairs* since 2000, served as associate director for Near East and South Asian affairs on the staff of the National Security Council and, from 1995 to 2000, was the Olin senior fellow and deputy director of national security studies at the Council of Foreign Relations.

MEENA BOSE is Peter S. Kalikow Chair in Presidential Studies at Hofstra University. She is the author of *Shaping and Signaling Presidential Policy: The National Security Decision Making of Eisenhower and Kennedy* (1998), co-editor (with Rosanna Perotti) of *From Cold War to New World Order: The Foreign Policy of George H.W. Bush* (2002), and co-editor (with Mark Landis) of *The Uses and Abuses of Presidential Ratings* (2003). She taught for six years at the United States Military Academy at West Point, where she also served as Director of American Politics in Spring 2006. She represented the American Political Science Association on the Department of State's Historical Advisory Committee from 2001-2004.

PETER LIBERMAN is associate professor of political science at Queens College and the Graduate Center of the City University of New York. He is the author of *Does Conquest Pay? The Exploitation of Occupied Industrial Societies* (Princeton, 1996), as well as journal articles on alliance politics, the causes of war, trade conflict, and nuclear proliferation, secrecy, and strategy. He serves on the editorial board of Security Studies.

DAVID SKIDMORE is a professor in the department of politics and international relations at Drake University. During the 1996-97 academic year, he taught at the Johns Hopkins-Nanjing University Center for Chinese and American Studies in Nanjing, China. Skidmore currently serves as director of the Center for Global Citizenship and is past director of the Drake Curriculum and First Year Seminar programs. Skidmore is author, coauthor, or editor of five books, including a forthcoming reader, entitled *U.S. Foreign Policy in a Unipolar Era* (Longman).

Contents

The Next War of the World

Niall Ferguson

ONE HUNDRED YEARS OF BUTCHERY

IN 1898, H. G. Wells wrote *The War of the Worlds,* a novel that imagined the destruction of a great city and the extermination of its inhabitants by ruthless invaders. The invaders in Wells' story were, of course, Martians. But no aliens were needed to make such devastation a reality. In the decades that followed the book's publication, human beings repeatedly played the part of the inhuman marauders, devastating city after city in what may justly be regarded as a single hundred-year "war of the world."

The twentieth century was the bloodiest era in history. World War I killed between 9 million and 10 million people, more if the influenza pandemic of 1918–19 is seen as a consequence of the war. Another 59 million died in World War II. And those conflicts were only two of the more deadly ones in the last hundred years. By one estimate, there were 16 conflicts throughout the last century that cost more than a million lives, a further six that claimed between 500,000 and a million, and 14 that killed between 250,000 and 500,000. In all, between 167 million and 188 million people died because of organized violence in the twentieth century—as many as one in every 22 deaths in that period.

Other periods matched the twentieth century's rate of killing, if not its magnitude: consider the reigns of tyrants such as Genghis Khan and Tamerlane; some crises in imperial China, such as the An Lushan

---

NIALL FERGUSON is Laurence A. Tisch Professor of History at Harvard University and a Senior Fellow at the Hoover Institution at Stanford University. His latest book is *The War of the World.*

Rebellion in the eighth century and the Taiping Rebellion in the mid-nineteenth century; and some cases of Western imperial conquest, such as Belgian rule in the Congo and the German war against the Herero in German Southwest Africa. Yet the twentieth century differs from those earlier ages in one key way: it was supposed to be—and in a great many ways was—a time of unparalleled material progress.

In real terms, average per capita GDP roughly quadrupled between 1913 and 1998. By the end of the twentieth century, human beings in many parts of the world enjoyed longer and better lives than had been possible at any time before, thanks mainly to improved nutrition and health care. Rising wealth meant that more and more people were able to flee what Karl Marx and Friedrich Engels had called "the idiocy of rural life": between 1900 and 1980, the proportion of the world's population that lived in large cities more than doubled. And by working more productively, people had more time available for leisure. Some spent their free time successfully campaigning for political representation and the redistribution of income. As a result, governments ceased to confine themselves to providing only basic public goods, such as national defense and a fair judicial system, but instead became welfare states that sought nothing less than the elimination of poverty.

It might have been expected that such prosperity would eliminate the causes of war. But much of the worst violence of the twentieth century involved the relatively wealthy countries at the opposite ends of Eurasia. The chief lesson of the twentieth century is that countries can provide their citizens with wealth, longevity, literacy, and even democracy but still descend into lethal conflict. Leon Trotsky nicely summed up the paradox when reflecting on the First Balkan War of 1912–13, which he covered as a reporter. The conflict, Trotsky wrote, "shows that we still haven't crawled out on all fours from the barbaric stage of our history. We have learned to wear suspenders, to write clever editorials, and to make chocolate milk, but when we have to decide seriously a question of the coexistence of a few tribes on a rich peninsula of Europe, we are helpless to find a way other than mutual mass slaughter." Trotsky later made his own contribution to the history of mass slaughter as the people's commissar for war and as the commander of the Red Army during the Russian Civil War.

Will the twenty-first century be as bloody as the twentieth? The answer depends partly on whether or not we can understand the causes of the last century's violence. Only if we can will we have a chance of avoiding a repetition of its horrors. If we cannot, there is a real possibility that we will relive the nightmare.

BLAME GAME

THERE ARE many unsatisfactory explanations for why the twentieth century was so destructive. One is the assertion that the availability of more powerful weapons caused bloodier conflicts. But there is no correlation between the sophistication of military technology and the lethality of conflict. Some of the worst violence of the century—the genocides in Cambodia in the 1970s and central Africa in the 1990s, for instance—was perpetrated with the crudest of weapons: rifles, axes, machetes, and knives.

Nor can economic crises explain the bloodshed. What may be the most familiar causal chain in modern historiography links the Great Depression to the rise of fascism and the outbreak of World War II. But that simple story leaves too much out. Nazi Germany started the war in Europe only after its economy had recovered. Not all the countries affected by the Great Depression were taken over by fascist regimes, nor did all such regimes start wars of aggression. In fact, no general relationship between economics and conflict is discernible for the century as a whole. Some wars came after periods of growth, others were the causes rather than the consequences of economic catastrophe, and some severe economic crises were not followed by wars.

Many trace responsibility for the butchery to extreme ideologies. The Marxist historian Eric Hobsbawm calls the years between 1914 and 1991 "an era of religious wars" but argues that "the most militant and bloodthirsty religions were secular ideologies." At the other end of the political spectrum, the conservative historian Paul Johnson blames the violence on "the rise of moral relativism, the decline of personal responsibility [and] the repudiation of Judeo-Christian values." But the rise of new ideologies or the decline of old values cannot be regarded as causes of violence in their own right. Extreme belief systems, such as anti-Semitism, have existed for most of modern history, but only at certain times and in certain places have they been widely embraced and translated into violence.

And as tempting as it is to blame tyrants such as Hitler, Stalin, and Mao for the century's bloodletting, to do so is to repeat the error on which Leo Tolstoy heaped so much scorn in *War and Peace.* Megalomaniacs may order men to invade Russia, but why do the men obey? Some historians have attempted to answer the novelist's question by indicting the modern nation-state. The nation-state does indeed possess unprecedented capabilities for mobilizing masses of people, but those means could just as easily be harnessed, and have been, to peaceful ends.

Others seek the cause of conflict in the internal political arrangements of states. It has become fashionable among political scientists to posit a causal link between democracy and peace, extrapolating from the observation that democracies tend not to go to war with one another. The corollary, of course, is that dictatorships generally are more bellicose. By that logic, the rise of democracy during the twentieth century should have made the world more peaceful. Democratization may well have reduced the incidence of war between states. But waves of democratization in the 1920s, 1960s, and 1980s seem to have multiplied the number of civil wars. Some of those (such as the conflicts in Afghanistan, Burundi, China, Korea, Mexico, Mozambique, Nigeria, Russia, Rwanda, and Vietnam) were among the deadliest conflicts of the century. Horrendous numbers of fatalities were also caused by genocidal or "politicidal" campaigns waged against civilian populations, such as those carried out by the Young Turks against the Armenians and the Greeks during World War I, the Soviet government from the 1920s until the 1950s, and the Nazis between 1933 and 1945—to say nothing of those perpetrated by the communist tyrannies of Mao in China and Pol Pot in Cambodia. Indeed, such civil strife has been the most common form of conflict during the past 50 years. Of the 24 armed conflicts recorded as "ongoing" by the University of Maryland's Ted Robert Gurr and George Mason University's Monty Marshall in early 2005, nearly all were civil wars.

Conventional explanations for the violence of the twentieth century are inadequate for another important reason. None is able to explain convincingly why lethal conflict happened when and where it did.

Ultimately, the interesting question is not, Why was the twentieth century more violent than the eighteenth or the nineteenth? but, Why did extreme violence happen in Poland and Serbia more than in Portugal and Sweden, and why was it more likely to happen between 1939 and 1945 than between 1959 and 1965?

In relative terms, Poland and Serbia were exceptionally prone to the ravages of warfare in the first half of the twentieth century. Polish Galicia was one of the killing fields of the eastern front between 1914 and 1917. Serbia had the highest mortality rate of any country during World War I; the war killed just under 6 percent of the country's prewar population. Far worse, the Polish mortality rate in World War II amounted to just under 19 percent; Polish Jews killed in the Holocaust accounted for a large share of that number. The Soviet rate was 11 percent, although the figure for Russians and Ukrainians, who dominated the ranks of the Red Army, was higher. Among other combatant countries, only Germany (including Austria) and Yugoslavia suffered war-induced mortality rates close to 10 percent. The next highest rates were for Hungary (8 percent) and Romania (6 percent). In no other country for which figures have been published did war mortality rise above 3 percent. Indeed, for four of the principal combatants—France, Italy, the United Kingdom, and the United States—total wartime mortality was less than 1 percent of the prewar population.

These figures give a good indication of the location and the timing of the worst twentieth-century violence. From around 1904 to 1953, the most dangerous place in the world was the triangle that lies between the Balkans, the Baltic Sea, and the Black Sea. Only slightly less dangerous over the same period was the region at the other end of Eurasia comprising Manchuria and the neighboring Korean Peninsula. Indeed, it was there that the era of large-scale modern warfare began, when Japan attacked Russia in 1904. It was also there that the era came to a close 50 years later, with the end of the Korean War. Thereafter, the location and the type of violence changed. Despite its reputation as having been a "long peace," the Cold War sparked a series of bitter proxy wars around the world, particularly in Central America, sub-Saharan Africa, and Indochina. Those conflicts in effect constituted a Third World War—or, more aptly, the Third World's War.

THE THREE E'S

THREE FACTORS explain the timing and the location of the extreme violence of the twentieth century: ethnic disintegration, economic volatility, and empires in decline.

Patterns of migration combined with the persistence of religious and cultural traditions have always made some areas of human settlement more ethnically homogeneous than others. In 1900, in parts of the world such as England or France it was possible to travel hundreds of miles without encountering anyone who looked, spoke, dressed, or worshiped in significantly different ways from everyone else. But an ethnic and linguistic map of central and eastern Europe at that time would have resembled a patchwork quilt, reflecting the region's diversity. There, ethnic groups lived next door to one another—sometimes literally. The many-named town known variously as Czernowitz, Cernauti, and Chernivtsi is a case in point. Located in what is now Ukraine, Chernivtsi was once a multiethnic city inhabited by German professors, Austrian civil servants, Jewish merchants, and workers from many other ethnicities. To the nineteenth-century poet Karl Emil Franzos, Chernivtsi was Czernowitz, "the courtyard of the German paradise," an island of *Kultur* within "Half Asia." Yet the multiethnic balance on which such places rested tipped over disastrously in the three decades after 1914.

Conflict in multiethnic societies was not and is not inevitable. In fact, central and eastern Europe in the early 1900s saw remarkable advances in the integration and assimilation of ethnic minorities. People of different ethnicities not only lived near one another but also worked, played, and studied together. They even intermarried. For example, in cities such as Hamburg and Trieste, rates of intermarriage between Jews and non-Jews reached remarkable heights. The same trend was apparent after the 1917 revolution in what soon became the Soviet Union, particularly in big cities.

Assimilation, however, can be violently reversed. It is no accident that ethnic tensions increased in places such as the then Romanian city Cernauti in the interwar period. Before World War I, four dynasties—the Hapsburg, the Hohenzollern, the Ottoman, and the Romanov—had governed central and eastern Europe. Such regimes cared less about their subjects' nationality than about their subjects' loyalty. After 1918, the political map of the region was redrawn to create or re-create nation-states. Yet the region's ethnic diversity made it impossible to set up homogeneous polities. As a result, in Czechoslovakia, Poland, Romania, and Yugoslavia, the majority population in each accounted for less than 80 percent of the total population. Ethnic minorities in such countries suddenly found themselves treated as second-class citizens. As part of postwar Romania, for instance, Cernauti became the scene of escalating ethnic conflict because of systematic discrimination against German educational institutions and landowners by the Romanian authorities. This was how ethnic disintegration happened.

The location and the timing of twentieth-century violence were determined by the decline and fall of empires.

Economic volatility exacerbated political frictions. The frequency and the amplitude of changes in output and prices peaked between 1919 and 1939. During those years, measures of standard deviation for growth and inflation were nearly double what they were in the preceding and succeeding periods and roughly seven times what they have been since 1990. From the mid-1920s to the mid-1930s, stock markets also experienced their highest levels of volatility of the century. Although it is obvious that low growth or a recession contributes to social instability, rapid growth can also be destabilizing. This is especially true in multiethnic societies, where booms can appear to benefit market-dominant minorities disproportionately, such as the Armenians in Turkey in the early 1900s or the Jews in central and eastern Europe. When booms turn to busts, the prosperous minority can become the target of reprisals by the impoverished majority. As Gregor von Rezzori recalled of his youth in Cernauti during this period, all of the city's other ethnic groups "despised the Jews, notwithstanding that Jews ... played an economically decisive role." If they could agree on nothing else, Germans and Romanians could agree that Jews were "the natural target of their aggression," Rezzori wrote in his memoir *The Snows of Yesteryear.*

Of course, not all multiethnic societies that experienced economic volatility in those years descended into sectarian violence. In the still relatively segregated United States, for example, the number of violent acts of racial hatred, such as lynchings, declined between the world wars. The critical third factor determining both the location and the timing of twentieth-century violence was the decline and fall of empires.

The twentieth century was characterized by a remarkably high rate of imperial dissolution. In 1913, around 65 percent of the world's land and 82 percent of its population were under some kind of imperial rule. Those empires soon disintegrated. The Qing dynasty in China was overthrown before World War I, and in 1917 the Romanov dynasty fell from power. They were quickly followed by the Hapsburgs, the Hohenzollerns, and the Ottomans. Little more than two decades later, the British, Dutch, and French empires in Asia were dealt heavy blows by imperial Japan, leaving damage that not even the Allied victory in World War II could repair. The Portuguese empire limped on, but by the early 1970s it too had collapsed. The new empires that grew among the ruins of the old were shorter lived than their predecessors. Whereas some early modern empires lasted for centuries (Ottoman rule, for instance, endured for 469 years), the Soviet Union fell apart after only 69 years, the Japanese overseas empire crumbled after just 50 years, and Hitler's empire beyond Germany's borders hung on for barely six years.

Violence is most likely to occur as empires decline. The late Romans understood well the unpleasantness associated with imperial dissolution. Modern commentators, on the other hand, have generally been too eager to see empires end and too credulous about the benefits of "self-determination" to realize the potentially high costs of any transition from a multiethnic polity to a homogeneous one. As imperial authority crumbles, local elites compete for the perquisites of power. The stakes are particularly high in ethnically heterogeneous provinces. From the point of view of minorities, the prospect of a new political order can be deeply alarming; members of a minority group that has collaborated with the imperial power frequently find that the empire's disappearance leaves them vulnerable to reprisals.

Anyone who doubts whether imperial decline can foment conflict need only reflect on how rarely empires broke up peacefully in the twentieth century. One of the last acts of the Ottoman Empire was to attempt genocide against the Armenians. The Austrian, German, and Russian empires all met bloody ends as World War I drew to a close; indeed, the civil war and ethnic strife that followed the Russian Revolution in 1917 was as costly to the tsar's former subjects as the preceding war against Austria and Germany was. The most violent year in the entire history of British India was 1947, when partition led to the deaths of more than a million people in communal clashes between Hindus and Muslims. Even the relatively calm dissolution of the Soviet Union bred bitter conflict between Armenia and Azerbaijan over the mainly Armenian enclave of Nagorno-Karabakh, as well as the war between Chechen separatists and the Russian government.

THE ROCKY ROAD AHEAD

IF THE combination of ethnic disintegration, economic volatility, and empires in decline is the basic formula for twentieth-century conflict, then what are the implications for the twenty-first century?

The good news is that global economic volatility has been significantly lower in recent years than at almost any time in the last century. By widening and deepening international markets for goods, labor, and capital, globalization appears to have made the world economy less prone to crisis. At the same time, financial innovations have improved the pricing and the distribution of risk, and policy innovations such as inflation targeting have helped governments to limit rises in consumer price (if not asset price) inflation. International organizations such as the World Trade Organization and the International Monetary Fund have helped to avert trade disputes and other sources of economic instability.

A second obvious point is that the old zones of conflict are unlikely to be the new ones. Those who engaged in ethnic cleansing in the twentieth century, whether by forced migration or genocide, did their work too well, so that today central and eastern Europe (and Manchuria and Korea) are no longer ethnically heterogeneous. Chernivtsi today is overwhelmingly Ukrainian, for instance, with only a tiny remnant of its once-thriving Jewish community still living there. And third, the world of 2006 is supposed to be a world without empires; the danger of imperial decline should accordingly be much less than in the past century.

Unfortunately, these appearances are deceptive. Today, one region displays in abundance all of the characteristics of the worst conflict zones of the twentieth century. Economic volatility has remained pronounced there even as it has diminished in the rest of the world. An empire (albeit one that dares not speak its name) is losing its grip over the region. Worst of all, ethnic disintegration is already well under way, even though many commentators still conceive of what is currently the main conflict there as an insurgency against foreign invaders or a "clash of civilizations" between Islam and the West.

That place is the Middle East.

Iraq has experienced severe economic volatility in recent years, first as a result of UN sanctions and then because of the U.S. invasion and the subsequent insecurity. Having declined by just under 8 percent in the last year of Saddam Hussein's reign, real GDP plummeted by more than 40 percent in 2003, the year the United States invaded. In 2004, output bounced back by an estimated 46 percent—but growth slowed last year to under 4 percent. That is about as extreme as volatility can get. Since oil production accounts for about two-thirds of Iraq's GDP, changes in the production and the price of oil have been the primary drivers of these economic swings. Oil prices are now up, meaning Iraq's exports are worth more, but inflation is stuck between 20 and 30 percent, and oil production is running at just 16 percent of its prewar level because of sabotage and other problems.

Other indicators are only slightly less dire. Power generation remains 28 percent below the target that was supposed to have been achieved in 2004. And the unemployment rate is estimated to be between 25 and 40 percent. It is true that there has been some economic good news since the war. More Iraqis now have cars, and many more Iraqis now have telephones thanks to the creation of a cell-phone network. Iraqis today also have a free press. Yet these improvements in communications have also helped insurgents and militias to mobilize.

Iraq is not the only Middle Eastern country with a volatile economy. All six countries that border Iraq have seen their own share of ups and downs. In the past five years, per capita GDP growth in Iran has ranged between 0.3 and 7.3 percent; in Jordan, between 0.3 and 5.1 percent; in Kuwait, between -5.5 and 6.9 percent; in Saudi Arabia, between -6.0 and 3.3 percent; in Syria, between -0.4 and 3.3 percent; and in Turkey, between -9.0 and 7.4 percent. Over the past decade, Kuwait's average annual GDP performance was the lowest (-0.9 percent), while Iran's was the highest (3.0 percent). On the other hand, the average Kuwaiti is nearly ten times richer than the average Iranian. Inflation in the region in 2004 ranged from 0.3 percent in Saudi Arabia to nearly 15 percent in Iran. Unemployment rates are in the low double digits everywhere but in Saudi Arabia (where it is around 5 percent), but youth unemployment rates are generally twice as high—just under 20 percent in Turkey, for example, compared with an overall rate of 10 percent. Youth unemployment matters because these are relatively youthful societies. Roughly 20 percent of the population of Iraq and its neighbors is between 15 and 24 years old; the equivalent figure for Europe and the United States is about 14 percent.

The Middle East also has the misfortune to be a zone of imperial conflict. Most Americans will probably always reject the proposition that the United States is (or operates) a de facto empire. Such squeamishness may be an integral part of the U.S. empire's problem. To be an empire in denial means resenting the costs of intervening in the affairs of foreign peoples and underestimating the benefits of doing so. It is remarkable that in June 2004, just over a year after U.S. troops toppled Saddam, a majority of Americans already said they regarded the invasion of Iraq as a mistake. Although support for the war has vacillated since then, at no time since September 2004 have more than 55 percent of poll respondents said they approved of it. What makes the U.S. public's misgivings especially remarkable is that the number of U.S. military personnel who have died in this war has been very small by historical standards. The total as of mid-July 2006 was 2,544, of whom 525 had died as a result of non-combat-related causes.

The Islamic Republic of Iran, by contrast, is heir to an imperial tradition dating back to the time of the Safavid dynasty, which ruled Persia from 1501, and beyond. Although Iran's leaders prefer the rhetoric of religious revolution and national liberation, the historian cannot fail to detect in their long-held ambition to acquire nuclear weapons—and thereby dominate the Middle East—a legacy of Persia's imperial past. The Iranian president, Mahmoud Ahmadinejad, is not only a devotee of the Hidden, or Twelfth, Imam (who devout Shiites believe will return to the world as the Mahdi, or messiah, for a final confrontation with the forces of evil); he is also a war veteran at the head of a youthful nation. It is not wholly fanciful to see in him a potential Caesar or Bonaparte.

The third and most striking feature of the Middle East today is the acceleration of ethnic disintegration, which is most obvious in Iraq. In 1993, Harvard's Samuel Huntington predicted that in the post–Cold War world, "the principal conflicts of global politics [would] occur between nations and groups of different civilizations," particularly between a decadent "Judeo-Christian" West and a demographically ascendant Islamic civilization. For a time, events seemed to be fulfilling his prophecy. Many Americans interpreted the terrorist attacks of September 11, 2001, in Huntington's terms, while Islamists interpreted the U.S. invasions of Afghanistan and Iraq as wars by Christian "crusaders" against Muslims.

Yet a closer inspection of events since 1993 suggests a post–Cold War trend of clashes within, rather than between, civilizations. Of the 30 major armed conflicts that either are going on now or have recently ended, only nine can be regarded as being in any sense between civilizations. But 19 are in some measure ethnic conflicts, the worst being the wars that continue to bedevil central Africa. Moreover, most of those conflicts that have a religious dimension are also ethnic conflicts.

Events in Iraq suggest that there, too, what is unfolding is not a clash between the West and Islam but, increasingly, a clash within Islamic civilization itself. By some accounts, ethnic disintegration there is already well under way. In a June 6, 2006, cable to Secretary of State Condoleezza Rice, which was leaked to the press, Zalmay Khalilzad, the U.S. ambassador to Iraq, cataloged the evidence of mounting sectarian tension in and around the Green Zone in Baghdad. "Personal fears are reinforcing divisive or sectarian channels," Khalilzad wrote. "Ethnic and sectarian faultlines are becoming part of the daily media fare. One Shia employee told us she can no longer watch TV news with her mother, who is a Sunni, because her mother blamed all the government failings on the fact that the Shia are in charge." Even more worrisome, Khalilzad reported that U.S. embassy employees had "become adept in modifying [their] behavior to avoid *Alasas*, informants who keep an eye out for 'outsiders' in neighborhoods. The *Alasa* mentality is becoming entrenched as Iraqi security forces fail to gain public confidence."

Such news should come as no surprise. Baghdad and the provinces around it—Babil, Diyala, and Salahuddin—are precisely the regions of Iraq where ethnic conflict could have been predicted to occur given the current conditions of economic volatility and imperial crisis. They are the most ethnically mixed parts of the country, where Sunnis and Shiites or Sunnis and Kurds live cheek by jowl. Under Saddam's secular tyranny, these communities coexisted more or less peacefully. Anecdotal evidence even suggests that there was some intermarriage. Since Saddam's fall, however, integration has been reversed. Around 92 percent of the votes in the December 2005 election were cast for sectarian parties. In such a fractious atmosphere, the odds seem dangerously stacked against the once-dominant Sunni Arab minority. Not only do current constitutional arrangements raise the prospect that Iraq's oil revenue will flow largely to Shiite and Kurdish provinces, but the Sunnis are badly underrepresented in the Iraqi security forces. According to the Brookings Institution, Sunnis make up less than ten percent of the enlisted forces.

Although the atmosphere has cooled somewhat since the Askariya shrine bombing in February, the trend is clearly toward ethnic or sectarian conflict. The number of incidents of sectarian violence recorded in May 2006 was 250, compared with just 20 in the same month the year before and ten in May 2004. There has been a threefold increase in the homicide rate in Baghdad since February 2006, much of it the result of sectarian violence. The assassination of Abu Musab al-Zarqawi, the leader of al Qaeda in Iraq, in June was therefore less of a milestone than President George W. Bush had hoped. As insurgency has given way to civil war, Zarqawi had already ceased to be a key player.

THE FIRE NEXT TIME

WHAT MAKES the escalating civil war in Iraq so disturbing is that it has the potential to spill over into neighboring countries. The Iranian government is already taking more than a casual interest in the politics of post-Saddam Iraq. And yet Iran, with its Sunni and Kurdish minorities, is no more homogeneous than Iraq. Jordan, Saudi Arabia, and Syria cannot be expected to look on insouciantly if the Sunni minority in central Iraq begins to lose out to what may seem to be an

Iranian-backed tyranny of the majority. The recent history of Lebanon offers a reminder that in the Middle East there is no such thing as a contained civil war. Neighbors are always likely to take an unhealthy interest in any country with fissiparous tendencies.

The obvious conclusion is that a new "war of the world" may already be brewing in a region that, incredible though it may seem, has yet to sate its appetite for violence. And the ramifications of such a Middle Eastern conflagration would be truly global. Economically, the world would have to contend with oil at above $100 a barrel. Politically, those countries in western Europe with substantial Muslim populations might also find themselves affected as sectarian tensions radiated outward. Meanwhile, the ethnic war between Jews and Arabs in Israel, the Gaza Strip, and the West Bank shows no sign of abating. Is it credible that the United States will remain unscathed if the Middle East erupts?

Although such an outcome may seem to be a low-probability, nightmare scenario, it is already more likely than the scenario of enduring peace in the region. If the history of the twentieth century is any guide, only economic stabilization and a credible reassertion of U.S. authority are likely to halt the drift toward chaos. Neither is a likely prospect. On the contrary, the speed with which responsibility for security in Iraq is being handed over to the predominantly Shiite and Kurdish security forces may accelerate the descent into internecine strife. Significantly, the audio statement released by Osama bin Laden in June excoriated not only the American-led "occupiers" of Iraq but also "certain sectors of the Iraqi people ... those who refused [neutrality] and stood to fight on the side of the crusaders." His allusions to "rejectionists," "traitors," and "agents of the Americans" were clearly intended to justify al Qaeda's policy of targeting Iraq's Shiites.

The war of the worlds that H. G. Wells imagined never came to pass. But a war of the world did. The sobering possibility we urgently need to confront is that another global conflict is brewing today—centered not on Poland or Manchuria, but more likely on Palestine and Mesopotamia.

The Coming Anarchy

How Scarcity, Crime, Overpopulation, Tribalism, and Disease are Rapidly Destroying the Social Fabric of our Planet

Robert D. Kaplan

The Minister's eyes were like egg yolks, an aftereffect of some of the many illnesses, malaria especially, endemic in his country. There was also an irrefutable sadness in his eyes. He spoke in a slow and creaking voice, the voice of hope about to expire. Flame trees, coconut palms, and a ballpoint-blue Atlantic composed the background. None of it seemed beautiful, though. "In forty-five years I have never seen things so bad. We did not manage ourselves well after the British departed. But what we have now is something worse—the revenge of the poor, of the social failures, of the people least able to bring up children in a modern society." Then he referred to the recent coup in the West African country Sierra Leone. "The boys who took power in Sierra Leone come from houses like this." The Minister jabbed his finger at a corrugated metal shack teeming with children. "In three months these boys confiscated all the official Mercedes, Volvos, and BMWs and willfully wrecked them on the road." The Minister mentioned one of the coup's leaders, Solomon Anthony Joseph Musa, who shot the people who had paid for his schooling, "in order to erase the humiliation and mitigate the power his middle-class sponsors held over him."

Reprinted by permission from *The Atlantic Monthly* (February 1994).

Tyranny is nothing new in Sierra Leone or in the rest of West Africa. But it is now part and parcel of an increasing lawlessness that is far more significant than any coup, rebel incursion, or episodic experiment in democracy. Crime was what my friend—a top-ranking African official whose life would be threatened were I to identify him more precisely—really wanted to talk about. Crime is what makes West Africa a natural point of departure for my report on what the political character of our planet is likely to be in the twenty-first century.

Sierra Leone is a microcosm of what is occurring in West Africa and much of the underdeveloped world: the withering away of central governments, the rise of tribal and regional domains, the unchecked spread of disease, and the growing pervasiveness of war.

The cities of West Africa at night are some of the unsafest places in the world. Streets are unlit; the police often lack gasoline for their vehicles; armed burglars, carjackers, and muggers proliferate. "The government in Sierra Leone has no writ after dark," says a foreign resident, shrugging. When I was in the capital, Freetown, last September, eight men armed with AK-47s broke into the house of an American man. They tied him up and stole everything of value. Forget Miami: direct flights between the United States and the Murtala Muhammed Airport, in neighboring Nigeria's largest city, Lagos, have been suspended by order of the U.S. Secretary of Transportation because of ineffective security at the terminal and its environs. A State Department report cited the airport for "extortion by law-enforcement and immigration officials." This is one of the few times that the U.S. government has embargoed a foreign airport for reasons that are linked purely to crime. In Abidjan, effectively the capital of the Côte d'Ivoire, or Ivory Coast, restaurants have stick- and gun-wielding guards who walk you the fifteen feet or so between your car and the entrance, giving you an eerie taste of what American cities might be like in the future. An Italian ambassador was killed by gunfire when robbers invaded an Abidjan restaurant. The family of the Nigerian ambassador was tied

THE ATLANTIC MONTHLY · *Volume 273 No. 2*

up and robbed at gunpoint in the ambassador's residence. After university students in the Ivory Coast caught bandits who had been plaguing their dorms, they executed them by hanging tires around their necks and setting the tires on fire. In one instance Ivorian policemen stood by and watched the "necklacings," afraid to intervene. Each time I went to the Abidjan bus terminal, groups of young men with restless, scanning eyes surrounded my taxi, putting their hands all over the windows, demanding "tips" for carrying my luggage even though I had only a rucksack. In cities in six West African countries I saw similar young men everywhere—hordes of them. They were like loose molecules in a very unstable social fluid, a fluid that was clearly on the verge of igniting.

"You see," my friend the Minister told me, "in the villages of Africa it is perfectly natural to feed at any table and lodge in any hut. But in the cities this communal existence no longer holds. You must pay for lodging and be invited for food. When young men find out that their relations cannot put them up, they become lost. They join other migrants and slip gradually into the criminal process."

"In the poor quarters of Arab North Africa," he continued, "there is much less crime, because Islam provides a social anchor: of education and indoctrination. Here in West Africa we have a lot of superficial Islam and superficial Christianity. Western religion is undermined by animist beliefs not suitable to a moral society, because they are based on irrational spirit power. Here spirits are used to wreak vengeance by one person against another, or one group against another." Many of the atrocities in the Liberian civil war have been tied to belief in *juju* spirits, and the BBC has reported, in its magazine *Focus on Africa,* that in the civil fighting in adjacent Sierra Leone, rebels were said to have "a young woman with them who would go to the front naked, always walking backwards and looking in a mirror to see where she was going. This made her invisible, so that she could cross to the army's positions and there bury charms ... to improve the rebels' chances of success."

Finally my friend the Minister mentioned polygamy. Designed for a pastoral way of life, polygamy continues to thrive in sub-Saharan Africa even though it is increasingly uncommon in Arab North Africa. Most youths I met on the road in West Africa told me that they were from "extended" families, with a mother in one place and a father in another. Translated to an urban environment, loose family structures are largely responsible for the world's highest birth rates and the explosion of the HIV virus on the continent. Like the communalism and animism, they provide a weak shield against the corrosive social effects of life in cities. In those cities African culture is being redefined while desertification and deforestation—also tied to overpopulation—drive more and more African peasants out of the countryside.

A PREMONITION OF THE FUTURE

West Africa is becoming *the* symbol of worldwide demographic, environmental, and societal stress, in which criminal anarchy emerges as the real "strategic" danger. Disease, overpopulation, unprovoked crime, scarcity of resources, refugee migrations, the increasing erosion of nation-states and international borders, and the empowerment of private armies, security firms, and international drug cartels are now most tellingly demonstrated through a West African prism. West Africa provides an appropriate introduction to the issues, often extremely unpleasant to discuss, that will soon confront our civilization. To remap the political earth the way it will be a few decades hence—as I intend to do in this article—I find I must begin with West Africa.

There is no other place on the planet where political maps are so deceptive—where, in fact, they tell such lies—as in West Africa. Start with Sierra Leone. According to the map, it is a nation-state of defined borders, with a government in control of its territory. In truth the Sierra Leonian government, run by a twenty-seven-year-old army captain, Valentine Strasser, controls Freetown by day and by day also controls part of the rural interior. In the government's territory the national army is an unruly rabble threatening drivers and passengers at most checkpoints. In the other part of the country units of two separate armies from the war in Liberia have taken up residence, as has an army of Sierra Leonian rebels. The government force fighting the rebels is full of renegade commanders who have aligned themselves with disaffected village chiefs. A pre-modern formlessness governs the battlefield, evoking the wars in medieval Europe prior to the 1648 Peace of Westphalia, which ushered in the era of organized nation-states.

As a consequence, roughly 400,000 Sierra Leonians are internally displaced, 280,000 more have fled to neighboring Guinea, and another 100,000 have fled to Liberia, even as 400,000 Liberians have fled to Sierra Leone. The third largest city in Sierra Leone, Gondama, is a displaced-persons camp. With an additional 600,000 Liberians in Guinea and 250,000 in the Ivory Coast, the borders dividing these four countries have become largely meaningless. Even in quiet zones none of the governments except the Ivory Coast's maintains the schools, bridges, roads, and police forces in a manner necessary for functional sovereignty. The Koranko ethnic group in northeastern Sierra Leone does all its trading in Guinea. Sierra Leonian diamonds are more likely to be sold in Liberia than in Freetown. In the eastern provinces of Sierra Leone you can buy Liberian beer but not the local brand.

In Sierra Leone, as in Guinea, as in the Ivory Coast, as in Ghana, most of the primary rain forest and the secondary bush is being destroyed at an alarming rate. I saw convoys of trucks bearing majestic hardwood trunks to coastal ports. When Sierra Leone achieved its independence, in 1961, as much as 60 percent of the country was primary rain forest. Now six percent is. In the Ivory Coast the proportion has fallen from 38 percent to eight percent. The deforestation has led to soil erosion, which has led to more flooding and more mosquitoes. Virtually everyone in the West African interior has some form of malaria.

Sierra Leone is a microcosm of what is occurring, albeit in a more tempered and gradual manner, throughout West Africa and much of the underdeveloped world: the withering away of central governments, the rise of tribal and regional domains, the unchecked spread of disease, and the growing pervasiveness of war. West Africa is reverting to the Africa of the Victorian atlas. It consists now of a series of coastal trading posts, such as Freetown and Conakry, and an interior that, owing to violence, volatility, and disease, is again becoming, as Graham Greene once observed, "blank" and "unexplored." However, whereas Greene's vision implies a certain romance, as in the somnolent and charmingly seedy Freetown of his celebrated novel *The Heart of the Matter*, it is Thomas Malthus, the philosopher of demographic doomsday, who is now the prophet of West Africa's future. And West Africa's future, eventually, will also be that of most of the rest of the world.

Consider "Chicago." I refer not to Chicago, Illinois, but to a slum district of Abidjan, which the young toughs in the area have named after the American city. ("Washington" is another poor section of Abidjan.) Although Sierra Leone is widely regarded as beyond salvage, the Ivory Coast has been considered an African success story, and Abidjan has been called "the Paris of West Africa." Success, however, was built on two artificial factors: the high price of cocoa, of which the Ivory Coast is the world's leading producer, and the talents of a French expatriate community, whose members have helped run the government and the private sector. The expanding cocoa economy made the Ivory Coast a magnet for migrant workers from all over West Africa: between a third and a half of the country's population is now non-Ivorian, and the figure could be as high as 75 percent in Abidjan. During the 1980s cocoa prices fell and the French began to leave. The skyscrapers of the Paris of West Africa are a façade. Perhaps 15 percent of Abidjan's population of three million people live in shantytowns like Chicago and Washington, and the vast majority live in places that are not much better. Not all of these places appear on any of the readily available maps. This is another indication of how political maps are the products of tired conventional wisdom and, in the Ivory Coast's case, of an elite that will ultimately be forced to relinquish power.

Chicago, like more and more of Abidjan, is a slum in the bush: a checkerwork of corrugated zinc roofs and walls made of cardboard and black plastic wrap. It is located in a gully teeming with coconut palms and oil palms, and is ravaged by flooding. Few residents have easy access to electricity, a sewage system, or a clean water supply. The crumbly red laterite earth crawls with foot-long lizards both inside and outside the shacks. Children defecate in a stream filled with garbage and pigs, droning with malarial mosquitoes. In this stream women do the washing. Young unemployed men spend their time drinking beer, palm wine, and gin while gambling on pinball games constructed out of rotting wood and rusty nails. These are the same youths who rob houses in more prosperous Ivorian neighborhoods at night. One man I met, Damba Tesele, came to Chicago from Burkina Faso in 1963. A cook by profession, he has four wives and thirty-two children, not one of whom has made it to high school. He has seen his shanty community destroyed by municipal authorities seven times since coming to the area. Each time he and his neighbors rebuild. Chicago is the latest incarnation.

Fifty-five percent of the Ivory Coast's population is urban, and the proportion is expected to reach 62 percent by 2000. The yearly net population growth is 3.6 percent. This means that the Ivory Coast's 13.5 million people will become 39 million by 2025, when much of the population will consist of urbanized peasants like those of Chicago. But don't count on the Ivory Coast's still existing then. Chicago, which is more indicative of Africa's and the Third World's demographic present—and even more of the future—than any idyllic junglescape of women balancing earthen jugs on their heads, illustrates why the Ivory Coast, once a model of Third World success, is becoming a case study in Third World catastrophe.

President Félix Houphouët-Boigny, who died last December at the age of about ninety, left behind a weak cluster of political parties and a leaden bureaucracy that discourages foreign investment. Because the military is small and the non-Ivorian population large, there is neither an obvious force to maintain order nor a sense of nationhood that would lessen the need for such enforcement. The economy has been shrinking since the mid-1980s. Though the French are working assiduously to preserve stability, the Ivory Coast faces a possibility worse than a coup: an anarchic implosion of criminal violence—an urbanized version of what has already happened in Somalia. Or it may become an African Yugoslavia, but one without mini-states to replace the whole.

Because the demographic reality of West Africa is a countryside draining into dense slums by the coast, ultimately the region's rulers will come to reflect the values of these shanty-towns. There are signs of this already in Sierra Leone—and in Togo, where the dictator Etienne Eyadema, in power since 1967, was nearly toppled in 1991, not by democrats but by thousands of youths whom the London-based magazine *West Africa* described as "Soweto-like stone-throwing adolescents." Their behavior may herald a regime more brutal than Eyadema's repressive one.

The fragility of these West African "countries" impressed itself on me when I took a series of bush taxis along the Gulf of Guinea, from the Togolese capital of Lomé, across Ghana, to Abidjan. The 400-mile journey required two full days of driving, because of stops at two border crossings and an additional eleven customs stations, at each of which my fellow passengers had their bags searched. I had to change money twice and repeatedly fill in currency-declaration forms. I had to bribe a Togolese immigration official with the equivalent of eighteen dollars before he would agree to put an exit stamp on my passport. Nevertheless, smuggling across these borders is rampant. *The London Observer* has reported that in 1992 the equivalent of $856 million left West Africa for Europe in the form of "hot cash" assumed to be laundered drug money. International cartels have discovered the utility of weak, financially strapped West African regimes.

The more fictitious the actual sovereignty, the more severe border authorities seem to be in trying to prove otherwise. Getting visas for these states can be as hard as crossing their borders. The Washington embassies of Sierra Leone and Guinea—the two poorest nations on earth, according to a 1993 United Nations report on "human development"—asked for letters from my bank (in lieu of prepaid round-trip tickets) and also personal references, in order to prove that I had sufficient means to sustain myself during my visits. I was reminded of my visa and currency hassles while traveling to the communist states of Eastern Europe, particularly East Germany and Czechoslovakia, before those states collapsed.

Ali A. Mazrui, the director of the Institute of Global Cultural Studies at the State University of New York at Binghamton, predicts that West Africa—indeed, the whole continent—is on the verge of large-scale border upheaval. Mazrui writes,

> In the 21st century France will be withdrawing from West Africa as she gets increasingly involved in the affairs [of Europe]. France's West African sphere of influence will be filled by Nigeria—a more natural hegemonic power.... It will be under those circumstances that Nigeria's own boundaries are likely to expand to incorporate the Republic of Niger (the Hausa link), the Republic of Benin (the Yoruba link) and conceivably Cameroon.

The future could be more tumultuous, and bloodier, than Mazrui dares to say. France *will* withdraw from former colonies like Benin, Togo, Niger, and the Ivory Coast, where it has been propping up local currencies. It will do so not only because its attention will be diverted to new challenges in Europe and Russia but also because younger French officials lack the older generation's emotional ties to the ex-colonies. However, even as Nigeria attempts to expand, it, too, is likely to split into several pieces. The State Department's Bureau of Intelligence and Research recently made the following points in an analysis of Nigeria:

> Prospects for a transition to civilian rule and democratization are slim.... The repressive apparatus of the state security service ... will be difficult for any future civilian government to control.... The country is becoming increasingly ungovernable.... Ethnic and regional splits are deepening, a situation made worse by an increase in the number of states from 19 to 30 and a doubling in the number of local governing authorities; religious cleavages are more serious; Muslim fundamentalism and evangelical Christian militancy are on the rise; and northern Muslim anxiety over southern [Christian] control of the economy is intense ... the will to keep Nigeria together is now very weak.

Given that oil-rich Nigeria is a bellwether for the region—its population of roughly 90 million equals the populations of all the other West African states combined—it is apparent that Africa faces cataclysms that could make the Ethiopian and Somalian famines pale in comparison. This is especially so because Nigeria's population, including that of its largest city, Lagos, whose crime, pollution, and overcrowding make it the cliché par excellence of Third World urban dysfunction, is set to double during the next twenty-five years, while the country continues to deplete its natural resources.

Part of West Africa's quandary is that although its population belts are horizontal, with habitation densities increasing as one travels south away from the Sahara and toward the tropical abundance of the Atlantic littoral, the borders erected by European colonialists are vertical, and therefore at cross-purposes with demography and topography. Satellite photos depict the same reality I experienced in the bush taxi: the Lomé-Abidjan coastal corridor—indeed, the entire stretch of coast from Abidjan eastward to Lagos—is one burgeoning megalopolis that by any rational economic and geographical standard should constitute a single sovereignty, rather than the five (the Ivory Coast, Ghana, Togo, Benin, and Nigeria) into which it is currently divided.

As many internal African borders begin to crumble, a more impenetrable boundary is being erected that threatens to isolate the continent as a whole: the wall of disease. Merely to visit West Africa in some degree of safety, I spent about $500 for a hepatitis B vaccination series and other disease prophylaxis. Africa may today be more dangerous in this regard than it was in 1862, before antibiotics, when the explorer Sir Richard Francis Burton described the health situation on the continent as "deadly, a Golgotha, a Jehannum." Of the approximately 12 million people worldwide whose blood is HIV-positive, 8 million are in Africa. In the capital of the Ivory Coast, whose modern road system only helps to spread the disease, 10 percent of the population is HIV-positive. And war and refugee movements help the virus break through to more-remote areas of Africa. Alan Greenberg, M.D., a representative of the Centers for Disease Control in Abidjan, explains that in Africa the HIV virus and tuberculosis are now "fast-forwarding each other." Of the approximately 4,000 newly diagnosed tuberculosis patients in Abidjan, 45 percent were also found to be HIV-positive. As African birth rates soar and slums proliferate, some experts worry that viral mutations and hybridizations might, just conceivably, result in a form of the AIDS virus that is easier to catch than the present strain.

It is malaria that is most responsible for the disease wall that threatens to separate Africa and other parts of the Third World from more-developed regions of the planet in the twenty-first century. It is mutating into increasingly deadly forms.

It is malaria that is most responsible for the disease wall that threatens to separate Africa and other parts of the Third World from more-developed regions of the planet in the twenty-first century. Carried by mosquitoes, malaria, unlike AIDS, is easy to catch. Most people in sub-Saharan Africa have recurring bouts of the disease throughout their entire lives, and it is mutating into increasingly deadly forms. "The great gift of Malaria is utter apathy," wrote Sir Richard Burton, accurately portraying the situation in much of the Third World today. Visitors to malaria-afflicted parts of the planet are protected by a new drug, mefloquine, a side effect of which is vivid, even violent, dreams. But a strain of cerebral malaria resistant to mefloquine is now on the offensive. Consequently, defending oneself against malaria in Africa is becoming more and more like defending oneself against violent crime. You engage in "behavior modification": not going out at dusk, wearing mosquito repellent all the time.

And the cities keep growing. I got a general sense of the future while driving from the airport to downtown Conakry, the capital of Guinea. The forty-five-minute journey in heavy traffic was through one never-ending shanty-town: a nightmarish Dickensian spectacle to which Dickens himself would never have given credence. The corrugated metal shacks and scabrous walls were coated with black slime. Stores were built out of rusted shipping containers, junked cars, and jumbles of wire mesh. The streets were one long puddle of floating garbage. Mosquitoes and flies were everywhere. Children, many of whom had protruding bellies, seemed as numerous as ants. When the tide went out, dead rats and the skeletons of cars were exposed on the mucky beach. In twenty-eight years Guinea's population will double if growth goes on at current rates. Hardwood logging continues at a madcap speed, and people flee the Guinean countryside for Conakry. It seemed to me that here, as elsewhere in Africa and the Third World, man is challenging nature far beyond its limits, and nature is now beginning to take its revenge.

Africa may be as relevant to the future character of world politics as the Balkans were a hundred years ago, prior to the two Balkan wars and the First World War. Then the threat was the collapse of empires and the birth of nations based solely on tribe. Now the threat is more elemental: *nature unchecked.* Africa's immediate future could be very bad. The coming upheaval, in which foreign embassies are shut down, states collapse, and contact with the outside world takes place through dangerous, disease-ridden coastal trading posts, will loom large in the century we are entering. (Nine of twenty-one U.S. foreign-aid missions to be closed over the next three years are in Africa—a prologue to a consolidation of U.S. embassies themselves.) Precisely because much of Africa is set to go over the edge at a time when the Cold War has ended, when environmental and demographic stress in other parts of the globe is becoming critical, and when the post–First World War system of nation-states—not just in the Balkans but perhaps also in the Middle East—is about to be toppled, Africa suggests what war, borders, and ethnic politics will be like a few decades hence.

To understand the events of the next fifty years, then, one must understand environmental scarcity, cultural and racial clash, geographic destiny, and the transformation of war. The order in which I have named these is not accidental. Each concept except the first relies partly on the one or ones before it, meaning that the last two—new approaches to mapmaking and to warfare—are the most important. They are also the least understood. I will now look at each idea, drawing upon the work of specialists and also my own travel experiences in various parts of the globe besides Africa, in order to fill in the blanks of a new political atlas.

THE ENVIRONMENT AS A HOSTILE POWER

For a while the media will continue to ascribe riots and other violent upheavals abroad mainly to ethnic and religious conflict. But as these conflicts multiply, it will become apparent that something else is afoot, making more and more places like Nigeria, India, and Brazil ungovernable.

Mention "the environment" or "diminishing natural resources" in foreign-policy circles and you meet a brick wall of skepticism or boredom. To conservatives especially, the very terms seem flaky. Public-policy foundations have contributed to the lack of interest, by funding narrowly focused environmental studies replete with technical jargon which foreign-affairs experts just let pile up on their desks.

It is time to understand "the environment" for what it is: *the* national-security issue of the early twenty-first century. The political and strategic impact of surging populations, spreading disease, deforestation and soil erosion, water depletion, air pollution, and, possibly, rising sea levels in critical, overcrowded regions like the Nile Delta and Bangladesh—developments that will prompt mass migrations and, in turn, incite group conflicts—will be the core foreign-policy challenge form which most others will ultimately emanate, arousing the public and uniting assorted interests left over from the Cold War. In the twenty-first century water will be in dangerously short supply in such diverse locales as Saudi Arabia, Central Asia, and the southwestern United States. A war could erupt between Egypt and Ethiopia over Nile River water. Even in Europe tensions have arisen between Hungary and Slovakia over the damming of the Danube, a classic case of how environmental disputes fuse with ethnic and historical ones. The political scientist and erstwhile Clinton adviser Michael Mandelbaum has said, "We have a foreign policy today in the shape of a doughnut—lots of peripheral interests but nothing at the center." The environment, I will argue, is part of a terrifying array of problems that will define a new threat to our security, filling the hole in Mandelbaum's doughnut and allowing a post–Cold War foreign policy to emerge inexorably by need rather than by design.

Our Cold War foreign policy truly began with George F. Kennan's famous article, signed "X," published in *Foreign Affairs* in July of 1947, in which Kennan argued for a "firm and vigilant containment" of a Soviet Union that was imperially, rather than ideologically, motivated. It may be that our post-Cold War foreign policy will one day be seen to have had its beginnings in an even bolder and more detailed piece of written analysis: one that appeared in the journal *International Security*. The article, published in the fall of 1991 by Thomas Fraser Homer-Dixon, who is the head of the Peace and Conflict Studies Program at the University of Toronto, was titled "On the Threshold: Environmental Changes as Causes of Acute Conflict." Homer-Dixon has, more successfully than other analysts, integrated two hitherto separate fields—military-conflict studies and the study of the physical environment.

In Homer-Dixon's view, future wars and civil violence will often arise from scarcities of resources such as water, cropland, forests, and fish. Just as there will be environmentally driven wars and refugee flows, there will be environmentally induced praetorian regimes—or, as he puts it, "hard regimes." Countries with the highest probability of acquiring hard regimes, according to Homer-Dixon, are those that are threatened by a declining resource base yet also have "a history of state [read 'military'] strength." Candidates include Indonesia, Brazil, and, of course, Nigeria. Though each of these nations has exhibited democratizing tendencies of late, Homer-Dixon argues that such tendencies are likely to be superficial "epiphenomena" having nothing to do with longterm processes that include soaring populations and shrinking raw materials. Democracy is problematic; scarcity is more certain.

Indeed, the Saddam Husseins of the future will have more, not fewer, opportunities. In addition to engendering tribal strife, scarcer resources will place a great strain on many peoples who never had much of a democratic or institutional tradition to begin with. Over the next fifty years the earth's population will soar from 5.5 billion to more than nine billion. Though optimists have hopes for new resource technologies and free-market development in the global village, they fail to note that, as the National Academy of Sciences has pointed out, 95 percent of the population increase will be in the poorest regions of the world, where governments now—just look at Africa—show little ability to function, let alone to implement even marginal improvements. Homer-Dixon writes, ominously, "Neo-Malthusians may underestimate human adaptability in *today's* environmental-social system, but as time passes their analysis may become ever more compelling."

While a minority of the human population will be, as Francis Fukuyama would put it, sufficiently sheltered so as to enter a "post-historical" realm, living in cities and suburbs in which the environment has been mastered and ethnic animosities have been quelled by bourgeois prosperity, an increasingly large number of people will be stuck in history, living in shantytowns where attempts to rise above poverty, cultural dysfunction, and ethnic strife will be doomed by a lack of water to drink, soil to till, and space to survive in. In the developing world environmental stress will present people with a choice that is increasingly among totalitarianism (as in Iraq), fascist-tending mini-states (as in Serb-held Bosnia), and road-warrior cultures (as in Somalia). Homer-Dixon concludes that "as environmental degradation proceeds, the size of the potential social disruption will increase."

Tad Homer-Dixon is an unlikely Jeremiah. Today a boyish thirty-seven, he grew up amid the sylvan majesty of Vancouver Island, attending private day schools. His speech is calm, perfectly even, and crisply enunciated. There is nothing in his background or manner that would indicate a bent toward pessimism. A Canadian Anglican who spends his summers canoeing on the lakes of northern Ontario, and who talks about the benign mountains, black bears, and Douglas firs of his youth, he is the opposite of the intellectually severe neoconservative, the kind at home with conflict scenarios. Nor is he an environmentalist who opposes development. "My father was a logger who thought about ecologically safe forestry before others," he says. "He logged, planted, logged, and planted. He got out of the business just as the issue was being polarized by environmentalists. They hate changed ecosystems. But human beings, just by carrying seeds around, change the natural world." As an only child whose playground was a virtually untouched wilderness and seacoast, Homer-Dixon has a familiarity with the natural world that permits him to see a reality that most policy analysts—children of suburbia and city streets—are blind to.

"We need to bring nature back in," he argues. "We have to stop separating politics from the physical world—the climate, public health, and the environment." Quoting Daniel Deudney, another pioneering expert on the security aspects of the environment, Homer-Dixon says that "for too long we've been prisoners of 'social-social' theory, which assumes there are only social causes for social and political changes, rather than natural causes, too. This social-social mentality emerged with the Industrial Revolution, which separated us from nature. But nature is coming back with a vengeance, tied to population growth. It will have incredible security implications.

"Think of a stretch limo in the potholed streets of New York City, where homeless beggars live. Inside the limo are the air-conditioned post-industrial regions of North America, Europe, the emerging Pacific Rim, and a few other isolated places, with their trade summitry and computer-information highways. Outside is the rest of mankind, going in a completely different direction."

We are entering a bifurcated world. Part of the globe is inhabited by Hegel's and Fukuyama's Last Man, healthy, well fed, and pampered by technology. The other, larger, part is inhabited by Hobbes's First Man, condemned to a life that is "poor, nasty, brutish, and short." Although both parts will be threatened by environmental stress, the Last Man will be able to master it; the First Man will not.

The Last Man will adjust to the loss of underground water tables in the western United States. He will build dikes to save Cape

Hatteras and the Chesapeake beaches from rising sea levels, even as the Maldive Islands, off the coast of India, sink into oblivion, and the shorelines of Egypt, Bangladesh, and Southeast Asia recede, driving tens of millions of people inland where there is no room for them, and thus sharpening ethnic divisions.

Homer-Dixon points to a world map of soil degradation in his Toronto office. "The darker the map color, the worse the degradation," he explains. The West African coast, the Middle East, the Indian subcontinent, China, and Central America have the darkest shades, signifying all manner of degradation, related to winds, chemicals, and water problems. "The worst degradation is generally where the population is highest. The population is generally highest where the soil is the best. So we're degrading earth's best soil."

China, in Homer-Dixon's view, is the quintessential example of environmental degradation. Its current economic "success" masks deeper problems. "China's fourteen percent growth rate does not mean it's going to be a world power. It means that coastal China, where the economic growth is taking place, is joining the rest of the Pacific Rim. The disparity with inland China is intensifying." Referring to the environmental research of his colleague, the Czech-born ecologist Vaclav Smil, Homer-Dixon explains how the per capita availability of arable land in interior China has rapidly declined at the same time that the quality of that land has been destroyed by deforestation, loss of topsoil, and salinization. He mentions the loss and contamination of water supplies, the exhaustion of wells, the plugging of irrigation systems and reservoirs with eroded silt, and a population of 1.54 billion by the year 2025: it is a misconception that China has gotten its population under control. Large-scale population movements are under way, from inland China to coastal China and from villages to cities, leading to a crime surge like the one in Africa and to growing regional disparities and conflicts in a land with a strong tradition of warlordism and a weak tradition of central government—again as in Africa. "We will probably see the center challenged and fractured, and China will not remain the same on the map," Homer-Dixon says.

Environmental scarcity will inflame existing hatreds and affect power relationships, at which we now look.

SKINHEAD COSSACKS, JUJU WARRIORS

In the summer, 1993, issue of *Foreign Affairs,* Samuel P. Huntington, of Harvard's Olin Institute for Strategic Studies, published a thought-provoking article called "The Clash of Civilizations?" The world, he argues, has been moving during the course of this century from nation-state conflict to ideological conflict to, finally, cultural conflict. I would add that as refugee flows increase and as peasants continue migrating to cities around the world—turning them into sprawling villages—national borders will mean less, even as more power will fall into the hands of less educated, less sophisticated groups. In the eyes of these uneducated but newly empowered millions, the real borders are the most tangible and intractable ones: those of culture and tribe. Huntington writes, "First, differences among civilizations are not only real; they are basic," involving, among other things, history, language, and religion. "Second ... interactions between peoples of different civilizations are increasing; these increasing interactions intensify civilization consciousness." Economic modernization is not necessarily a panacea, since it fuels individual and group ambitions while weakening traditional loyalties to the state. It is worth noting, for example, that it is precisely the wealthiest and fastest-developing city in India. Bombay, that has seen the worst intercommunal violence between Hindus and Muslims. Consider that Indian cities, like African and Chinese ones, are ecological time bombs—Delhi and Calcutta, and also Beijing, suffer the worst air quality of any cities in the world—and it is apparent how surging populations, environmental degradation, and ethnic conflict are deeply related.

Huntington points to interlocking conflicts among Hindu, Muslim, Slavic Orthodox, Western, Japanese, Confucian, Latin American, and possibly African civilizations: for instance, Hindus clashing with Muslims in India, Turkic Muslims clashing with Slavic Orthodox Russians in Central Asian cities, the West clashing with Asia. (Even in the United States, African-Americans find themselves besieged by an influx of competing Latinos.) Whatever the laws, refugees find a way to crash official borders, bringing their passions with them, meaning that Europe and the United States will be weakened by cultural disputes.

Because Huntington's brush is broad, his specifics are vulnerable to attack. In a rebuttal of Huntington's argument the Johns Hopkins professor Fouad Ajami, a Lebanese-born Shi'ite who certainly knows the world beyond suburbia, writes in the September–October, 1993, issue of *Foreign Affairs,*

> The world of Islam divides and subdivides. The battle lines in the Caucasus ... are not coextensive with civilizational fault lines. The lines follow the interests of states. Where Huntington sees a civilizational duel between Armenia and Azerbaijan, the Iranian state has cast religious zeal ... to the wind ... in that battle the Iranians have tilted toward Christian Armenia.

True, Huntington's hypothesized war between Islam and Orthodox Christianity is not borne out by the alliance network in the Caucasus. But that is only because he has misidentified *which* cultural war is occurring there. A recent visit to Azerbaijan made clear to me that Azeri Turks, the world's most secular Shi'ite Muslims, see their cultural identity in terms not of religion but of their Turkic race. The Armenians, likewise, fight the Azeris not because the latter are Muslims but because they are Turks, related to the same Turks who massacred Armenians in 1915. Turkic culture (secular and based on languages employing a Latin script) is battling Iranian culture (religiously militant as defined by Tehran, and wedded to an Arabic script) across the whole swath of Central Asia and the Caucasus. The Armenians are, therefore, natural allies of their fellow Indo-Europeans the Iranians.

Huntington is correct that the Caucasus is a flashpoint of cultural and racial war. But, as Ajami observes, Huntington's plate tectonics are too simple. Two months of recent travel throughout Turkey revealed to me that although the Turks are developing a deep distrust, bordering on hatred, of fellow-Muslim Iran, they are also, especially in the shantytowns that are coming to dominate Turkish public opinion, revising their group identity, increasingly seeing themselves as Muslims being deserted by a West that does little to help besieged Muslims in Bosnia and that attacks Turkish Muslims in the streets of Germany.

In other words, the Balkans, a powder keg for nation-state war at the beginning of the twentieth century, could be a powder keg for cultural war at the turn of the twenty-first: between Orthodox Christianity (represented by the Serbs and a classic Byzantine configuration of Greeks, Russians, and Romanians) and the House of Islam. Yet in the Caucasus that House of Islam is falling into a clash between Turkic and Iranian civilizations. Ajami asserts that this very subdivision, not to mention all the divisions within the Arab world, indicates that the West, including the United States, is not threatened by Huntington's scenario. As the Gulf War demonstrated, the West has proved capable of playing one part of the House of Islam against another.

True. However, whether he is aware of it or not, Ajami is describing a world even more dangerous than the one Huntington envisions, especially when one takes into account Homer-Dixon's research on environmental scarcity. Outside the stretch limo would be a rundown, crowded planet of skinhead Cossacks and *juju* warriors, influenced by the worst refuse of Western pop culture and ancient tribal hatreds, and battling over scraps of overused earth in guerrilla conflicts that ripple across continents and intersect in no discernible pattern—meaning there's no easy-to-define threat. Kennan's world of one adversary seems as distant as the world of Herodotus.

Most people believe that the political earth since 1989 has undergone immense change. But it is minor compared with what is yet to come. The breaking apart and remaking of the atlas is only now beginning. The crack-up of the Soviet empire and the coming end of Arab-Israeli military confrontation are merely prologues to the really big changes that lie ahead. Michael Vlahos, a long-range thinker for the U.S. Navy, warns, "We are not in charge of the environment and the world is not following us. It is going in many directions. Do not assume that democratic capitalism is the last word in human social evolution."

Before addressing the questions of maps and of warfare, I want to take a closer look at the interaction of religion, culture, demographic shifts, and the distribution of natural resources in a specific area of the world: the Middle East.

THE PAST IS DEAD

Built on steep, muddy hills, the shantytowns of Ankara, the Turkish capital, exude visual drama. Altindag, or "Golden Mountain," is a pyramid of dreams, fashioned from cinder blocks and corrugated iron, rising as though each shack were built on top of another, all reaching awkwardly and painfully toward heaven—the heaven of wealthier Turks who live elsewhere in the city. Nowhere else on the planet have I found such a poignant architectural symbol of man's striving, with gaps in house walls plugged with rusted cans, and leeks and onions growing on verandas assembled from planks of rotting wood. For reasons that I will explain, the Turkish shacktown is a psychological universe away from the African one.

To see the twenty-first century truly, one's eyes must learn a different set of aesthetics. One must reject the overly stylized images of travel magazines, with their inviting photographs of exotic villages and glamorous downtowns. There are far too many millions whose dreams are more vulgar, more real—whose raw energies and desires will overwhelm the visions of the elites, remaking the future into something frighteningly new. But in Turkey I learned that shantytowns are not all bad.

Slum quarters in Abidjan terrify and repel the outsider. In Turkey it is the opposite. The closer I got to Golden Mountain the better it looked, and the safer I felt. I had $1,500 worth of Turkish lira in one pocket and $1,000 in traveler's checks in the other, yet I felt no fear. Golden Mountain was a real neighborhood. The inside of one house told the story: The architectural bedlam of cinder block and sheet metal and cardboard walls was deceiving. Inside was a *home*—order, that is, bespeaking dignity. I saw a working refrigerator, a television, a wall cabinet with a few books and lots of family pictures, a few plants by a window, and a stove. Though the streets become rivers of mud when it rains, the floors inside this house were spotless.

Other houses were like this too. Schoolchildren ran along with briefcases strapped to their backs, trucks delivered cooking gas, a few men sat inside a café sipping tea. One man sipped beer. Alcohol is easy to obtain in Turkey, a secular state where 99 percent of the population is Muslim. Yet there is little problem of alcoholism. Crime against persons is infinitesimal. Poverty and illiteracy are watered-down versions of what obtains in Algeria and Egypt (to say nothing of West Africa), making it that much harder for religious extremists to gain a foothold.

My point in bringing up a rather wholesome, crime-free slum is this: its existence demonstrates how formidable is the fabric of which Turkish Muslim culture is made. A culture this strong has the potential to dominate the Middle East once again. Slums are litmus tests for innate cultural strengths and weaknesses. Those peoples whose cultures can harbor extensive slum life without decomposing will be, relatively speaking, the future's winners. Those whose cultures cannot will be the future's victims. Slums—in the sociological sense—do not exist in Turkish cities. The mortar between people and family groups is stronger here than in Africa. Resurgent Islam and Turkic cultural identity have produced a civilization with natural muscle tone. Turks, history's perennial nomads, take disruption in stride.

The future of the Middle East is quietly being written inside the heads of Golden Mountain's inhabitants. Think of an Ottoman military encampment on the eve of the destruction of Greek Constantinople in 1453. That is Golden Mountain. "We brought the village here. But in the village we worked harder—in the field, all day. So we couldn't fast during [the holy month of] Ramadan. Here we fast. Here we are more religious." Aishe Tanrikulu, along with half a dozen other women, was stuffing rice into vine leaves from a crude plastic bowl. She asked me to join her under the shade of a piece of sheet metal. Each of these women had her hair covered by a kerchief. In the city they were encountering television for the first time. "We are traditional, religious people. The programs offend us," Aishe said. Another woman complained about the schools. Though her children had educational options unavailable in the village, they had to compete with wealthier, secular Turks. "The kids from rich families with connections—they get all the places." More opportunities, more tensions, in other words.

Saddam Husseins of the future will have more, not fewer, opportunities. In addition to engendering tribal strife, scarcer resources will place a great strain on many peoples who never had much of a democratic or institutional tradition to begin with.

My guidebook to Golden Mountain was an untypical one: *Tales From the Garbage Hills*, a brutally realistic novel by a Turkish writer,

Latife Tekin, about life in the shantytowns, which in Turkey are called *gecekondus* ("built in a night"). "He listened to the earth and wept unceasingly for water, for work and for the cure of the illnesses spread by the garbage and the factory waste," Tekin writes. In the most revealing passage of *Tales From the Garbage Hills* the squatters are told "about a certain 'Ottoman Empire'... that where they now lived there had once been an empire of this name." This history "confounded" the squatters. It was the first they had heard of it. Though one of them knew "that his grandfather and his dog died fighting the Greeks," nationalism and an encompassing sense of Turkish history are the province of the Turkish middle and upper classes, and of foreigners like me who feel required to have a notion of "Turkey."

But what did the Golden Mountain squatters know about the armies of Turkish migrants that had come before their own—namely, Seljuks and Ottomans? For these recently urbanized peasants, and their counterparts in African, the Arab world, India, and so many other places, the world is new, to adapt V.S. Naipaul's phrase. As Naipaul wrote of urban refugees in *India: A Wounded Civilization,* "They saw themselves at the beginning of things: unaccommodated men making a claim on their land for the first time, and out of chaos evolving their own philosophy of community and self-help. For them the past was dead; they had left it behind in the villages."

Everywhere in the developing world at the turn of the twenty-first century these new men and women, rushing into the cities, are remaking civilizations and redefining their identities in terms of religion and tribal ethnicity which do not coincide with the borders of existing states.

In Turkey several things are happening at once. In 1980, 44 percent of Turks lived in cities; in 1990 it was 61 percent. By the year 2000 the figure is expected to be 67 percent. Villages are emptying out as concentric rings of *gecekondu* developments grow around Turkish cities. This is the real political and demographic revolution in Turkey and elsewhere, and foreign correspondents usually don't write about it.

Whereas rural poverty is age-old and almost a "normal" part of the social fabric, urban poverty is socially destabilizing. As Iran has shown, Islamic extremism is the psychological defense mechanism of many urbanized peasants threatened with the loss of traditions in pseudo-modern cities where their values are under attack, where basic services like water and electricity are unavailable, and where they are assaulted by a physically unhealthy environment. The American ethnologist and orientalist Carleton Stevens Coon wrote in 1951 that Islam "has made possible the optimum survival and happiness of millions of human beings in an increasingly impoverished environment over a fourteen-hundred-year period." Beyond its stark, clearly articulated message, Islam's very militancy makes it attractive to the downtrodden. It is the one religion that is prepared to *fight.* A political era driven by environmental stress, increased cultural sensitivity, unregulated urbanization, and refugee migrations is an era divinely created for the spread and intensification of Islam, already the world's fastest-growing religion. (Though Islam is spreading in West Africa, it is being hobbled by syncretization with animism: this makes new converts less apt to become anti-Western extremists, but it also makes for a weakened version of the faith, which is less effective as an antidote to crime.)

In Turkey, however, Islam is painfully and awkwardly forging a consensus with modernization, a trend that is less apparent in the Arab and Persian worlds (and virtually invisible in Africa). In Iran the oil boom—because it put development and urbanization on a fast track, making the culture shock more intense—fueled the 1978 Islamic Revolution. But Turkey, unlike Iran and the Arab world, has little oil. Therefore its development and urbanization have been more gradual. Islamists have been integrated into the parliamentary system for decades. The tensions I noticed in Golden Mountain are natural, creative ones: the kind immigrants face the world over. While the world has focused on religious perversity in Algeria, a nation rich in natural gas, and in Egypt, parts of whose capital city, Cairo, evince worse crowding than I have seen even in Calcutta, Turkey has been living through the Muslim equivalent of the Protestant Reformation.

Resource distribution is strengthening Turks in another way vis-à-vis Arabs and Persians. Turks may have little oil, but their Anatolian heartland has lots of water—the most important fluid of the twenty-first century. Turkey's Southeast Anatolia Project, involving twenty-two major dams and irrigation systems, is impounding the waters of the Tigris and Euphrates rivers. Much of the water that Arabs and perhaps Israelis will need to drink in the future is controlled by Turks. The project's centerpiece is the mile-wide, sixteenstory Atatürk Dam, upon which are emblazoned the words of modern Turkey's founder: "*Ne Mutlu Turkum Diyene*" ("Lucky is the one who is a Turk").

Unlike Egypt's Aswan High Dam, on the Nile, and Syria's Revolution Dam, on the Euphrates, both of which were built largely by Russians, the Atatürk Dam is a predominantly Turkish affair, with Turkish engineers and companies in charge. On a recent visit my eyes took in the immaculate offices and their gardens, the high-voltage electric grids and phone switching stations, the dizzying sweep of giant humming transformers, the poured-concrete spillways, and the prim unfolding suburbia, complete with schools, for dam employees. The emerging power of the Turks was palpable.

Erduhan Bayindir, the site manger at the dam, told me that "while oil can be shipped abroad to enrich only elites, water has to be spread more evenly within the society.... It is true, we can stop the flow of water into Syria and Iraq for up to eight months without the same water overflowing our dams, in order to regulate their political behavior."

Power is certainly moving north in the Middle East, from the oil fields of Dhahran, on the Persian Gulf, to the water plain of Harran, in southern Anatolia—near the site of the Atatürk Dam. But will the nation-state of Turkey, as presently constituted, be the inheritor of this wealth?

I very much doubt it.

THE LIES OF MAPMAKERS

Whereas West Africa represents the least stable part of political reality outside Homer-Dixon's stretch limo, Turkey, an organic outgrowth of two Turkish empires that ruled Anatolia for 850 years, has been among the most stable. Turkey's borders were established not by colonial powers but in a war of independence, in the early 1920s. Kemal Atatürk provided Turkey with a secular nation-building myth that most Arab and African states, burdened by artificially drawn borders, lack. That lack will leave many Arab states defenseless against a wave of Islam that will eat away at their legitimacy and frontiers in coming years. Yet even as regards Turkey, maps deceive.

It is not only African shantytowns that don't appear on urban maps. Many shantytowns in Turkey and elsewhere are also missing—as are the considerable territories controlled by guerrilla armies and urban mafias. Traveling with Eritrean guerrillas in what, according to the map, was northern Ethiopia, traveling in "northern Iraq" with Kurdish guerrillas, and staying in a hotel in the Caucasus controlled by a local mafia—to say nothing of my experiences in West Africa—led me to develop a healthy skepticism toward maps, which, I began to realize, create a conceptual barrier that prevents us from comprehending the political crack-up just beginning to occur worldwide.

Consider the map of the world, with its 190 or so countries, each signified by a bold and uniform color: this map, with which all of us have grown up, is generally an invention of modernism, specifically of European colonialism. Modernism, in the sense of which I speak, began with the rise of nation-states in Europe and was confirmed by the death of feudalism at the end of the Thirty Years' War—an event that was interposed between the Renaissance and the Enlightenment, which together gave birth to modern science. People were suddenly flush with an enthusiasm to categorize, to define. The map, based on scientific techniques of measurement, offered a way to classify new national organisms, making a jigsaw puzzle of neat pieces without transition zones between them. "Frontier" is itself a modern concept that didn't exist in the feudal mind. And as European nations carved out far-flung domains at the same time that print technology was making the reproduction of maps cheaper, cartography came into its own as a way of creating facts by ordering the way we look at the world.

In his book *Imagined Communities: Reflections on the Origin and Spread of Nationalism*, Benedict Anderson, of Cornell University, demonstrates that the map enabled colonialists to think about their holdings in terms of a "totalizing classificatory grid.... It was bounded, determinate, and therefore—in principle—countable." To the colonialist, country maps were the equivalent of an accountant's ledger books. Maps, Anderson explains, "shaped the grammar" that would make possible such questionable concepts as Iraq, Indonesia, Sierra Leone, and Nigeria. The state, recall, is a purely Western notion, one that until the twentieth century applied to countries covering only three percent of the earth's land area. Nor is the evidence compelling that the state, as a governing ideal, can be successfully transported to areas outside the industrialized world. Even the United Sates of America, in the words of one of our best living poets, Gary Snyder, consists of "arbitrary and inaccurate impositions on what is really here."

Yet this inflexible, artificial reality staggers on, not only in the United Nations but in various geographic and travel publications (themselves by-products of an age of elite touring which colonialism made possible) that still report on and photograph the world according to "country." Newspapers, this magazine, and this writer are not innocent of the tendency.

According to the map, the great hydropower complex emblemized by the Atatürk Dam is situated in Turkey. Forget the map. This southeastern region of Turkey is populated almost completely by Kurds. About half of the world's 20 million Kurds live in "Turkey." The Kurds are predominant in an ellipse of territory that overlaps not only with Turkey but also with Iraq, Iran, Syria, and the former Soviet Union. The Western-enforced Kurdish enclave in northern Iraq, a consequence of the 1991 Gulf War, has already exposed the fictitious nature of that supposed nation-state.

The savagery of the fighting points to a truth that we lack the stomach to contemplate: A large number of people on this planet, to whom the comfort and stability of a middle-class life is utterly unknown, find war and a barracks existence a step up.

On a recent visit to the Turkish-Iranian border, it occurred to me what a risky idea the nation-state is. Here I was on the legal fault line between two clashing civilizations, Turkic and Iranian. Yet the reality was more subtle: as in West Africa, the border was porous and smuggling abounded, but here the people doing the smuggling, on both sides of the border, were Kurds. In such a moonscape, over which peoples have migrated and settled in patterns that obliterate borders, the end of the Cold War will bring on a cruel process of natural selection among existing states. No longer will these states be so firmly propped up by the West or the Soviet Union. Because the Kurds overlap with nearly everybody in the Middle East, on account of their being cheated out of a state in the post–First World War peace treaties, they are emerging, in effect, as *the* natural selector—the ultimate reality check. They have destabilized Iraq and may continue to disrupt states that do not offer them adequate breathing space, while strengthening states that do.

Because the Turks, owing to their water resources, their growing economy, and the social cohesion evinced by the most crime-free slums I have encountered, are on the verge of big-power status, and because the 10 million Kurds within Turkey threaten that status, the outcome of the Turkish-Kurdish dispute will be more critical to the future of the Middle East than the eventual outcome of the recent Israeli-Palestinian agreement.

America's fascination with the Israeli-Palestinian issue, coupled with its lack of interest in the Turkish-Kurdish one, is a function of its own domestic and ethnic obsessions, not of the cartographic reality that is about to transform the Middle East. The diplomatic process involving Israelis and Palestinians will, I believe, have little effect on the early- and mid-twenty-first-century map of the region. Israel, with a 6.6 percent economic growth rate based increasingly on hightech exports, is about to enter Homer-Dixon's stretch limo, fortified by a well-defined political community that is an organic outgrowth of history and ethnicity. Like prosperous and peaceful Japan on the one hand, and war-torn and poverty-wracked Armenia on the other, Israel is a classic national-ethnic organism. Much of the Arab world, however, will undergo alteration, as Islam spreads across artificial frontiers, fueled by mass migrations into the cities and a soaring birth rate of more than 3.2 percent. Seventy percent of the Arab population has been born since 1970—youths with little historical memory of anticolonial independence struggles, postcolonial attempts at nation-building, or any of the Arab-Israeli wars. The most distant recollection of these youths will be the West's humiliation of colonially invented Iraq in 1991. Today seventeen out of twenty-two Arab states have a declining gross national product; in the next twenty years, at current growth rates, the population of many Arab countries will double. These states, like most African ones, will be ungovernable through conventional secular ideologies. The Middle East analyst Christine M. Helms explains.

> Declaring Arab nationalism "bankrupt," the political "disinherited" are not rationalizing the failure of Arabism... or reformulating it. Alternative solutions are not contemplated. They have simply opted for the political paradigm at the other end of the political spectrum with which they are familiar—Islam.

Like the borders of West Africa, the colonial borders of Syria, Iraq, Jordan, Algeria, and other Arab states are often contrary to cultural and political reality. As state control mechanisms wither in the face of environmental and demographic stress, "hard" Islamic city-states or shantytown-states are likely to emerge. The fiction that the impoverished city of Algiers, on the Mediterranean, controls Tamanrasset, deep in the Algerian Sahara, cannot obtain forever. Whatever the outcome of the peace process, Israel is destined to be a Jewish ethnic fortress amid a vast and volatile realm of Islam. In that realm, the violent youth culture of the Gaza shantytowns may be indicative of the coming era.

The destiny of Turks and Kurds is far less certain, but far more relevant to the kind of map that will explain our future world. The Kurds suggest a geographic reality that cannot be shown in two-dimensional space. The issue in Turkey is not simply a matter of giving autonomy or even independence to Kurds in the southeast. This isn't the Balkans or the Caucasus, where regions are merely subdividing into smaller units, Abkhazia breaking off from Georgia, and so on. Federalism is not the answer. Kurds are found everywhere in Turkey, including the shanty districts of Istanbul and Ankara. Turkey's problem is that its Anatolian land mass is the home of two cultures and languages, Turkish and Kurdish. Identity in Turkey, as in India, Africa, and elsewhere, is more complex and subtle than conventional cartography can display.

A NEW KIND OF WAR

To Appreciate fully the political and cartographic implications of postmodernism—an epoch of themeless juxtapositions, in which the classificatory grid of nation-states is going to be replaced by a jagged-glass pattern of city-states, shanty-states, nebulous and anarchic regionalisms—it is necessary to consider, finally, the whole question of war.

"Oh, what a relief to fight, to fight enemies who defend themselves, enemies who are awake!" André Malraux wrote in *Man's Fate*. I cannot think of a more suitable battle cry for many combatants in the early decades of the twenty-first century. The intense savagery of the fighting in such diverse cultural settings as Liberia, Bosnia, the Caucasus, and Sri Lanka—to say nothing of what obtains in American inner cities—indicates something very troubling that those of us inside the stretch limo, concerned with issues like middle-class entitlements and the future of interactive cable television, lack the stomach to contemplate. It is this: a large number of people on this planet, to whom the comfort and stability of a middle-class life is utterly unknown, find war and a barracks existence a step up rather than a step down.

"Just as it makes no sense to ask 'why people eat' or 'what they sleep for,'" writes Martin van Creveld, a military historian at the Hebrew University in Jerusalem, in *The Transformation of War*, "so fighting in many ways is not a means but an end. Throughout history, for every person who has expressed his horror of war there is another who found in it the most marvelous of all the experiences that are vouchsafed to man, even to the point that he later spent a lifetime boring his descendants by recounting his exploits." When I asked Pentagon officials about the nature of war in the twenty-first century, the answer I frequently got was "Read Van Creveld." The top brass are enamored of this historian not because his writings justify their existence but, rather, the opposite: Van Creveld warns them that huge state military machines like the Pentagon's are dinosaurs about to go extinct, and that something far more terrible awaits us.

The degree to which Van Creveld's *Transformation of War* complements Homer-Dixon's work on the environment, Huntington's thoughts on cultural clash, my own realizations in traveling by foot, bus, and bush taxi in more than sixty countries, and America's sobering comeuppances in intractable-culture zones like Haiti and Somalia is startling. The book begins by demolishing the notion that men don't like to fight. "By compelling the senses to focus themselves on the here and now," Van Creveld writes, war "can cause a man to take his leave of them." As anybody who has had experience with Chetniks in Serbia, "technicals" in Somalia, Tontons Macoutes in Haiti, or soldiers in Sierra Leone can tell you, in places where the Western Enlightenment has not penetrated and where there has always been mass poverty, people find liberation in violence. In Afghanistan and elsewhere, I vicariously experienced this phenomenon: worrying about mines and ambushes frees you from worrying about mundane details of daily existence. If my own experience is too subjective, there is a wealth of data showing the sheer frequency of war, especially in the developing world since the Second World War. Physical aggression is a part of being human. Only when people attain a certain economic, educational, and cultural standard is this trait tranquilized. In light of the fact that 95 percent of the earth's population growth will be in the poorest areas of the globe, the question is not whether there will be war (there will be a lot of it) but what kind of war. And who will fight whom?

Debunking the great military strategist Carl von Clausewitz, Van Creveld, who may be the most original thinker on war since that early-nineteenth-century Prussian, writes, "Clausewitz's ideas ... were wholly rooted in the fact that, ever since 1648, war had been waged overwhelmingly by states." But, as Van Creveld explains, the period of nation-states and, therefore, of state conflict is now ending, and with it the clear "threefold division into government, army, and people" which state-directed wars enforce. Thus, to see the future, the first step is to look back to the past immediately prior to the birth of modernism—the wars in medieval Europe which began during the Reformation and reached their culmination in the Thirty Years' War.

Van Creveld writes,

> In all these struggles political, social, economic, and religious motives were hopelessly entangled. Since this was an age when armies consisted of mercenaries, all were also attended by swarms of military entrepreneurs.... Many of them paid little but lip service to the organizations for whom they had contracted to fight. Instead, they robbed the countryside on their own behalf....
>
> Given such conditions, any fine distinctions... between armies on the one hand and peoples on the other were bound to break down. Engulfed by war, civilians suffered terrible atrocities.

Back then, in other words, there was no "politics" as we have come to understand the term, just as there is less and less "politics" today in Liberia, Sierra Leone, Somalia, Sri Lanka, the Balkans, and the Caucasus, among other places.

Because, as Van Creveld notes, the radius of trust within tribal societies is narrowed to one's immediate family and guerrilla comrades, truces arranged with one Bosnian commander, say may be broken immediately by another Bosnian commander. The plethora of short-lived ceasefires in the Balkans and the Caucasus constitute proof that we are no longer in a world where the old rules of state warfare apply. More evidence is provided by the destruction of medieval monuments in the Croatian port of Dubrovnik: when cultures, rather than states, fight, then cultural and religious monuments are weapons of war, making them fair game.

Also, war-making entities will no longer be restricted to a specific territory. Loose and shadowy organisms such as Islamic terrorist organizations suggest why borders will mean increasingly little and sedimentary layers of tribalistic identity and control will mean more. "From the vantage point of the present, there appears every prospect that religious ... fanaticisms will play a larger role in the motivation of armed conflict" in the West than at any time "for the last 300 years," Van Creveld writes. This is why analysts like Michael Vlahos are closely monitoring religious cults. Vlahos says, "An ideology that challenges us may not take familiar form, like the old Nazis or Commies. It may not even engage us initially in ways that fit old threat markings." Van Creveld concludes, "Armed conflict will be waged by men on earth, not robots in space. It will have more in common with the struggles of primitive tribes than with large-scale conventional war." While another military historian, John Keegan, in his new book *A History of Warfare*, draws a more benign portrait of primitive man, it is important to point out that what Van Creveld really means is *re-primitivized* man: warrior societies operating at a time of unprecedented resource scarcity and planetary overcrowding.

Van Creveld's pre-Westphalian vision of worldwide low-intensity conflict is not a superficial "back to the future" scenario. First of all, technology will be used toward primitive ends. In Liberia the guerrilla leader Prince Johnson didn't just cut off the ears of President

Samuel Doe before Doe was tortured to death in 1990—Johnson made a video of it, which has circulated throughout West Africa. In December of 1992, when plotters of a failed coup against the Strasser regime in Sierra Leone had their ears cut off at Freetown's Hamilton Beach prior to being killed, it was seen by many to be a copycat execution. Considering, as I've explained earlier, that the Strasser regime is not really a government and that Sierra Leone is not really a nation-state, listen closely to Van Creveld: "Once the legal monopoly of armed force, long claimed by the state, is wrested out of its hands, existing distinctions between war and crime will break down much as is already the case today in … Lebanon, Sri Lanka, El Salvador, Peru, or Colombia."

If crime and war become indistinguishable, then "national defense" may in the future be viewed as a local concept. As crime continues to grow in our cities and the ability of state governments and criminal-justice systems to protect their citizens diminishes, urban crime may, according to Van Creveld, "develop into low-intensity conflict by coalescing along racial, religious, social, and political lines." As small-scale violence multiplies at home and abroad, state armies will continue to shrink, being gradually replaced by a booming private security business, as in West Africa, and by urban mafias, especially in the former communist world, who may be better equipped than municipal police forces to grant physical protection to local inhabitants.

Future wars will be those of communal survival, aggravated or, in many cases, caused by environmental scarcity. These wars will be subnational, meaning that it will be hard for states and local governments to protect their own citizens physically. This is how many states will ultimately die. As state power fades—and with it the state's ability to help weaker groups within society, not to mention other states—peoples and cultures around the world will be thrown back upon their own strengths and weaknesses, with fewer equalizing mechanisms to protect them. Whereas the distant future will probably see the emergence of a racially hybrid, globalized man, the coming decades will see us more aware of our differences than of our similarities. To the average person, political values will mean less, personal security more. The belief that we are all equal is liable to be replaced by the overriding obsession of the ancient Greek travelers: Why the differences between peoples?

THE LAST MAP

In *Geography and the Human Spirit*, Anne Buttimer, a professor at University College, Dublin, recalls the work of an early-nineteenth-century German geographer. Carl Ritter, whose work implied "a divine plan for humanity" based on regionalism and a constant, living flow of forms. The map of the future, to the extent that a map is even possible, will represent a perverse twisting of Ritter's vision. Imagine cartography in three dimensions, as if in a hologram. In this hologram would be the overlapping sediments of group and other identities atop the merely two-dimensional color markings of city-states and the remaining nations, themselves confused in places by shadowy tentacles, hovering overhead, indicating the power of drug cartels, mafias, and private security agencies. Instead of borders, there would be moving "centers" of power, as in the Middle Ages. Many of these layers would be in motion. Replacing fixed and abrupt lines on a flat space would be a shifting pattern of buffer entities, like the Kurdish and Azeri buffer entities between Turkey and Iran, the Turkic Uighur buffer entity between Central Asia and Inner China (itself distinct from coastal China), and the Latino buffer entity replacing a precise U.S.-Mexican border. To this protean cartographic hologram one must add other factors, such as migrations of populations, explosions of birth rates, vectors of disease. Henceforward the map of the world will never be static. This future map—in a sense, the "Last Map"—will be an ever-mutating representation of chaos.

The Indian subcontinent offers examples of what is happening. For different reasons, both India and Pakistan are increasingly dysfunctional. The argument over democracy in these places is less and less relevant to the larger issue of governability. In India's case the question arises, Is one unwieldy bureaucracy in New Delhi the best available mechanism for promoting the lives of 866 million people of diverse languages, religions, and ethnic groups? In 1950, when the Indian population was much less than half as large and nation-building idealism was still strong, the argument for democracy was more impressive than it is now. Given that in 2025 India's population could be close to 1.5 billion, that much of its economy rests on a shrinking natural-resource base, including dramatically declining water levels, and that communal violence and urbanization are spiraling upward, it is difficult to imagine that the Indian state will survive the next century. India's oft-trumpeted Green Revolution has been achieved by overworking its croplands and depleting its watershed. Norman Myers, a British development consultant, worries that Indians have "been feeding themselves today by borrowing against their children's food sources."

Pakistan's problem is more basic still: like much of Africa, the country makes no geographic or demographic sense. It was founded as a homeland for the Muslims of the subcontinent, yet there are more subcontinental Muslims outside Pakistan than within it. Like Yugoslavia, Pakistan is a patchwork of ethnic groups, increasingly in violent conflict with one another. While the Western media gushes over the fact that the country has a woman Prime Minister, Benazir Bhutto, Karachi is becoming a subcontinental version of Lagos. In eight visits to Pakistan, I have never gotten a sense of a cohesive national identity. With as much as 65 percent of its land dependent of intensive irrigation, with wide-scale deforestation, and with a yearly population growth of 2.7 percent (which ensures that the amount of cultivated land per rural inhabitant will plummet), Pakistan is becoming a more and more desperate place. As irrigation in the Indus River basin intensifies to serve two growing populations, Muslim-Hindu strife over falling water tables may be unavoidable.

"India and Pakistan will probably fall apart." Homer-Dixon predicts. "Their secular governments have less and less legitimacy as well as less management ability over people and resources." Rather than one bold line dividing the subcontinent into two parts, the future will likely see a lot of thinner lines and smaller parts, with the ethnic entities of Pakhtunistan and Punjab gradually replacing Pakistan in the space between the Central Asian plateau and the heart of the subcontinent.

None of this even takes into account climatic change, which, if it occurs in the next century, will further erode the capacity of existing states to cope. India, for instance, receives 70 percent of its precipitation from the monsoon cycle, which planetary warming could disrupt.

Not only will the three-dimensional aspects of the Last Map be in constant motion, but its two-dimensional base may change too. The National Academy of Sciences reports that

> as many as one billion people, or 20 per cent of the world's population, live on lands likely to be inundated or dramatically changed by rising waters.... Low-lying countries in the developing world such as Egypt and Bangladesh, where rivers are large and the deltas extensive and densely populated, will be hardest hit.... Where the rivers are dammed, as in the case of the Nile, the effects ... will be especially severe.

Egypt could be where climatic upheaval—to say nothing of the more immediate threat of increasing population—will incite religious upheaval in truly biblical fashion. Natural catastrophes, such as the October, 1992, Cairo earthquake, in which the government failed to deliver relief aid and slum residents were in many instances helped by their local mosques, can only strengthen the position of Islamic factions. In a statement about greenhouse warming which could refer to any of a variety of natural catastrophes, the environmental expert Jessica Tuchman Matthews warns that many of us underestimate the extent to which political systems, in affluent societies as well as in places like Egypt, "depend on the underpinning of natural systems." She adds, "The fact that one can move with ease form Vermont to Miami has nothing to say about the consequences of Vermont acquiring Miami's climate."

Indeed, it is not clear that the United States will survive the next century in exactly its present form. Because America is a multi-ethnic society, the nation-state has always been more fragile here than it is in more homogeneous societies like Germany and Japan. James Kurth, in an article published in *The National Interest* in 1992, explains that whereas nation-state societies tend to be built around a mass-conscription army and a standardized public school system, "multicultural regimes" feature a high-tech, all-volunteer army (and, I would add, private schools that teach competing values), operating in a culture in which the international media and entertainment industry has more influence than the "national political class." In other words, a nation-state is a place where everyone has been educated along similar lines, where people take their cue from national leaders, and where everyone (every male, at least) has gone through the crucible of military service, making patriotism a simpler issue. Writing about his immigrant family in turn-of-the-century Chicago, Saul Bellow states, "The country took us over. It *was* a country then, not a collection of 'cultures.' "

During the Second World War and the decade following it, the United States reached its apogee as a classic nation-state. During the 1960s, as is now clear, America began a slow but unmistakable process of transformation. The signs hardly need belaboring: racial polarity, educational dysfunction, social fragmentation of many and various kinds. William Irwin Thompson, in *Passages About Earth: An Exploration of the New Planetary Culture*, writes, "The educational system that had worked on the Jews or the Irish could no longer work on the blacks; and when Jewish teachers in New York tried to take black children away from their parents exactly in the way they had been taken from theirs, they were shocked to encounter a violent affirmation of negritude."

Issues like West Africa could yet emerge as a new kind of foreign-policy issue, further eroding America's domestic peace. The spectacle of several West African nations collapsing at once could reinforce the worst racial stereotypes here at home. That is another reason why Africa matters. We must not kid ourselves: the sensitivity factor is higher than ever. The Washington, D.C., public school system is already experimenting with an Afrocentric curriculum. Summits between African leaders and prominent African-Americans are becoming frequent, as are Pollyanna-ish prognostications about multiparty elections in Africa that do not factor in crime, surging birth rates, and resource depletion. The Congressional Black Caucus was among those urging U.S. involvement in Somalia and in Haiti. At the *Los Angeles Times* minority staffers have protested against, among other things, what they allege to be the racist tone of the newspaper's Africa coverage, allegations that the editor of the "World Report" section, Dan Fisher, denies, saying essentially that Africa should be viewed through the same rigorous analytical lens as other parts of the world.

Africa may be marginal in terms of conventional late-twentieth-century conceptions of strategy, but in an age of cultural and racial clash, when national defense is increasingly local, Africa's distress will exert a destabilizing influence on the United States.

This and many other factors will make the United States less of a nation than it is today, even as it gains territory following the peaceful dissolution of Canada. Quebec, based on the bedrock of Roman Catholicism and Francophone ethnicity, could yet turn out to be North America's most cohesive and crime-free nation-state. (It may be a smaller Quebec, though, since aboriginal peoples may lop off northern parts of the province.) "Patriotism" will become increasingly regional as people in Alberta and Montana discover that they have far more in common with each other than they do with Ottawa or Washington, and Spanish-speakers in the Southwest discover a greater commonality with Mexico City. (*The Nine Nations of North America,* by Joel Garreau, a book about the continent's regionalization, is more relevant now than when it was published, in 1981.) As Washington's influence wanes, and with it the traditional symbols of American patriotism, North Americans will take psychological refuge in their insulated communities and cultures.

Returning from West Africa last fall was an illuminating ordeal. After leaving Abidjan, my Air Afrique flight landed in Dakar, Senegal, where all passengers had to disembark in order to go through another security check, this one demanded by U.S. authorities before they would permit the flight to set out for New York. Once we were in New York, despite the midnight hour, immigration officials at Kennedy Airport held up disembarkation by conducting quick interrogations of the aircraft's passengers—this was in addition to all the normal immigration and customs procedures. It was apparent that drug smuggling, disease, and other factors had contributed to the toughest security procedures I have ever encountered when returning from overseas.

Then, for the first time in over a month, I spotted businesspeople with attaché cases and laptop computers. When I had left New York for Abidjan, all the businesspeople were boarding planes for Seoul and Tokyo, which departed from gates near Air Afrique's. The only non-Africans off to West Africa had been relief workers in T-shirts and khakis. Although the borders within West Africa are increasingly unreal, those separating West Africa from the outside world are in various ways becoming more impenetrable.

But Afrocentrists are right in one respect: we ignore this dying region at our own risk. When the Berlin Wall was falling, in November of 1989, I happened to be in Kosovo, covering a riot between Serbs and Albanians. The future was in Kosovo, I told myself that night, not in Berlin. The same day that Yitzhak Rabin and Yasser Arafat clasped hands on the White House lawn, my Air Afrique plane was approaching Bamako, Mali, revealing corrugated-zinc shacks at the edge of an expanding desert. The real news wasn't at the White House, I realized. It was right below.

The End of History?

Francis Fukuyama

In watching the flow of events over the past decade or so, it is hard to avoid the feeling that something very fundamental has happened in world history. The past year has seen a flood of articles commemorating the end of the Cold War, and the fact that "peace" seems to be breaking out in many regions of the world. Most of these analyses lack any larger conceptual framework for distinguishing between what is essential and what is contingent or accidental in world history, and are predictably superficial. If Mr. Gorbachev were ousted from the Kremlin or a new Ayatollah proclaimed the millennium from a desolate Middle Eastern capital, these same commentators would scramble to announce the rebirth of a new era of conflict.

And yet, all of these people sense dimly that there is some larger process at work, a process that gives coherence and order to the daily headlines. The twentieth century saw the developed world descend into a paroxysm of ideological violence, as liberalism contended first with the remnants of absolutism, then bolshevism and fascism, and finally an updated Marxism that threatened to lead to the ultimate apocalypse of nuclear war. But the century that began full of self-confidence in the ultimate triumph of Western liberal democracy seems at its close to be returning full circle to where it started: not to an "end of ideology" or a

---

FRANCIS FUKUYAMA is deputy director of the State Department's policy planning staff and former analyst at the RAND Corporation. This article is based on a lecture presented at the University of Chicago's John M. Olin Center for Inquiry Into the Theory and Practice of Democracy. The author would like to pay special thanks to the Olin Center and to Nathan Tarcov and Allan Bloom for their support in this and many earlier endeavors. The opinions expressed in this article do not reflect those of the RAND Corporation or of any agency of the U.S. government.

---

convergence between capitalism and socialism, as earlier predicted, but to an unabashed victory of economic and political liberalism.

The triumph of the West, of the Western *idea*, is evident first of all in the total exhaustion of viable systematic alternatives to Western liberalism. In the past decade, there have been unmistakable changes in the intellectual climate of the world's two largest communist countries, and the beginnings of significant reform movements in both. But this phenomenon extends beyond high politics and it can be seen also in the ineluctable spread of consumerist Western culture in such diverse contexts as the peasants' markets and color television sets now omnipresent throughout China, the cooperative restaurants and clothing stores opened in the past year in Moscow, the Beethoven piped into Japanese department stores, and the rock music enjoyed alike in Prague, Rangoon, and Tehran.

What we may be witnessing is not just the end of the Cold War, or the passing of a particular period of postwar history, but the end of history as such: that is, the end point of mankind's ideological evolution and the universalization of Western liberal democracy as the final form of human government. This is not to say that there will no longer be events to fill the pages of *Foreign Affairs*'s yearly summaries of international relations, for the victory of liberalism has occurred primarily in the realm of ideas or consciousness and is as yet incomplete in the real or material world. But there are powerful reasons for believing that it is the ideal that will govern the material world *in the long run*. To understand how this is so, we must first consider some theoretical issues concerning the nature of historical change.

I

The notion of the end of history is not an original one. Its best known propagator was Karl Marx, who believed that the direction of historical development was a purposeful one determined by the interplay of material forces, and would come to an end only with the achievement of a communist utopia that would finally resolve all prior contradictions. But the concept of history as a dialectical process with a beginning, a middle, and an end was borrowed by Marx from his great German predecessor, Georg Wilhelm Friedrich Hegel.

For better or worse, much of Hegel's historicism has become part of our contemporary intellectual baggage. The notion that mankind has progressed through a series of primitive stages of consciousness on his path to the present, and that these stages corresponded to concrete forms of social organization, such as tribal, slave-owning, theocratic, and finally democratic-egalitarian societies, has become inseparable from the modern understanding of man. Hegel was the first philosopher to speak the language of modern social science, insofar as man for him was the product of his concrete historical and social environment and not, as earlier natural right theorists would have it, a collection of more or less fixed "natural" attributes. The mastery and transformation of man's natural environment through the application of science and technology was originally not a Marxist concept, but a Hegelian one. Unlike later historicists whose historical relativism degenerated into relativism *tout court*, however, Hegel believed that history culminated in an absolute moment—a moment in which a final, rational form of society and state became victorious.

It is Hegel's misfortune to be known now primarily as Marx's precursor, and it is our misfortune that few of us are familiar with Hegel's work from direct study, but only as it has been filtered through the distorting lens of Marxism. In France, however, there has been an effort to save Hegel from his Marxist interpreters and to resurrect him as the philosopher who most correctly speaks to our time. Among those modern French interpreters of Hegel, the greatest was certainly Alexandre Kojève, a brilliant Russian emigre who taught a highly influential series of seminars in Paris in the 1930's at the *Ecole Practique des Hautes Etudes*.[1] While largely unknown in the United States, Kojève had a major impact on the intellectual life of the continent. Among his students ranged such future luminaries as Jean-Paul Sartre on the Left and Raymond Aron on the Right; postwar existentialism borrowed many of its basic categories from Hegel via Kojève.

[1]Kojève's best-known work is his *Introduction à la lecture de Hegel* (Paris: Editions Gallimard, 1947), which is a transcript of the *Ecole Practique* lectures from the 1930's. This book is available in English entitled *Introduction to the Reading of Hegel* arranged by Raymond Queneau, edited by Allan Bloom, and translated by James Nichols (New York: Basic Books, 1969).

Kojève sought to resurrect the Hegel of the *Phenomenology of Mind*, the Hegel who proclaimed history to be at an end in 1806. For as early as this Hegel saw in Napoleon's defeat of the Prussian monarchy at the Battle of Jena the victory of the ideals of the French Revolution, and the imminent universalization of the state incorporating the principles of liberty and equality. Kojève, far from rejecting Hegel in light of the turbulent events of the next century and a half, insisted that the latter had been essentially correct.[2] The Battle of Jena marked the end of history because it was at that point that the *vanguard* of humanity (a term quite familiar to Marxists) actualized the principles of the French Revolution. While there was considerable work to be done after 1806—abolishing slavery and the slave trade, extending the franchise to workers, women, blacks, and other racial minorities, etc.—the basic *principles* of the liberal democratic state could not be improved upon. The two world wars in this century and their attendant revolutions and upheavals simply had the effect of extending those principles spatially, such that the various provinces of human civilization were brought up to the level of its most advanced outposts, and of forcing those societies in Europe and North America at the vanguard of civilization to implement their liberalism more fully.

The state that emerges at the end of history is liberal insofar as it recognizes and protects through a system of law man's universal right to freedom, and democratic insofar as it exists only with the consent of the governed. For Kojève, this so-called "universal homogenous state" found real-life embodiment in the countries of postwar Western Europe—precisely those flabby, prosperous, self-satisfied, inward-looking, weak-willed states whose grandest project was nothing more heroic than the creation of the Common Market.[3] But this was only to be expected. For human history and the conflict that characterized it was based on the existence of "contradictions": primitive

[2]In this respect Kojève stands in sharp contrast to contemporary German interpreters of Hegel like Herbert Marcuse who, being more sympathetic to Marx, regarded Hegel ultimately as an historically bound and incomplete philosopher.

[3]Kojève alternatively identified the end of history with the postwar "American way of life," toward which he thought the Soviet Union was moving as well.

man's quest for mutual recognition, the dialectic of the master and slave, the transformation and mastery of nature, the struggle for the universal recognition of rights, and the dichotomy between proletarian and capitalist. But in the universal homogenous state, all prior contradictions are resolved and all human needs are satisfied. There is no struggle or conflict over "large" issues, and consequently no need for generals or statesmen; what remains is primarily economic activity. And indeed, Kojève's life was consistent with his teaching. Believing that there was no more work for philosophers as well, since Hegel (correctly understood) had already achieved absolute knowledge, Kojève left teaching after the war and spent the remainder of his life working as a bureaucrat in the European Economic Community, until his death in 1968.

To his contemporaries at mid-century, Kojève's proclamation of the end of history must have seemed like the typical eccentric solipsism of a French intellectual, coming as it did on the heels of World War II and at the very height of the Cold War. To comprehend how Kojève could have been so audacious as to assert that history has ended, we must first of all understand the meaning of Hegelian idealism.

II

For Hegel, the contradictions that drive history exist first of all in the realm of human consciousness, i.e. on the level of ideas[4]—not the trivial election year proposals of American politicians, but ideas in the sense of large unifying world views that might best be understood under the rubric of ideology. Ideology in this sense is not restricted to the secular and explicit political doctrines we usually associate with the term, but can include religion, culture, and the complex of moral values underlying any society as well.

Hegel's view of the relationship between the ideal and the real or material worlds was an extremely complicated one, beginning with the

[4]This notion was expressed in the famous aphorism from the preface to the *Philosophy of History* to the effect that "everything that is rational is real, and everything that is real is rational."

fact that for him the distinction between the two was only apparent.[5] He did not believe that the real world conformed or could be made to conform to ideological preconceptions of philosophy professors in any simple-minded way, or that the "material" world could not impinge on the ideal. Indeed, Hegel the professor was temporarily thrown out of work as a result of a very material event, the Battle of Jena. But while Hegel's writing and thinking could be stopped by a bullet from the material world, the hand on the trigger of the gun was motivated in turn by the ideas of liberty and equality that had driven the French Revolution.

For Hegel, all human behavior in the material world, and hence all human history, is rooted in a prior state of consciousness—an idea similar to the one expressed by John Maynard Keynes when he said that the views of men of affairs were usually derived from defunct economists and academic scribblers of earlier generations. This consciousness may not be explicit and self-aware, as are modern political doctrines, but may rather take the form of religion or simple cultural or moral habits. And yet this realm of consciousness *in the long run* necessarily becomes manifest in the material world, indeed creates the material world in its own image. Consciousness is cause and not effect, and can develop autonomously from the material world; hence the real subtext underlying the apparent jumble of current events is the history of ideology.

Hegel's idealism has fared poorly at the hands of later thinkers. Marx reversed the priority of the real and the ideal completely, relegating the entire realm of consciousness—religion, art, culture, philosophy itself—to a "superstructure" that was determined entirely by the prevailing material mode of production. Yet another unfortunate legacy of Marxism is our tendency to retreat into materialist or utilitarian explanations of political or historical phenomena, and our disinclination to believe in the autonomous power of ideas. A recent example of this is Paul Kennedy's hugely successful *The Rise and Fall of the Great Powers*, which ascribes the decline of great powers to simple

[5]Indeed, for Hegel the very dichotomy between the ideal and material worlds was itself only an apparent one that was ultimately overcome by the self-conscious subject; in his system, the material world is itself only an aspect of mind.

economic overextension. Obviously, this is true on some level: an empire whose economy is barely above the level of subsistence cannot bankrupt its treasury indefinitely. But whether a highly productive modern industrial society chooses to spend 3 or 7 percent of its GNP on defense rather than consumption is entirely a matter of that society's political priorities, which are in turn determined in the realm of consciousness.

The materialist bias of modern thought is characteristic not only of people on the Left who may be sympathetic to Marxism, but of many passionate anti-Marxists as well. Indeed, there is on the Right what one might label the *Wall Street Journal* school of deterministic materialism that discounts the importance of ideology and culture and sees man as essentially a rational, profit-maximizing individual. It is precisely this kind of individual and his pursuit of material incentives that is posited as the basis for economic life as such in economic textbooks.[6] One small example will illustrate the problematic character of such materialist views.

Max Weber begins his famous book, *The Protestant Ethic and the Spirit of Capitalism*, by noting the different economic performance of Protestant and Catholic communities throughout Europe and America, summed up in the proverb that Protestants eat well while Catholics sleep well. Weber notes that according to any economic theory that posited man as a rational profit-maximizer, raising the piece-work rate should increase labor productivity. But in fact, in many traditional peasant communities, raising the piece-work rate actually had the opposite effect of *lowering* labor productivity: at the higher rate, a peasant accustomed to earning two and one-half marks per day found he could earn the same amount by working less, and did so because he valued leisure more than income. The choices of leisure over income, or of the militaristic life of the Spartan hoplite over the wealth of the Athenian trader, or even the ascetic life of the early capitalist entrepreneur over that of a traditional leisured aristocrat, cannot possibly be explained by the impersonal working of material forces,

---

[6]In fact, modern economists, recognizing that man does not always behave as a *profit*-maximizer, posit a "utility" function, utility being either income or some other good that can be maximized: leisure, sexual satisfaction, or the pleasure of philosophizing. That profit must be replaced with a value like utility indicates the cogency of the idealist perspective.

but come preeminently out of the sphere of consciousness—what we have labeled here broadly as ideology. And indeed, a central theme of Weber's work was to prove that contrary to Marx, the material mode of production, far from being the "base," was itself a "superstructure" with roots in religion and culture, and that to understand the emergence of modern capitalism and the profit motive one had to study their antecedents in the realm of the spirit.

As we look around the contemporary world, the poverty of materialist theories of economic development is all too apparent. The *Wall Street Journal* school of deterministic materialism habitually points to the stunning economic success of Asia in the past few decades as evidence of the viability of free market economics, with the implication that all societies would see similar development were they simply to allow their populations to pursue their material self-interest freely. Surely free markets and stable political systems are a necessary precondition to capitalist economic growth. But just as surely the cultural heritage of those Far Eastern societies, the ethic of work and saving and family, a religious heritage that does not, like Islam, place restrictions on certain forms of economic behavior, and other deeply ingrained moral qualities, are equally important in explaining their economic performance.[7] And yet the intellectual weight of materialism is such that not a single respectable contemporary theory of economic development addresses consciousness and culture seriously as the matrix within which economic behavior is formed.

Failure to understand that the roots of economic behavior lie in the realm of consciousness and culture leads to the common mistake of attributing material causes to phenomena that are essentially ideal in nature. For example, it is commonplace in the West to interpret the reform movements first in China and most recently in the Soviet Union as the victory of the material over the ideal—that is, a recognition that ideological incentives could not replace material ones in stimulating a highly productive modern economy, and that if one

---

[7]One need look no further than the recent performance of Vietnamese immigrants in the U.S. school system when compared to their black or Hispanic classmates to realize that culture and consciousness are absolutely crucial to explain not only economic behavior but virtually every other important aspect of life as well.

wanted to prosper one had to appeal to baser forms of self-interest. But the deep defects of socialist economies were evident thirty or forty years ago to anyone who chose to look. Why was it that these countries moved away from central planning only in the 1980's? The answer must be found in the consciousness of the elites and leaders ruling them, who decided to opt for the "Protestant" life of wealth and risk over the "Catholic" path of poverty and security.[8] That change was in no way made inevitable by the material conditions in which either country found itself on the eve of the reform, but instead came about as the result of the victory of one idea over another.[9]

For Kojève, as for all good Hegelians, understanding the underlying processes of history requires understanding developments in the realm of consciousness or ideas, since consciousness will ultimately remake the material world in its own image. To say that history ended in 1806 meant that mankind's ideological evolution ended in the ideals of the French or American Revolutions: while particular regimes in the real world might not implement these ideals fully, their theoretical truth is absolute and could not be improved upon. Hence it did not matter to Kojève that the consciousness of the postwar generation of Europeans had not been universalized throughout the world; if ideological development had in fact ended, the homogenous state would eventually become victorious throughout the material world.

I have neither the space nor, frankly, the ability to defend in depth Hegel's radical idealist perspective. The issue is not whether Hegel's system was right, but whether his perspective might uncover the problematic nature of many materialist explanations we often take for granted. This is not to deny the role of material factors as such. To

---

[8]I understand that a full explanation of the origins of the reform movements in China and Russia is a good deal more complicated than this simple formula would suggest. The Soviet reform, for example, was motivated in good measure by Moscow's sense of *insecurity* in the technological-military realm. Nonetheless, neither country on the eve of its reforms was in such a state of *material* crisis that one could have predicted the surprising reform paths ultimately taken.

[9]It is still not clear whether the Soviet peoples are as "Protestant" as Gorbachev and will follow him down that path.

a literal-minded idealist, human society can be built around any arbitrary set of principles regardless of their relationship to the material world. And in fact men have proven themselves able to endure the most extreme material hardships in the name of ideas that exist in the realm of the spirit alone, be it the divinity of cows or the nature of the Holy Trinity.[10]

But while man's very perception of the material world is shaped by his historical consciousness of it, the material world can clearly affect in return the viability of a particular state of consciousness. In particular, the spectacular abundance of advanced liberal economies and the infinitely diverse consumer culture made possible by them seem to both foster and preserve liberalism in the political sphere. I want to avoid the materialist determinism that says that liberal economics inevitably produces liberal politics, because I believe that both economics and politics presuppose an autonomous prior state of consciousness that makes them possible. But that state of consciousness that permits the growth of liberalism seems to stabilize in the way one would expect at the end of history if it is underwritten by the abundance of a modern free market economy. We might summarize the content of the universal homogenous state as liberal democracy in the political sphere combined with easy access to VCRs and stereos in the economic.

III

Have we in fact reached the end of history? Are there, in other words, any fundamental "contradictions" in human life that cannot be resolved in the context of modern liberalism, that would be resolvable by an alternative political-economic structure? If we accept the

---

[10]The internal politics of the Byzantine Empire at the time of Justinian revolved around a conflict between the so-called monophysites and monothelites, who believed that the unity of the Holy Trinity was alternatively one of nature or of will. This conflict corresponded to some extent to one between proponents of different racing teams in the Hippodrome in Byzantium and led to a not insignificant level of political violence. Modern historians would tend to seek the roots of such conflicts in antagonisms between social classes or some other modern economic category, being unwilling to believe that men would kill each other over the nature of the Trinity.

idealist premises laid out above, we must seek an answer to this question in the realm of ideology and consciousness. Our task is not to answer exhaustively the challenges to liberalism promoted by every crackpot messiah around the world, but only those that are embodied in important social or political forces and movements, and which are therefore part of world history. For our purposes, it matters very little what strange thoughts occur to people in Albania or Burkina Faso, for we are interested in what one could in some sense call the common ideological heritage of mankind.

In the past century, there have been two major challenges to liberalism, those of fascism and of communism. The former[11] saw the political weakness, materialism, anomie, and lack of community of the West as fundamental contradictions in liberal societies that could only be resolved by a strong state that forged a new "people" on the basis of national exclusiveness. Fascism was destroyed as a living ideology by World War II. This was a defeat, of course, on a very material level, but it amounted to a defeat of the idea as well. What destroyed fascism as an idea was not universal moral revulsion against it, since plenty of people were willing to endorse the idea as long as it seemed the wave of the future, but its lack of success. After the war, it seemed to most people that German fascism as well as its other European and Asian variants were bound to self-destruct. There was no material reason why new fascist movements could not have sprung up again after the war in other locales, but for the fact that expansionist ultranationalism, with its promise of unending conflict leading to disastrous military defeat, had completely lost its appeal. The ruins of the Reich chancellory as well as the atomic bombs dropped on Hiroshima and Nagasaki killed this ideology on the level of consciousness as well as materially, and all of the proto-fascist

[11]I am not using the term "fascism" here in its most precise sense, fully aware of the frequent misuse of this term to denounce anyone to the right of the user. "Fascism" here denotes any organized ultra-nationalist movement with universalistic pretensions—not universalistic with regard to its nationalism, of course, since the latter is exclusive by definition, but with regard to the movement's belief in its right to rule other people. Hence Imperial Japan would qualify as fascist while former strongman Stoessner's Paraguay or Pinochet's Chile would not. Obviously fascist ideologies cannot be universalistic in the sense of Marxism or liberalism, but the structure of the doctrine can be transferred from country to country.

movements spawned by the German and Japanese examples like the Peronist movement in Argentina or Subhas Chandra Bose's Indian National Army withered after the war.

The ideological challenge mounted by the other great alternative to liberalism, communism, was far more serious. Marx, speaking Hegel's language, asserted that liberal society contained a fundamental contradiction that could not be resolved within its context, that between capital and labor, and this contradiction has constituted the chief accusation against liberalism ever since. But surely, the class issue has actually been successfully resolved in the West. As Kojève (among others) noted, the egalitarianism of modern America represents the essential achievement of the classless society envisioned by Marx. This is not to say that there are not rich people and poor people in the United States, or that the gap between them has not grown in recent years. But the root causes of economic inequality do not have to do with the underlying legal and social structure of our society, which remains fundamentally egalitarian and moderately redistributionist, so much as with the cultural and social characteristics of the groups that make it up, which are in turn the historical legacy of premodern conditions. Thus black poverty in the United States is not the inherent product of liberalism, but is rather the "legacy of slavery and racism" which persisted long after the formal abolition of slavery.

As a result of the receding of the class issue, the appeal of communism in the developed Western world, it is safe to say, is lower today than any time since the end of the First World War. This can be measured in any number of ways: in the declining membership and electoral pull of the major European communist parties, and their overtly revisionist programs; in the corresponding electoral success of conservative parties from Britain and Germany to the United States and Japan, which are unabashedly pro-market and anti-statist; and in an intellectual climate whose most "advanced" members no longer believe that bourgeois society is something that ultimately needs to be overcome. This is not to say that the opinions of progressive intellectuals in Western countries are not deeply pathological in any number of ways. But those who believe that the future must inevitably be socialist tend to be very old, or very marginal to the real political discourse of their societies.

One may argue that the socialist alternative was never terribly plausible for the North Atlantic world, and was sustained for the last several decades primarily by its success outside of this region. But it is precisely in the non-European world that one is most struck by the occurrence of major ideological transformations. Surely the most remarkable changes have occurred in Asia. Due to the strength and adaptability of the indigenous cultures there, Asia became a battleground for a variety of imported Western ideologies early in this century. Liberalism in Asia was a very weak reed in the period after World War I; it is easy today to forget how gloomy Asia's political future looked as recently as ten or fifteen years ago. It is easy to forget as well how momentous the outcome of Asian ideological struggles seemed for world political development as a whole.

The first Asian alternative to liberalism to be decisively defeated was the fascist one represented by Imperial Japan. Japanese fascism (like its German version) was defeated by the force of American arms in the Pacific war, and liberal democracy was imposed on Japan by a victorious United States. Western capitalism and political liberalism when transplanted to Japan were adapted and transformed by the Japanese in such a way as to be scarcely recognizable.[12] Many Americans are now aware that Japanese industrial organization is very different from that prevailing in the United States or Europe, and it is questionable what relationship the factional maneuvering that takes place with the governing Liberal Democratic Party bears to democracy. Nonetheless, the very fact that the essential elements of economic and political liberalism have been so successfully grafted onto uniquely Japanese traditions and institutions guarantees their survival in the long run. More important is the contribution that Japan has made in turn to world history by following in the footsteps of the United States to create a truly universal consumer culture that has become both a symbol and an underpinning of the universal homogenous state. V.S. Naipaul travelling in Khomeini's Iran shortly

[12]I use the example of Japan with some caution, since Kojève late in his life came to conclude that Japan, with its culture based on purely formal arts, proved that the universal homogenous state was not victorious and that history had perhaps not ended. See the long note at the end of the second edition of *Introduction à la Lecture de Hegel*, 462–3.

after the revolution noted the omnipresent signs advertising the products of Sony, Hitachi, and JVC, whose appeal remained virtually irresistible and gave the lie to the regime's pretensions of restoring a state based on the rule of the *Shariah*. Desire for access to the consumer culture, created in large measure by Japan, has played a crucial role in fostering the spread of economic liberalism throughout Asia, and hence in promoting political liberalism as well.

The economic success of the other newly industrializing countries (NICs) in Asia following on the example of Japan is by now a familiar story. What is important from a Hegelian standpoint is that political liberalism has been following economic liberalism, more slowly than many had hoped but with seeming inevitability. Here again we see the victory of the idea of the universal homogenous state. South Korea had developed into a modern, urbanized society with an increasingly large and well-educated middle class that could not possibly be isolated from the larger democratic trends around them. Under these circumstances it seemed intolerable to a large part of this population that it should be ruled by an anachronistic military regime while Japan, only a decade or so ahead in economic terms, had parliamentary institutions for over forty years. Even the former socialist regime in Burma, which for so many decades existed in dismal isolation from the larger trends dominating Asia, was buffeted in the past year by pressures to liberalize both its economy and political system. It is said that unhappiness with strongman Ne Win began when a senior Burmese officer went to Singapore for medical treatment and broke down crying when he saw how far socialist Burma had been left behind by its ASEAN neighbors.

But the power of the liberal idea would seem much less impressive if it had not infected the largest and oldest culture in Asia, China. The simple existence of communist China created an alternative pole of ideological attraction, and as such constituted a threat to liberalism. But the past fifteen years have seen an almost total discrediting of Marxism-Leninism as an economic system. Beginning with the famous third plenum of the Tenth Central Committee in 1978, the Chinese Communist party set about decollectivizing agriculture for the 800 million Chinese who still lived in the countryside. The role of the state in agriculture was reduced to that of a tax collector, while production of consumer goods was sharply increased in order to give peasants a taste of the universal homogenous state and thereby an incentive to work. The reform doubled Chinese grain output in only five years, and in the process created for Deng Xiao-ping a solid political base from which he was able to extend the reform to other parts of the economy. Economic statistics do not begin to describe the dynamism, initiative, and openness evident in China since the reform began.

China could not now be described in any way as a liberal democracy. At present, no more than 20 percent of its economy has been marketized, and most importantly it continues to be ruled by a self-appointed Communist party which has given no hint of wanting to devolve power. Deng has made none of Gorbachev's promises regarding democratization of the political system and there is no Chinese equivalent of *glasnost*. The Chinese leadership has in fact been much more circumspect in criticizing Mao and Maoism than Gorbachev with respect to Brezhnev and Stalin, and the regime continues to pay lip service to Marxism-Leninism as its ideological underpinning. But anyone familiar with the outlook and behavior of the new technocratic elite now governing China knows that Marxism and ideological principle have become virtually irrelevant as guides to policy, and that bourgeois consumerism has a real meaning in that country for the first time since the revolution. The various slowdowns in the pace of reform, the campaigns against "spiritual pollution" and crackdowns on political dissent are more properly seen as tactical adjustments made in the process of managing what is an extraordinarily difficult political transition. By ducking the question of political reform while putting the economy on a new footing, Deng has managed to avoid the breakdown of authority that has accompanied Gorbachev's *perestroika*. Yet the pull of the liberal idea continues to be very strong as economic power devolves and the economy becomes more open to the outside world. There are currently over 20,000 Chinese students studying in the U.S. and other Western countries, almost all of them the children of the Chinese elite. It is hard to believe that when they return home to run the country they will be content for China to be the only country in Asia unaffected by the larger democratizing trend. The student demonstrations in Beijing that broke out first in December 1986 and recurred recently on the occasion of Hu Yao-bang's death were only the beginning of what will inevitably be mounting pressure for change in the political system as well.

What is important about China from the standpoint of world history is not the present state of the reform or even its future prospects. The central issue is the fact that the People's Republic of China can no longer act as a beacon for illiberal forces around the world, whether they be guerrillas in some Asian jungle or middle class students in Paris. Maoism, rather than being the pattern for Asia's future, became an anachronism, and it was the mainland Chinese who in fact were decisively influenced by the prosperity and dynamism of their overseas co-ethnics—the ironic ultimate victory of Taiwan.

Important as these changes in China have been, however, it is developments in the Soviet Union—the original "homeland of the world proletariat"—that have put the final nail in the coffin of the Marxist-Leninist alternative to liberal democracy. It should be clear that in terms of formal institutions, not much has changed in the four years since Gorbachev has come to power: free markets and the cooperative movement represent only a small part of the Soviet economy, which remains centrally planned; the political system is still dominated by the Communist party, which has only begun to democratize internally and to share power with other groups; the regime continues to assert that it is seeking only to modernize socialism and that its ideological basis remains Marxism-Leninism; and, finally, Gorbachev faces a potentially powerful conservative opposition that could undo many of the changes that have taken place to date. Moreover, it is hard to be too sanguine about the chances for success of Gorbachev's proposed reforms, either in the sphere of economics or politics. But my purpose here is not to analyze events in the short-term, or to make predictions for policy purposes, but to look at underlying trends in the sphere of ideology and consciousness. And in that respect, it is clear that an astounding transformation has occurred.

Emigres from the Soviet Union have been reporting for at least the last generation now that virtually nobody in that country truly believed in Marxism-Leninism any longer, and that this was nowhere more true than in the Soviet elite, which continued to mouth Marxist slogans out of sheer cynicism. The corruption and decadence of the late Brezhnev-era Soviet state seemed to matter little, however, for as long as the state itself refused to throw into question any of the fundamental principles underlying Soviet society, the system was capable of functioning adequately out of sheer inertia and could even muster some dynamism in the realm of foreign and defense policy. Marxism-Leninism was like a magical incantation which, however absurd and devoid of meaning, was the only common basis on which the elite could agree to rule Soviet society.

What has happened in the four years since Gorbachev's coming to power is a revolutionary assault on the most fundamental institutions and principles of Stalinism, and their replacement by other principles which do not amount to liberalism *per se* but whose only connecting thread is liberalism. This is most evident in the economic sphere, where the reform economists around Gorbachev have become steadily more radical in their support for free markets, to the point where some like Nikolai Shmelev do not mind being compared in public to Milton Friedman. There is a virtual consensus among the currently dominant school of Soviet economists now that central planning and the command system of allocation are the root cause of economic inefficiency, and that if the Soviet system is ever to heal itself, it must permit free and decentralized decision-making with respect to investment, labor, and prices. After a couple of initial years of ideological confusion, these principles have finally been incorporated into policy with the promulgation of new laws on enterprise autonomy, cooperatives, and finally in 1988 on lease arrangements and family farming. There are, of course, a number of fatal flaws in the current implementation of the reform, most notably the absence of a thoroughgoing price reform. But the problem is no longer a *conceptual* one: Gorbachev and his lieutenants seem to understand the economic logic of marketization well enough, but like the leaders of a Third World country facing the IMF, are afraid of the social consequences of ending consumer subsidies and other forms of dependence on the state sector.

In the political sphere, the proposed changes to the Soviet constitution, legal system, and party rules amount to much less than the establishment of a liberal state. Gorbachev has spoken of democratization primarily in the sphere of internal party affairs, and has shown little intention of ending the Communist party's monopoly of power; indeed, the political reform seeks to legitimize and therefore strengthen the CPSU's rule.[13] Nonetheless, the general principles underlying many of the reforms—that the "people" should be truly responsible for their own affairs, that higher political bodies should be answerable to lower ones, and not vice versa, that the rule of law should prevail over arbitrary police actions, with separation of powers and an independent judiciary, that there should be legal protection for property rights, the need for open discussion of public issues and the right of public dissent, the empowering of the Soviets as a forum in which the whole Soviet people can participate, and of a political culture that is more tolerant and pluralistic—come from a source fundamentally alien to the USSR's Marxist-Leninist tradition, even if they are incompletely articulated and poorly implemented in practice.

Gorbachev's repeated assertions that he is doing no more than trying to restore the original meaning of Leninism are themselves a kind of Orwellian doublespeak. Gorbachev and his allies have consistently maintained that intraparty democracy was somehow the essence of Leninism, and that the various liberal practices of open debate, secret ballot elections, and rule of law were all part of the Leninist heritage, corrupted only later by Stalin. While almost anyone would look good compared to Stalin, drawing so sharp a line between Lenin and his successor is questionable. The essence of Lenin's democratic centralism was centralism, not democracy; that is, the absolutely rigid, monolithic, and disciplined dictatorship of a hierarchically organized vanguard Communist party, speaking in the name of the *demos*. All of Lenin's vicious polemics against Karl Kautsky, Rosa Luxemburg, and various other Menshevik and Social Democratic rivals, not to mention his contempt for "bourgeois legality" and freedoms,

---

[13]This is not true in Poland and Hungary, however, whose Communist parties have taken moves toward true power-sharing and pluralism.

centered around his profound conviction that a revolution could not be successfully made by a democratically run organization.

Gorbachev's claim that he is seeking to return to the true Lenin is perfectly easy to understand: having fostered a thorough denunciation of Stalinism and Brezhnevism as the root of the USSR's present predicament, he needs some point in Soviet history on which to anchor the legitimacy of the CPSU's continued rule. But Gorbachev's tactical requirements should not blind us to the fact that the democratizing and decentralizing principles which he has [illegible] both the economic and political spheres are highly [illegible] some of the most fundamental precepts of both [illegible]eninism. Indeed, if the bulk of the present economic [illegible]s were put into effect, it is hard to know how the [illegible] would be more socialist than those of other Western [illegible]ge public sectors.

[illegible]nion could in no way be described as a liberal or [illegible]ry now, nor do I think that it is terribly likely that [illegible]ceed such that the label will be thinkable any time [illegible] near future. But at the end of history it is not necessary that all societies become successful liberal societies, merely that they end their ideological pretensions of representing different and higher forms of human society. And in this respect I believe that something very important has happened in the Soviet Union in the past few years: the criticisms of the Soviet system sanctioned by Gorbachev have been so thorough and devastating that there is very little chance of going back to either Stalinism or Brezhnevism in any simple way. Gorbachev has finally permitted people to say what they had privately understood for many years, namely, that the magical incantations of Marxism-Leninism were nonsense, that Soviet socialism was not superior to the West in any respect but was in fact a monumental failure. The conservative opposition in the USSR, consisting both of simple workers afraid of unemployment and inflation and of party officials fearful of losing their jobs and privileges, is outspoken and may be strong enough to force Gorbachev's ouster in the next few years. But what both groups desire is tradition, order, and authority; they manifest no deep commitment to Marxism-Leninism, except insofar as they have invested much of their own lives in it.[14] For authority to be restored in the Soviet Union after Gorbachev's demolition work, it must be on the basis of some new and vigorous ideology which has not yet appeared on the horizon.

If we admit for the moment that the fascist and communist challenges to liberalism are dead, are there any other ideological competitors left? Or put another way, are there contradictions in liberal society beyond that of class that are not resolvable? Two possibilities suggest themselves, those of religion and nationalism.

The rise of religious fundamentalism in recent years within the Christian, Jewish, and Muslim traditions has been widely noted. One is inclined to say that the revival of religion in some way attests to a broad unhappiness with the impersonality and spiritual vacuity of liberal consumerist societies. Yet while the emptiness at the core of liberalism is most certainly a defect in the ideology—indeed, a flaw that one does not need the perspective of religion to recognize[15]—it is not at all clear that it is remediable through politics. Modern liberalism itself was historically a consequence of the weakness of religiously-based societies which, failing to agree on the nature of the good life, could not provide even the minimal preconditions of peace and stability. In the contemporary world only Islam has offered a theocratic state as a political alternative to both liberalism and communism. But the doctrine has little appeal for non-Muslims, and it is hard to believe that the movement will take on any universal significance. Other less organized religious impulses have been successfully satisfied within the sphere of personal life that is permitted in liberal societies.

The other major "contradiction" potentially unresolvable by liberalism is the one posed by nationalism and other forms of racial and ethnic consciousness. It is certainly true that a very large degree

[14]This is particularly true of the leading Soviet conservative, former Second Secretary Yegor Ligachev, who has publicly recognized many of the deep defects of the Brezhnev period.

[15]I am thinking particularly of Rousseau and the Western philosophical tradition that flows from him that was highly critical of Lockean or Hobbesian liberalism, though one could criticize liberalism from the standpoint of classical political philosophy as well.

of conflict since the Battle of Jena has had its roots in nationalism. Two cataclysmic world wars in this century have been spawned by the nationalism of the developed world in various guises, and if those passions have been muted to a certain extent in postwar Europe, they are still extremely powerful in the Third World. Nationalism has been a threat to liberalism historically in Germany, and continues to be one in isolated parts of "post-historical" Europe like Northern Ireland.

But it is not clear that nationalism represents an irreconcilable contradiction in the heart of liberalism. In the first place, nationalism is not one single phenomenon but several, ranging from mild cultural nostalgia to the highly organized and elaborately articulated doctrine of National Socialism. Only systematic nationalisms of the latter sort can qualify as a formal ideology on the level of liberalism or communism. The vast majority of the world's nationalist movements do not have a political program beyond the negative desire of independence *from* some other group or people, and do not offer anything like a comprehensive agenda for socio-economic organization. As such, they are compatible with doctrines and ideologies that do offer such agendas. While they may constitute a source of conflict for liberal societies, this conflict does not arise from liberalism itself so much as from the fact that the liberalism in question is incomplete. Certainly a great deal of the world's ethnic and nationalist tension can be explained in terms of peoples who are forced to live in unrepresentative political systems that they have not chosen.

While it is impossible to rule out the sudden appearance of new ideologies or previously unrecognized contradictions in liberal societies, then, the present world seems to confirm that the fundamental principles of socio-political organization have not advanced terribly far since 1806. Many of the wars and revolutions fought since that time have been undertaken in the name of ideologies which claimed to be more advanced than liberalism, but whose pretensions were ultimately unmasked by history. In the meantime, they have helped to spread the universal homogenous state to the point where it could have a significant effect on the overall character of international relations.

IV

What are the implications of the end of history for international relations? Clearly, the vast bulk of the Third World remains very much mired in history, and will be a terrain of conflict for many years to come. But let us focus for the time being on the larger and more developed states of the world who after all account for the greater part of world politics. Russia and China are not likely to join the developed nations of the West as liberal societies any time in the foreseeable future, but suppose for a moment that Marxism-Leninism ceases to be a factor driving the foreign policies of these states—a prospect which, if not yet here, the last few years have made a real possibility. How will the overall characteristics of a de-ideologized world differ from those of the one with which we are familiar at such a hypothetical juncture?

The most common answer is—not very much. For there is a very widespread belief among many observers of international relations that underneath the skin of ideology is a hard core of great power national interest that guarantees a fairly high level of competition and conflict between nations. Indeed, according to one academically popular school of international relations theory, conflict inheres in the international system as such, and to understand the prospects for conflict one must look at the shape of the system—for example, whether it is bipolar or multipolar—rather than at the specific character of the nations and regimes that constitute it. This school in effect applies a Hobbesian view of politics to international relations, and assumes that aggression and insecurity are universal characteristics of human societies rather than the product of specific historical circumstances.

Believers in this line of thought take the relations that existed between the participants in the classical nineteenth century European balance of power as a model for what a de-ideologized contemporary world would look like. Charles Krauthammer, for example, recently explained that if as a result of Gorbachev's reforms the USSR is shorn of Marxist-Leninist ideology, its behavior will revert to that of nineteenth century imperial Russia.[16] While he

[16] See his article, "Beyond the Cold War," *New Republic*, December 19, 1988.

finds this more reassuring than the threat posed by a communist Russia, he implies that there will still be a substantial degree of competition and conflict in the international system, just as there was say between Russia and Britain or Wilhelmine Germany in the last century. This is, of course, a convenient point of view for people who want to admit that something major is changing in the Soviet Union, but do not want to accept responsibility for recommending the radical policy redirection implicit in such a view. But is it true?

In fact, the notion that ideology is a superstructure imposed on a substratum of permanent great power interest is a highly questionable proposition. For the way in which any state defines its national interest is not universal but rests on some kind of prior ideological basis, just as we saw that economic behavior is determined by a prior state of consciousness. In this century, states have adopted highly articulated doctrines with explicit foreign policy agendas legitimizing expansionism, like Marxism-Leninism or National Socialism.

The expansionist and competitive behavior of nineteenth-century European states rested on no less ideal a basis; it just so happened that the ideology driving it was less explicit than the doctrines of the twentieth century. For one thing, most "liberal" European societies were illiberal insofar as they believed in the legitimacy of imperialism, that is, the right of one nation to rule over other nations without regard for the wishes of the ruled. The justifications for imperialism varied from nation to nation, from a crude belief in the legitimacy of force, particularly when applied to non-Europeans, to the White Man's Burden and Europe's Christianizing mission, to the desire to give people of color access to the culture of Rabelais and Molière. But whatever the particular ideological basis, every "developed" country believed in the acceptability of higher civilizations ruling lower ones—including, incidentally, the United States with regard to the Philippines. This led to a drive for pure territorial aggrandizement in the latter half of the century and played no small role in causing the Great War.

The radical and deformed outgrowth of nineteenth-century imperialism was German fascism, an ideology which justified Germany's right not only to rule over non-European peoples, but over *all* non-German ones. But in retrospect it seems that Hitler represented a diseased bypath in the general course of European development, and since his fiery defeat, the legitimacy of any kind of territorial aggrandizement has been thoroughly discredited.[17] Since the Second World War, European nationalism has been defanged and shorn of any real relevance to foreign policy, with the consequence that the nineteenth-century model of great power behavior has become a serious anachronism. The most extreme form of nationalism that any Western European state has mustered since 1945 has been Gaullism, whose self-assertion has been confined largely to the realm of nuisance politics and culture. International life for the part of the world that has reached the end of history is far more preoccupied with economics than with politics or strategy.

The developed states of the West do maintain defense establishments and in the postwar period have competed vigorously for influence to meet a worldwide communist threat. This behavior has been driven, however, by an external threat from states that possess overtly expansionist ideologies, and would not exist in their absence. To take the "neo-realist" theory seriously, one would have to believe that "natural" competitive behavior would reassert itself among the OECD states were Russia and China to disappear from the face of the earth. That is, West Germany and France would arm themselves against each other as they did in the 1930's, Australia and New Zealand would send military advisers to block each others' advances in Africa, and the U.S.-Canadian border would become fortified. Such a prospect is, of course, ludicrous: minus Marxist-Leninist ideology, we are far more likely to see the "Common Marketization" of world politics than the disintegration of the EEC into nineteenth-century competitiveness. Indeed, as our experience in dealing with Europe on matters such as terrorism or Libya prove, they are much further gone than we down the road that denies the legitimacy of the use of force in international politics, even in self-defense.

---

[17]It took European colonial powers like France several years after the war to admit the illegitimacy of their empires, but decolonialization was an inevitable consequence of the Allied victory which had been based on the promise of a restoration of democratic freedoms.

The automatic assumption that Russia shorn of its expansionist communist ideology should pick up where the czars left off just prior to the Bolshevik Revolution is therefore a curious one. It assumes that the evolution of human consciousness has stood still in the meantime, and that the Soviets, while picking up currently fashionable ideas in the realm of economics, will return to foreign policy views a century out of date in the rest of Europe. This is certainly not what happened to China after it began its reform process. Chinese competitiveness and expansionism on the world scene have virtually disappeared: Beijing no longer sponsors Maoist insurgencies or tries to cultivate influence in distant African countries as it did in the 1960's. This is not to say that there are not troublesome aspects to contemporary Chinese foreign policy, such as the reckless sale of ballistic missile technology in the Middle East; and the PRC continues to manifest traditional great power behavior in its sponsorship of the Khmer Rouge against Vietnam. But the former is explained by commercial motives and the latter is a vestige of earlier ideologically-based rivalries. The new China far more resembles Gaullist France than pre-World War I Germany.

The real question for the future, however, is the degree to which Soviet elites have assimilated the consciousness of the universal homogenous state that is post-Hitler Europe. From their writings and from my own personal contacts with them, there is no question in my mind that the liberal Soviet intelligentsia rallying around Gorbachev has arrived at the end-of-history view in a remarkably short time, due in no small measure to the contacts they have had since the Brezhnev era with the larger European civilization around them. "New political thinking," the general rubric for their views, describes a world dominated by economic concerns, in which there are no ideological grounds for major conflict between nations, and in which, consequently, the use of military force becomes less legitimate. As Foreign Minister Shevardnadze put it in mid-1988:

> The struggle between two opposing systems is no longer a determining tendency of the present-day era. At the modern stage, the ability to build up material wealth at an accelerated rate on the basis of front-ranking science and high-level techniques and technology, and to distribute it fairly,

> and through joint efforts to restore and protect the resources necessary for mankind's survival acquires decisive importance.[18]

The post-historical consciousness represented by "new thinking" is only one possible future for the Soviet Union, however. There has always been a very strong current of great Russian chauvinism in the Soviet Union, which has found freer expression since the advent of *glasnost*. It may be possible to return to traditional Marxism-Leninism for a while as a simple rallying point for those who want to restore the authority that Gorbachev has dissipated. But as in Poland, Marxism-Leninism is dead as a mobilizing ideology: under its banner people cannot be made to work harder, and its adherents have lost confidence in themselves. Unlike the propagators of traditional Marxism-Leninism, however, ultra-nationalists in the USSR believe in their Slavophile cause passionately, and one gets the sense that the fascist alternative is not one that has played itself out entirely there.

The Soviet Union, then, is at a fork in the road: it can start down the path that was staked out by Western Europe forty-five years ago, a path that most of Asia has followed, or it can realize its own uniqueness and remain stuck in history. The choice it makes will be highly important for us, given the Soviet Union's size and military strength, for that power will continue to preoccupy us and slow our realization that we have already emerged on the other side of history.

V

The passing of Marxism-Leninism first from China and then from the Soviet Union will mean its death as a living ideology of world historical significance. For while there may be some isolated true believers left in places like Managua, Pyongyang, or Cambridge, Massachusetts, the fact that there is not a single large state in which it is a going concern undermines completely its pretensions to being in the vanguard of human history. And the death of this ideology means

---

[18] *Vestnik Ministerstva Inostrannikh Del SSSR* no. 15 (August 1988), 27–46. "New thinking" does of course serve a propagandistic purpose in persuading Western audiences of Soviet good intentions. But the fact that it is good propaganda does not mean that its formulators do not take many of its ideas seriously.

the growing "Common Marketization" of international relations, and the diminution of the likelihood of large-scale conflict between states.

This does not by any means imply the end of international conflict *per se*. For the world at that point would be divided between a part that was historical and a part that was post-historical. Conflict between states still in history, and between those states and those at the end of history, would still be possible. There would still be a high and perhaps rising level of ethnic and nationalist violence, since those are impulses incompletely played out, even in parts of the post-historical world. Palestinians and Kurds, Sikhs and Tamils, Irish Catholics and Walloons, Armenians and Azeris, will continue to have their unresolved grievances. This implies that terrorism and wars of national liberation will continue to be an important item on the international agenda. But large-scale conflict must involve large states still caught in the grip of history, and they are what appear to be passing from the scene.

The end of history will be a very sad time. The struggle for recognition, the willingness to risk one's life for a purely abstract goal, the worldwide ideological struggle that called forth daring, courage, imagination, and idealism, will be replaced by economic calculation, the endless solving of technical problems, environmental concerns, and the satisfaction of sophisticated consumer demands. In the post-historical period there will be neither art nor philosophy, just the perpetual caretaking of the museum of human history. I can feel in myself, and see in others around me, a powerful nostalgia for the time when history existed. Such nostalgia, in fact, will continue to fuel competition and conflict even in the post-historical world for some time to come. Even though I recognize its inevitability, I have the most ambivalent feelings for the civilization that has been created in Europe since 1945, with its north Atlantic and Asian offshoots. Perhaps this very prospect of centuries of boredom at the end of history will serve to get history started once again.

The Clash of Civilizations?

Samuel P. Huntington

THE NEXT PATTERN OF CONFLICT

WORLD POLITICS IS entering a new phase, and intellectuals have not hesitated to proliferate visions of what it will be—the end of history, the return of traditional rivalries between nation states, and the decline of the nation state from the conflicting pulls of tribalism and globalism, among others. Each of these visions catches aspects of the emerging reality. Yet they all miss a crucial, indeed a central, aspect of what global politics is likely to be in the coming years.

It is my hypothesis that the fundamental source of conflict in this new world will not be primarily ideological or primarily economic. The great divisions among humankind and the dominating source of conflict will be cultural. Nation states will remain the most powerful actors in world affairs, but the principal conflicts of global politics will occur between nations and groups of different civilizations. The clash of civilizations will dominate global politics. The fault lines between civilizations will be the battle lines of the future.

Conflict between civilizations will be the latest phase in the evolution of conflict in the modern world. For a century and a half after the emergence of the modern international system with the Peace of Westphalia, the conflicts of the Western world were largely among

---

SAMUEL P. HUNTINGTON is the Eaton Professor of the Science of Government and Director of the John M. Olin Institute for Strategic Studies at Harvard University. This article is the product of the Olin Institute's project on "The Changing Security Environment and American National Interests."

Reprinted by permission from *Foreign Affairs*, 72:3 (Summer 1993).

princes—emperors, absolute monarchs and constitutional monarchs attempting to expand their bureaucracies, their armies, their mercantilist economic strength and, most important, the territory they ruled. In the process they created nation states, and beginning with the French Revolution the principal lines of conflict were between nations rather than princes. In 1793, as R. R. Palmer put it, "The wars of kings were over; the wars of peoples had begun." This nineteenth-century pattern lasted until the end of World War I. Then, as a result of the Russian Revolution and the reaction against it, the conflict of nations yielded to the conflict of ideologies, first among communism, fascism-Nazism and liberal democracy, and then between communism and liberal democracy. During the Cold War, this latter conflict became embodied in the struggle between the two superpowers, neither of which was a nation state in the classical European sense and each of which defined its identity in terms of its ideology.

These conflicts between princes, nation states and ideologies were primarily conflicts within Western civilization, "Western civil wars," as William Lind has labeled them. This was as true of the Cold War as it was of the world wars and the earlier wars of the seventeenth, eighteenth and nineteenth centuries. With the end of the Cold War, international politics moves out of its Western phase, and its centerpiece becomes the interaction between the West and non-Western civilizations and among non-Western civilizations. In the politics of civilizations, the peoples and governments of non-Western civilizations no longer remain the objects of history as targets of Western colonialism but join the West as movers and shapers of history.

THE NATURE OF CIVILIZATIONS

DURING THE COLD WAR the world was divided into the First, Second and Third Worlds. Those divisions are no longer relevant. It is far more meaningful now to group countries not in terms of their political or economic systems or in terms of their level of economic development but rather in terms of their culture and civilization.

What do we mean when we talk of a civilization? A civilization is a cultural entity. Villages, regions, ethnic groups, nationalities, religious groups, all have distinct cultures at different levels of cultural heterogeneity. The culture of a village in southern Italy may be different from that of a village in northern Italy, but both will share in a common Italian culture that distinguishes them from German villages. European communities, in turn, will share cultural features that distinguish them from Arab or Chinese communities. Arabs, Chinese and Westerners, however, are not part of any broader cultural entity. They constitute civilizations. A civilization is thus the highest cultural grouping of people and the broadest level of cultural identity people have short of that which distinguishes humans from other species. It is defined both by common objective elements, such as language, history, religion, customs, institutions, and by the subjective self-identification of people. People have levels of identity: a resident of Rome may define himself with varying degrees of intensity as a Roman, an Italian, a Catholic, a Christian, a European, a Westerner. The civilization to which he belongs is the broadest level of identification with which he intensely identifies. People can and do redefine their identities and, as a result, the composition and boundaries of civilizations change.

Civilizations may involve a large number of people, as with China ("a civilization pretending to be a state," as Lucian Pye put it), or a very small number of people, such as the Anglophone Caribbean. A civilization may include several nation states, as is the case with Western, Latin American and Arab civilizations, or only one, as is the case with Japanese civilization. Civilizations obviously blend and overlap, and may include subcivilizations. Western civilization has two major variants, European and North American, and Islam has its Arab, Turkic and Malay subdivisions. Civilizations are nonetheless meaningful entities, and while the lines between them are seldom sharp, they are real. Civilizations are dynamic; they rise and fall; they divide and merge. And, as any student of history knows, civilizations disappear and are buried in the sands of time.

Westerners tend to think of nation states as the principal actors in global affairs. They have been that, however, for only a few centuries. The broader reaches of human history have been the history of civilizations. In *A Study of History*, Arnold Toynbee identified 21 major civilizations; only six of them exist in the contemporary world.

WHY CIVILIZATIONS WILL CLASH

CIVILIZATION IDENTITY will be increasingly important in the future, and the world will be shaped in large measure by the interactions among seven or eight major civilizations. These include Western, Confucian, Japanese, Islamic, Hindu, Slavic-Orthodox, Latin American and possibly African civilization. The most important conflicts of the future will occur along the cultural fault lines separating these civilizations from one another.

Why will this be the case?

First, differences among civilizations are not only real; they are basic. Civilizations are differentiated from each other by history, language, culture, tradition and, most important, religion. The people of different civilizations have different views on the relations between God and man, the individual and the group, the citizen and the state, parents and children, husband and wife, as well as differing views of the relative importance of rights and responsibilities, liberty and authority, equality and hierarchy. These differences are the product of centuries. They will not soon disappear. They are far more fundamental than differences among political ideologies and political regimes. Differences do not necessarily mean conflict, and conflict does not necessarily mean violence. Over the centuries, however, differences among civilizations have generated the most prolonged and the most violent conflicts.

> The conflicts of the future will occur along the cultural fault lines separating civilizations.

Second, the world is becoming a smaller place. The interactions between peoples of different civilizations are increasing; these increasing interactions intensify civilization consciousness and awareness of differences between civilizations and commonalities within civilizations. North African immigration to France generates hostility among Frenchmen and at the same time increased receptivity to immigration by "good" European Catholic Poles. Americans react far more negatively to Japanese investment than to larger investments from Canada and European countries. Similarly, as Donald Horowitz has pointed out, "An Ibo may be ... an Owerri Ibo or an Onitsha Ibo in what was the Eastern region of Nigeria. In Lagos, he is simply an Ibo. In London, he is a Nigerian. In New York, he is an African." The interactions among peoples of different civilizations enhance the civilization-consciousness of people that, in turn, invigorates differences and animosities stretching or thought to stretch back deep into history.

Third, the processes of economic modernization and social change throughout the world are separating people from longstanding local identities. They also weaken the nation state as a source of identity. In much of the world religion has moved in to fill this gap, often in the form of movements that are labeled "fundamentalist." Such movements are found in Western Christianity, Judaism, Buddhism and Hinduism, as well as in Islam. In most countries and most religions the people active in fundamentalist movements are young, college-educated, middle-class technicians, professionals and business persons. The "unsecularization of the world," George Weigel has remarked, "is one of the dominant social facts of life in the late twentieth century." The revival of religion, "la revanche de Dieu," as Gilles Kepel labeled it, provides a basis for identity and commitment that transcends national boundaries and unites civilizations.

Fourth, the growth of civilization-consciousness is enhanced by the dual role of the West. On the one hand, the West is at a peak of power. At the same time, however, and perhaps as a result, a return to the roots phenomenon is occurring among non-Western civilizations. Increasingly one hears references to trends toward a turning inward and "Asianization" in Japan, the end of the Nehru legacy and the "Hinduization" of India, the failure of Western ideas of socialism and nationalism and hence "re-Islamization" of the Middle East, and now a debate over Westernization versus Russianization in Boris Yeltsin's country. A West at the peak of its power confronts non-Wests that increasingly have the desire, the will and the resources to shape the world in non-Western ways.

In the past, the elites of non-Western societies were usually the people who were most involved with the West, had been educated at Oxford, the Sorbonne or Sandhurst, and had absorbed Western attitudes and values. At the same time, the populace in non-Western countries often remained deeply imbued with the indigenous culture. Now, however, these relationships are being reversed. A de-Westernization and indigenization of elites is occurring in many non-Western countries at the same time that Western, usually American, cultures, styles and habits become more popular among the mass of the people.

Fifth, cultural characteristics and differences are less mutable and hence less easily compromised and resolved than political and economic ones. In the former Soviet Union, communists can become democrats, the rich can become poor and the poor rich, but Russians cannot become Estonians and Azeris cannot become Armenians. In class and ideological conflicts, the key question was "Which side are you on?" and people could and did choose sides and change sides. In conflicts between civilizations, the question is "What are you?" That is a given that cannot be changed. And as we know, from Bosnia to the Caucasus to the Sudan, the wrong answer to that question can mean a bullet in the head. Even more than ethnicity, religion discriminates sharply and exclusively among people. A person can be half-French and half-Arab and simultaneously even a citizen of two countries. It is more difficult to be half-Catholic and half-Muslim.

Finally, economic regionalism is increasing. The proportions of total trade that were intraregional rose between 1980 and 1989 from 51 percent to 59 percent in Europe, 33 percent to 37 percent in East Asia, and 32 percent to 36 percent in North America. The importance of regional economic blocs is likely to continue to increase in the future. On the one hand, successful economic regionalism will reinforce civilization-consciousness. On the other hand, economic regionalism may succeed only when it is rooted in a common civilization. The European Community rests on the shared foundation of European culture and Western Christianity. The success of the North American Free Trade Area depends on the convergence now underway of Mexican, Canadian and American cultures. Japan, in contrast, faces difficulties in creating a comparable economic entity in East Asia because Japan is a society and civilization unique to itself. However strong the trade and investment links Japan may develop with other East Asian countries, its cultural differences with those countries inhibit and perhaps preclude its promoting regional economic integration like that in Europe and North America.

Common culture, in contrast, is clearly facilitating the rapid expansion of the economic relations between the People's Republic of China and Hong Kong, Taiwan, Singapore and the overseas Chinese communities in other Asian countries. With the Cold War over, cultural commonalities increasingly overcome ideological differences, and mainland China and Taiwan move closer together. If cultural commonality is a prerequisite for economic integration, the principal East Asian economic bloc of the future is likely to be centered on China. This bloc is, in fact, already coming into existence. As Murray Weidenbaum has observed,

> Despite the current Japanese dominance of the region, the Chinese-based economy of Asia is rapidly emerging as a new epicenter for industry, commerce and finance. This strategic area contains substantial amounts of technology and manufacturing capability (Taiwan), outstanding entrepreneurial, marketing and services acumen (Hong Kong), a fine communications network (Singapore), a tremendous pool of financial capital (all three), and very large endowments of land, resources and labor (mainland China).... From Guangzhou to Singapore, from Kuala Lumpur to Manila, this influential network—often based on extensions of the traditional clans—has been described as the backbone of the East Asian economy.[1]

Culture and religion also form the basis of the Economic Cooperation Organization, which brings together ten non-Arab Muslim countries: Iran, Pakistan, Turkey, Azerbaijan, Kazakhstan, Kyrgyzstan, Turkmenistan, Tadjikistan, Uzbekistan and Afghanistan. One impetus to the revival and expansion of this organization, founded originally in the 1960s by Turkey, Pakistan and Iran, is the realization by the leaders of several of these countries that they had no chance of admission to the European Community. Similarly, Caricom, the Central American Common Market and Mercosur rest

[1]Murray Weidenbaum, *Greater China: The Next Economic Superpower?*, St. Louis: Washington University Center for the Study of American Business, Contemporary Issues, Series 57, February 1993, pp. 2-3.

on common cultural foundations. Efforts to build a broader Caribbean-Central American economic entity bridging the Anglo-Latin divide, however, have to date failed.

As people define their identity in ethnic and religious terms, they are likely to see an "us" versus "them" relation existing between themselves and people of different ethnicity or religion. The end of ideologically defined states in Eastern Europe and the former Soviet Union permits traditional ethnic identities and animosities to come to the fore. Differences in culture and religion create differences over policy issues, ranging from human rights to immigration to trade and commerce to the environment. Geographical propinquity gives rise to conflicting territorial claims from Bosnia to Mindanao. Most important, the efforts of the West to promote its values of democracy and liberalism as universal values, to maintain its military predominance and to advance its economic interests engender countering responses from other civilizations. Decreasingly able to mobilize support and form coalitions on the basis of ideology, governments and groups will increasingly attempt to mobilize support by appealing to common religion and civilization identity.

The clash of civilizations thus occurs at two levels. At the micro-level, adjacent groups along the fault lines between civilizations struggle, often violently, over the control of territory and each other. At the macro-level, states from different civilizations compete for relative military and economic power, struggle over the control of international institutions and third parties, and competitively promote their particular political and religious values.

THE FAULT LINES BETWEEN CIVILIZATIONS

THE FAULT LINES between civilizations are replacing the political and ideological boundaries of the Cold War as the flash points for crisis and bloodshed. The Cold War began when the Iron Curtain divided Europe politically and ideologically. The Cold War ended with the end of the Iron Curtain. As the ideological division of Europe has disappeared, the cultural division of Europe between Western Christianity, on the one hand, and Orthodox Christianity

Source: W. Wallace, THE TRANSFORMATION OF WESTERN EUROPE, London: Pinter, 1990.
Map by Ib Ohlsson for FOREIGN AFFAIRS.

and Islam, on the other, has reemerged. The most significant dividing line in Europe, as William Wallace has suggested, may well be the eastern boundary of Western Christianity in the year 1500. This line runs along what are now the boundaries between Finland and Russia and between the Baltic states and Russia, cuts through Belarus and Ukraine separating the more Catholic western Ukraine from Orthodox eastern Ukraine, swings westward separating Transylvania from the rest of Romania, and then goes through Yugoslavia almost exactly along the line now separating Croatia and Slovenia from the rest of Yugoslavia. In the Balkans this line, of course, coincides with the historic boundary between the Hapsburg and Ottoman empires. The peoples to the north and west of this line are Protestant or Catholic; they shared the common experiences of European history—feudalism, the Renaissance, the Reformation, the Enlightenment, the French Revolution, the Industrial Revolution; they are generally economically better off than the peoples to the east; and they may now look forward to increasing involvement in a common European economy and to the consolidation of democratic political systems. The peoples to the east and south of this line are Orthodox or Muslim; they historically belonged to the Ottoman or Tsarist empires and were only lightly touched by the shaping events in the rest of Europe; they are generally less advanced economically; they seem much less likely to develop stable democratic political systems. The Velvet Curtain of culture has replaced the Iron Curtain of ideology as the most significant dividing line in Europe. As the events in Yugoslavia show, it is not only a line of difference; it is also at times a line of bloody conflict.

Conflict along the fault line between Western and Islamic civilizations has been going on for 1,300 years. After the founding of Islam, the Arab and Moorish surge west and north only ended at Tours in 732. From the eleventh to the thirteenth century the Crusaders attempted with temporary success to bring Christianity and Christian rule to the Holy Land. From the fourteenth to the seventeenth century, the Ottoman Turks reversed the balance, extended their sway over the Middle East and the Balkans, captured Constantinople, and twice laid siege to Vienna. In the nineteenth and early twentieth centuries as Ottoman power declined Britain, France, and Italy established Western control over most of North Africa and the Middle East.

After World War II, the West, in turn, began to retreat; the colonial empires disappeared; first Arab nationalism and then Islamic fundamentalism manifested themselves; the West became heavily dependent on the Persian Gulf countries for its energy; the oil-rich Muslim countries became money-rich and, when they wished to, weapons-rich. Several wars occurred between Arabs and Israel (created by the West). France fought a bloody and ruthless war in Algeria for most of the 1950s; British and French forces invaded Egypt in 1956; American forces went into Lebanon in 1958; subsequently American forces returned to Lebanon, attacked Libya, and engaged in various military encounters with Iran; Arab and Islamic terrorists, supported by at least three Middle Eastern governments, employed the weapon of the weak and bombed Western planes and installations and seized Western hostages. This warfare between Arabs and the West culminated in 1990, when the United States sent a massive army to the Persian Gulf to defend some Arab countries against aggression by another. In its aftermath NATO planning is increasingly directed to potential threats and instability along its "southern tier."

This centuries-old military interaction between the West and

Islam is unlikely to decline. It could become more virulent. The Gulf War left some Arabs feeling proud that Saddam Hussein had attacked Israel and stood up to the West. It also left many feeling humiliated and resentful of the West's military presence in the Persian Gulf, the West's overwhelming military dominance, and their apparent inability to shape their own destiny. Many Arab countries, in addition to the oil exporters, are reaching levels of economic and social development where autocratic forms of government become inappropriate and efforts to introduce democracy become stronger. Some openings in Arab political systems have already occurred. The principal beneficiaries of these openings have been Islamist movements. In the Arab world, in short, Western democracy strengthens anti-Western political forces. This may be a passing phenomenon, but it surely complicates relations between Islamic countries and the West.

Those relations are also complicated by demography. The spectacular population growth in Arab countries, particularly in North Africa, has led to increased migration to Western Europe. The movement within Western Europe toward minimizing internal boundaries has sharpened political sensitivities with respect to this development. In Italy, France and Germany, racism is increasingly open, and political reactions and violence against Arab and Turkish migrants have become more intense and more widespread since 1990.

On both sides the interaction between Islam and the West is seen as a clash of civilizations. The West's "next confrontation," observes M. J. Akbar, an Indian Muslim author, "is definitely going to come from the Muslim world. It is in the sweep of the Islamic nations from the Maghreb to Pakistan that the struggle for a new world order will begin." Bernard Lewis comes to a similar conclusion:

> We are facing a mood and a movement far transcending the level of issues and policies and the governments that pursue them. This is no less than a clash of civilizations—the perhaps irrational but surely historic reaction of an ancient rival against our Judeo-Christian heritage, our secular present, and the worldwide expansion of both.[2]

---

[2]Bernard Lewis, "The Roots of Muslim Rage," *The Atlantic Monthly*, vol. 266, September 1990, p. 60; *Time*, June 15, 1992, pp. 24–28.

Historically, the other great antagonistic interaction of Arab Islamic civilization has been with the pagan, animist, and now increasingly Christian black peoples to the south. In the past, this antagonism was epitomized in the image of Arab slave dealers and black slaves. It has been reflected in the on-going civil war in the Sudan between Arabs and blacks, the fighting in Chad between Libyan-supported insurgents and the government, the tensions between Orthodox Christians and Muslims in the Horn of Africa, and the political conflicts, recurring riots and communal violence between Muslims and Christians in Nigeria. The modernization of Africa and the spread of Christianity are likely to enhance the probability of violence along this fault line. Symptomatic of the intensification of this conflict was the Pope John Paul II's speech in Khartoum in February 1993 attacking the actions of the Sudan's Islamist government against the Christian minority there.

On the northern border of Islam, conflict has increasingly erupted between Orthodox and Muslim peoples, including the carnage of Bosnia and Sarajevo, the simmering violence between Serb and Albanian, the tenuous relations between Bulgarians and their Turkish minority, the violence between Ossetians and Ingush, the unremitting slaughter of each other by Armenians and Azeris, the tense relations between Russians and Muslims in Central Asia, and the deployment of Russian troops to protect Russian interests in the Caucasus and Central Asia. Religion reinforces the revival of ethnic identities and restimulates Russian fears about the security of their southern borders. This concern is well captured by Archie Roosevelt:

> Much of Russian history concerns the struggle between the Slavs and the Turkic peoples on their borders, which dates back to the foundation of the Russian state more than a thousand years ago. In the Slavs' millennium-long confrontation with their eastern neighbors lies the key to an understanding not only of Russian history, but Russian character. To understand Russian realities today one has to have a concept of the great Turkic ethnic group that has preoccupied Russians through the centuries.[3]

The conflict of civilizations is deeply rooted elsewhere in Asia. The historic clash between Muslim and Hindu in the subcontinent

---

[3]Archie Roosevelt, *For Lust of Knowing*, Boston: Little, Brown, 1988, pp. 332-333.

manifests itself now not only in the rivalry between Pakistan and India but also in intensifying religious strife within India between increasingly militant Hindu groups and India's substantial Muslim minority. The destruction of the Ayodhya mosque in December 1992 brought to the fore the issue of whether India will remain a secular democratic state or become a Hindu one. In East Asia, China has outstanding territorial disputes with most of its neighbors. It has pursued a ruthless policy toward the Buddhist people of Tibet, and it is pursuing an increasingly ruthless policy toward its Turkic-Muslim minority. With the Cold War over, the underlying differences between China and the United States have reasserted themselves in areas such as human rights, trade and weapons proliferation. These differences are unlikely to moderate. A "new cold war," Deng Xaioping reportedly asserted in 1991, is under way between China and America.

The crescent-shaped Islamic bloc, from the bulge of Africa to central Asia, has bloody borders.

The same phrase has been applied to the increasingly difficult relations between Japan and the United States. Here cultural difference exacerbates economic conflict. People on each side allege racism on the other, but at least on the American side the antipathies are not racial but cultural. The basic values, attitudes, behavioral patterns of the two societies could hardly be more different. The economic issues between the United States and Europe are no less serious than those between the United States and Japan, but they do not have the same political salience and emotional intensity because the differences between American culture and European culture are so much less than those between American civilization and Japanese civilization.

The interactions between civilizations vary greatly in the extent to which they are likely to be characterized by violence. Economic competition clearly predominates between the American and European subcivilizations of the West and between both of them and Japan. On the Eurasian continent, however, the proliferation of ethnic conflict, epitomized at the extreme in "ethnic cleansing," has not been totally random. It has been most frequent and most violent between groups belonging to different civilizations. In Eurasia the great historic fault lines between civilizations are once more aflame. This is particularly true along the boundaries of the crescent-shaped Islamic bloc of nations from the bulge of Africa to central Asia. Violence also occurs between Muslims, on the one hand, and Orthodox Serbs in the Balkans, Jews in Israel, Hindus in India, Buddhists in Burma and Catholics in the Philippines. Islam has bloody borders.

CIVILIZATION RALLYING: THE KIN-COUNTRY SYNDROME

GROUPS OR STATES belonging to one civilization that become involved in war with people from a different civilization naturally try to rally support from other members of their own civilization. As the post-Cold War world evolves, civilization commonality, what H. D. S. Greenway has termed the "kin-country" syndrome, is replacing political ideology and traditional balance of power considerations as the principal basis for cooperation and coalitions. It can be seen gradually emerging in the post-Cold War conflicts in the Persian Gulf, the Caucasus and Bosnia. None of these was a full-scale war between civilizations, but each involved some elements of civilizational rallying, which seemed to become more important as the conflict continued and which may provide a foretaste of the future.

First, in the Gulf War one Arab state invaded another and then fought a coalition of Arab, Western and other states. While only a few Muslim governments overtly supported Saddam Hussein, many Arab elites privately cheered him on, and he was highly popular among large sections of the Arab publics. Islamic fundamentalist movements universally supported Iraq rather than the Western-backed governments of Kuwait and Saudi Arabia. Forswearing Arab nationalism, Saddam Hussein explicitly invoked an Islamic appeal. He and his supporters attempted to define the war as a war between civilizations. "It is not the world against Iraq," as Safar Al-Hawali, dean of Islamic Studies at the Umm Al-Qura University in Mecca, put it in a widely circulated tape. "It is the West against Islam." Ignoring the rivalry between Iran and Iraq, the chief Iranian religious leader, Ayatollah Ali Khamenei, called for a holy war against the West: "The struggle against American aggression, greed, plans and policies will be counted as a jihad, and anybody who is killed on that path is a martyr." "This is a war," King Hussein of Jordan argued, "against all Arabs and all Muslims and not against Iraq alone."

The rallying of substantial sections of Arab elites and publics behind Saddam Hussein caused those Arab governments in the anti-Iraq coalition to moderate their activities and temper their public statements. Arab governments opposed or distanced themselves from subsequent Western efforts to apply pressure on Iraq, including enforcement of a no-fly zone in the summer of 1992 and the bombing of Iraq in January 1993. The Western-Soviet-Turkish-Arab anti-Iraq coalition of 1990 had by 1993 become a coalition of almost only the West and Kuwait against Iraq.

Muslims contrasted Western actions against Iraq with the West's failure to protect Bosnians against Serbs and to impose sanctions on Israel for violating U.N. resolutions. The West, they alleged, was using a double standard. A world of clashing civilizations, however, is inevitably a world of double standards: people apply one standard to their kin-countries and a different standard to others.

Second, the kin-country syndrome also appeared in conflicts in the former Soviet Union. Armenian military successes in 1992 and 1993 stimulated Turkey to become increasingly supportive of its religious, ethnic and linguistic brethren in Azerbaijan. "We have a Turkish nation feeling the same sentiments as the Azerbaijanis," said one Turkish official in 1992. "We are under pressure. Our newspapers are full of the photos of atrocities and are asking us if we are still serious about pursuing our neutral policy. Maybe we should show Armenia that there's a big Turkey in the region." President Turgut Özal agreed, remarking that Turkey should at least "scare the Armenians a little bit." Turkey, Özal threatened again in 1993, would "show its fangs." Turkish Air Force jets flew reconnaissance flights along the Armenian border; Turkey suspended food shipments and air flights to Armenia; and Turkey and Iran announced they would not accept dismemberment of Azerbaijan. In the last years of its existence, the Soviet government supported Azerbaijan because its government was dominated by former communists. With the end of the Soviet Union, however, political considerations gave way to religious ones. Russian troops fought on the side of the Armenians, and Azerbaijan accused the "Russian government of turning 180 degrees" toward support for Christian Armenia.

Third, with respect to the fighting in the former Yugoslavia, Western publics manifested sympathy and support for the Bosnian Muslims and the horrors they suffered at the hands of the Serbs. Relatively little concern was expressed, however, over Croatian attacks on Muslims and participation in the dismemberment of Bosnia-Herzegovina. In the early stages of the Yugoslav breakup, Germany, in an unusual display of diplomatic initiative and muscle, induced the other 11 members of the European Community to follow its lead in recognizing Slovenia and Croatia. As a result of the pope's determination to provide strong backing to the two Catholic countries, the Vatican extended recognition even before the Community did. The United States followed the European lead. Thus the leading actors in Western civilization rallied behind their coreligionists. Subsequently Croatia was reported to be receiving substantial quantities of arms from Central European and other Western countries. Boris Yeltsin's government, on the other hand, attempted to pursue a middle course that would be sympathetic to the Orthodox Serbs but not alienate Russia from the West. Russian conservative and nationalist groups, however, including many legislators, attacked the government for not being more forthcoming in its support for the Serbs. By early 1993 several hundred Russians apparently were serving with the Serbian forces, and reports circulated of Russian arms being supplied to Serbia.

Islamic governments and groups, on the other hand, castigated the West for not coming to the defense of the Bosnians. Iranian leaders urged Muslims from all countries to provide help to Bosnia; in violation of the U.N. arms embargo, Iran supplied weapons and men for the Bosnians; Iranian-supported Lebanese groups sent guerrillas to train and organize the Bosnian forces. In 1993 up to 4,000 Muslims from over two dozen Islamic countries were reported to be fighting in Bosnia. The governments of Saudi Arabia and other countries felt under increasing pressure from fundamentalist groups in their own societies to provide more vigorous support for the Bosnians. By the end of 1992, Saudi Arabia had reportedly supplied substantial funding for weapons and supplies for the Bosnians, which significantly increased their military capabilities vis-à-vis the Serbs.

In the 1930s the Spanish Civil War provoked intervention from countries that politically were fascist, communist and democratic. In the 1990s the Yugoslav conflict is provoking intervention from countries that are Muslim, Orthodox and Western Christian. The parallel has not gone unnoticed. "The war in Bosnia-Herzegovina has become the emotional equivalent of the fight against fascism in the Spanish Civil War," one Saudi editor observed. "Those who died there are regarded as martyrs who tried to save their fellow Muslims."

Conflicts and violence will also occur between states and groups within the same civilization. Such conflicts, however, are likely to be less intense and less likely to expand than conflicts between civilizations. Common membership in a civilization reduces the probability of violence in situations where it might otherwise occur. In 1991 and 1992 many people were alarmed by the possibility of violent conflict between Russia and Ukraine over territory, particularly Crimea, the Black Sea fleet, nuclear weapons and economic issues. If civilization is what counts, however, the likelihood of violence between Ukrainians and Russians should be low. They are two Slavic, primarily Orthodox peoples who have had close relationships with each other for centuries. As of early 1993, despite all the reasons for conflict, the leaders of the two countries were effectively negotiating and defusing the issues between the two countries. While there has been serious fighting between Muslims and Christians elsewhere in the former Soviet Union and much tension and some fighting between Western and Orthodox Christians in the Baltic states, there has been virtually no violence between Russians and Ukrainians.

Civilization rallying to date has been limited, but it has been growing, and it clearly has the potential to spread much further. As the conflicts in the Persian Gulf, the Caucasus and Bosnia continued, the positions of nations and the cleavages between them increasingly were along civilizational lines. Populist politicians, religious leaders and the media have found it a potent means of arousing mass support and of pressuring hesitant governments. In the coming years, the local conflicts most likely to escalate into major wars will be those, as in Bosnia and the Caucasus, along the fault lines between civilizations. The next world war, if there is one, will be a war between civilizations.

THE WEST VERSUS THE REST

THE WEST IS NOW at an extraordinary peak of power in relation to other civilizations. Its superpower opponent has disappeared from the map. Military conflict among Western states is unthinkable, and Western military power is unrivaled. Apart from Japan, the West faces no economic challenge. It dominates international political and security institutions and with Japan international economic institutions. Global political and security issues are effectively settled by a directorate of the United States, Britain and France, world economic issues by a directorate of the United States, Germany and Japan, all of which maintain extraordinarily close relations with each other to the exclusion of lesser and largely non-Western countries. Decisions made at the U.N. Security Council or in the International Monetary Fund that reflect the interests of the West are presented to the world as reflecting the desires of the world community. The very phrase "the world community" has become the euphemistic collective noun (replacing "the Free World") to give global legitimacy to actions reflecting the interests of the United States and other Western powers.[4] Through the IMF and other international economic institutions, the West promotes its economic interests and imposes on other nations the economic policies it thinks appropriate. In any poll of non-Western peoples, the IMF undoubtedly would win the support of finance ministers and a few others, but get an overwhelmingly unfavorable rating from just about everyone else, who would agree

[4]Almost invariably Western leaders claim they are acting on behalf of "the world community." One minor lapse occurred during the run-up to the Gulf War. In an interview on "Good Morning America," Dec. 21, 1990, British Prime Minister John Major referred to the actions "the West" was taking against Saddam Hussein. He quickly corrected himself and subsequently referred to "the world community." He was, however, right when he erred.

with Georgy Arbatov's characterization of IMF officials as "neo-Bolsheviks who love expropriating other people's money, imposing undemocratic and alien rules of economic and political conduct and stifling economic freedom."

Western domination of the U.N. Security Council and its decisions, tempered only by occasional abstention by China, produced U.N. legitimation of the West's use of force to drive Iraq out of Kuwait and its elimination of Iraq's sophisticated weapons and capacity to produce such weapons. It also produced the quite unprecedented action by the United States, Britain and France in getting the Security Council to demand that Libya hand over the Pan Am 103 bombing suspects and then to impose sanctions when Libya refused. After defeating the largest Arab army, the West did not hesitate to throw its weight around in the Arab world. The West in effect is using international institutions, military power and economic resources to run the world in ways that will maintain Western predominance, protect Western interests and promote Western political and economic values.

The very phrase "world community" has become a euphemism to give legitimacy to the actions of the West.

That at least is the way in which non-Westerners see the new world, and there is a significant element of truth in their view. Differences in power and struggles for military, economic and institutional power are thus one source of conflict between the West and other civilizations. Differences in culture, that is basic values and beliefs, are a second source of conflict. V. S. Naipaul has argued that Western civilization is the "universal civilization" that "fits all men." At a superficial level much of Western culture has indeed permeated the rest of the world. At a more basic level, however, Western concepts differ fundamentally from those prevalent in other civilizations. Western ideas of individualism, liberalism, constitutionalism, human rights, equality, liberty, the rule of law, democracy, free markets, the separation of church and state, often have little resonance in Islamic, Confucian, Japanese, Hindu, Buddhist or Orthodox cultures. Western efforts to propagate such ideas produce instead a reaction against "human rights imperialism" and a reaffirmation of indigenous values, as can be seen in the support for religious fundamentalism by the younger generation in non-Western cultures. The very notion that there could be a "universal civilization" is a Western idea, directly at odds with the particularism of most Asian societies and their emphasis on what distinguishes one people from another. Indeed, the author of a review of 100 comparative studies of values in different societies concluded that "the values that are most important in the West are least important worldwide."[5] In the political realm, of course, these differences are most manifest in the efforts of the United States and other Western powers to induce other peoples to adopt Western ideas concerning democracy and human rights. Modern democratic government originated in the West. When it has developed in non-Western societies it has usually been the product of Western colonialism or imposition.

The central axis of world politics in the future is likely to be, in Kishore Mahbubani's phrase, the conflict between "the West and the Rest" and the responses of non-Western civilizations to Western power and values.[6] Those responses generally take one or a combination of three forms. At one extreme, non-Western states can, like Burma and North Korea, attempt to pursue a course of isolation, to insulate their societies from penetration or "corruption" by the West, and, in effect, to opt out of participation in the Western-dominated global community. The costs of this course, however, are high, and few states have pursued it exclusively. A second alternative, the equivalent of "band-wagoning" in international relations theory, is to attempt to join the West and accept its values and institutions. The third alternative is to attempt to "balance" the West by developing economic and military power and cooperating with other non-Western societies against the West, while preserving indigenous values and institutions; in short, to modernize but not to Westernize.

---

[5]Harry C. Triandis, *The New York Times*, Dec. 25, 1990, p. 41, and "Cross-Cultural Studies of Individualism and Collectivism," Nebraska Symposium on Motivation, vol. 37, 1989, pp. 41-133.

[6]Kishore Mahbubani, "The West and the Rest," *The National Interest*, Summer 1992, pp. 3-13.

THE TORN COUNTRIES

IN THE FUTURE, as people differentiate themselves by civilization, countries with large numbers of peoples of different civilizations, such as the Soviet Union and Yugoslavia, are candidates for dismemberment. Some other countries have a fair degree of cultural homogeneity but are divided over whether their society belongs to one civilization or another. These are torn countries. Their leaders typically wish to pursue a bandwagoning strategy and to make their countries members of the West, but the history, culture and traditions of their countries are non-Western. The most obvious and prototypical torn country is Turkey. The late twentieth-century leaders of Turkey have followed in the Attatürk tradition and defined Turkey as a modern, secular, Western nation state. They allied Turkey with the West in NATO and in the Gulf War; they applied for membership in the European Community. At the same time, however, elements in Turkish society have supported an Islamic revival and have argued that Turkey is basically a Middle Eastern Muslim society. In addition, while the elite of Turkey has defined Turkey as a Western society, the elite of the West refuses to accept Turkey as such. Turkey will not become a member of the European Community, and the real reason, as President Özal said, "is that we are Muslim and they are Christian and they don't say that." Having rejected Mecca, and then being rejected by Brussels, where does Turkey look? Tashkent may be the answer. The end of the Soviet Union gives Turkey the opportunity to become the leader of a revived Turkic civilization involving seven countries from the borders of Greece to those of China. Encouraged by the West, Turkey is making strenuous efforts to carve out this new identity for itself.

During the past decade Mexico has assumed a position somewhat similar to that of Turkey. Just as Turkey abandoned its historic opposition to Europe and attempted to join Europe, Mexico has stopped defining itself by its opposition to the United States and is instead attempting to imitate the United States and to join it in the North American Free Trade Area. Mexican leaders are engaged in the great task of redefining Mexican identity and have introduced fundamental economic reforms that eventually will lead to fundamental political change. In 1991 a top adviser to President Carlos Salinas de Gortari described at length to me all the changes the Salinas government was making. When he finished, I remarked: "That's most impressive. It seems to me that basically you want to change Mexico from a Latin American country into a North American country." He looked at me with surprise and exclaimed: "Exactly! That's precisely what we are trying to do, but of course we could never say so publicly." As his remark indicates, in Mexico as in Turkey, significant elements in society resist the redefinition of their country's identity. In Turkey, European-oriented leaders have to make gestures to Islam (Özal's pilgrimage to Mecca); so also Mexico's North American-oriented leaders have to make gestures to those who hold Mexico to be a Latin American country (Salinas' Ibero-American Guadalajara summit).

Historically Turkey has been the most profoundly torn country. For the United States, Mexico is the most immediate torn country. Globally the most important torn country is Russia. The question of whether Russia is part of the West or the leader of a distinct Slavic-Orthodox civilization has been a recurring one in Russian history. That issue was obscured by the communist victory in Russia, which imported a Western ideology, adapted it to Russian conditions and then challenged the West in the name of that ideology. The dominance of communism shut off the historic debate over Westernization versus Russification. With communism discredited Russians once again face that question.

President Yeltsin is adopting Western principles and goals and seeking to make Russia a "normal" country and a part of the West. Yet both the Russian elite and the Russian public are divided on this issue. Among the more moderate dissenters, Sergei Stankevich argues that Russia should reject the "Atlanticist" course, which would lead it "to become European, to become a part of the world economy in rapid and organized fashion, to become the eighth member of the Seven, and to put particular emphasis on Germany and the United States as the two dominant members of the Atlantic alliance." While also rejecting an exclusively Eurasian policy, Stankevich nonetheless argues that Russia should give priority to the protection of Russians in other countries, emphasize its Turkic and Muslim connections, and promote "an appreciable redistribution of our resources, our options, our ties, and our interests in favor of Asia, of the eastern direction." People of this persuasion criticize Yeltsin for subordinating Russia's interests to those of the West, for reducing Russian military strength, for failing to support traditional friends such as Serbia, and for pushing economic and political reform in ways injurious to the Russian people. Indicative of this trend is the new popularity of the ideas of Petr Savitsky, who in the 1920s argued that Russia was a unique Eurasian civilization.[7] More extreme dissidents voice much more blatantly nationalist, anti-Western and anti-Semitic views, and urge Russia to redevelop its military strength and to establish closer ties with China and Muslim countries. The people of Russia are as divided as the elite. An opinion survey in European Russia in the spring of 1992 revealed that 40 percent of the public had positive attitudes toward the West and 36 percent had negative attitudes. As it has been for much of its history, Russia in the early 1990s is truly a torn country.

To redefine its civilization identity, a torn country must meet three requirements. First, its political and economic elite has to be generally supportive of and enthusiastic about this move. Second, its public has to be willing to acquiesce in the redefinition. Third, the dominant groups in the recipient civilization have to be willing to embrace the convert. All three requirements in large part exist with respect to Mexico. The first two in large part exist with respect to Turkey. It is not clear that any of them exist with respect to Russia's joining the West. The conflict between liberal democracy and Marxism-Leninism was between ideologies which, despite their major differences, ostensibly shared ultimate goals of freedom, equality and prosperity. A traditional, authoritarian, nationalist Russia could have quite different goals. A Western democrat could carry on an intellectual debate with a Soviet Marxist. It would be virtually

[7]Sergei Stankevich, "Russia in Search of Itself," *The National Interest*, Summer 1992, pp. 47-51; Daniel Schneider, "A Russian Movement Rejects Western Tilt," *Christian Science Monitor*, Feb. 5, 1993, pp. 5-7.

impossible for him to do that with a Russian traditionalist. If, as the Russians stop behaving like Marxists, they reject liberal democracy and begin behaving like Russians but not like Westerners, the relations between Russia and the West could again become distant and conflictual.[8]

THE CONFUCIAN-ISLAMIC CONNECTION

THE OBSTACLES TO non-Western countries joining the West vary considerably. They are least for Latin American and East European countries. They are greater for the Orthodox countries of the former Soviet Union. They are still greater for Muslim, Confucian, Hindu and Buddhist societies. Japan has established a unique position for itself as an associate member of the West: it is in the West in some respects but clearly not of the West in important dimensions. Those countries that for reason of culture and power do not wish to, or cannot, join the West compete with the West by developing their own economic, military and political power. They do this by promoting their internal development and by cooperating with other non-Western countries. The most prominent form of this cooperation is the Confucian-Islamic connection that has emerged to challenge Western interests, values and power.

Almost without exception, Western countries are reducing their military power; under Yeltsin's leadership so also is Russia. China, North Korea and several Middle Eastern states, however, are significantly expanding their military capabilities. They are doing this by the import of arms from Western and non-Western sources and by the development of indigenous arms industries. One result is the emergence of what Charles Krauthammer has called "Weapon

---

[8]Owen Harries has pointed out that Australia is trying (unwisely in his view) to become a torn country in reverse. Although it has been a full member not only of the West but also of the ABCA military and intelligence core of the West, its current leaders are in effect proposing that it defect from the West, redefine itself as an Asian country and cultivate close ties with its neighbors. Australia's future, they argue, is with the dynamic economies of East Asia. But, as I have suggested, close economic cooperation normally requires a common cultural base. In addition, none of the three conditions necessary for a torn country to join another civilization is likely to exist in Australia's case.

States," and the Weapon States are not Western states. Another result is the redefinition of arms control, which is a Western concept and a Western goal. During the Cold War the primary purpose of arms control was to establish a stable military balance between the United States and its allies and the Soviet Union and its allies. In the post-Cold War world the primary objective of arms control is to prevent the development by non-Western societies of military capabilities that could threaten Western interests. The West attempts to do this through international agreements, economic pressure and controls on the transfer of arms and weapons technologies.

The conflict between the West and the Confucian-Islamic states focuses largely, although not exclusively, on nuclear, chemical and biological weapons, ballistic missiles and other sophisticated means for delivering them, and the guidance, intelligence and other electronic capabilities for achieving that goal. The West promotes nonproliferation as a universal norm and nonproliferation treaties and inspections as means of realizing that norm. It also threatens a variety of sanctions against those who promote the spread of sophisticated weapons and proposes some benefits for those who do not. The attention of the West focuses, naturally, on nations that are actually or potentially hostile to the West.

A Confucian-Islamic connection has emerged to challenge Western interests, values and power.

The non-Western nations, on the other hand, assert their right to acquire and to deploy whatever weapons they think necessary for their security. They also have absorbed, to the full, the truth of the response of the Indian defense minister when asked what lesson he learned from the Gulf War: "Don't fight the United States unless you have nuclear weapons." Nuclear weapons, chemical weapons and missiles are viewed, probably erroneously, as the potential equalizer of superior Western conventional power. China, of course, already has nuclear weapons; Pakistan and India have the capability to deploy them. North Korea, Iran, Iraq, Libya and Algeria appear to be attempting to acquire them. A top Iranian official has declared that all Muslim states should acquire nuclear weapons, and in 1988 the president of

Iran reportedly issued a directive calling for development of "offensive and defensive chemical, biological and radiological weapons."

Centrally important to the development of counter-West military capabilities is the sustained expansion of China's military power and its means to create military power. Buoyed by spectacular economic development, China is rapidly increasing its military spending and vigorously moving forward with the modernization of its armed forces. It is purchasing weapons from the former Soviet states; it is developing long-range missiles; in 1992 it tested a one-megaton nuclear device. It is developing power-projection capabilities, acquiring aerial refueling technology, and trying to purchase an aircraft carrier. Its military buildup and assertion of sovereignty over the South China Sea are provoking a multilateral regional arms race in East Asia. China is also a major exporter of arms and weapons technology. It has exported materials to Libya and Iraq that could be used to manufacture nuclear weapons and nerve gas. It has helped Algeria build a reactor suitable for nuclear weapons research and production. China has sold to Iran nuclear technology that American officials believe could only be used to create weapons and apparently has shipped components of 300-mile-range missiles to Pakistan. North Korea has had a nuclear weapons program under way for some while and has sold advanced missiles and missile technology to Syria and Iran. The flow of weapons and weapons technology is generally from East Asia to the Middle East. There is, however, some movement in the reverse direction; China has received Stinger missiles from Pakistan.

A Confucian-Islamic military connection has thus come into being, designed to promote acquisition by its members of the weapons and weapons technologies needed to counter the military power of the West. It may or may not last. At present, however, it is, as Dave McCurdy has said, "a renegades' mutual support pact, run by the proliferators and their backers." A new form of arms competition is thus occurring between Islamic-Confucian states and the West. In an old-fashioned arms race, each side developed its own arms to balance or to achieve superiority against the other side. In this new form of arms competition, one side is developing its arms and the other side is attempting not to balance but to limit and prevent that arms build-up while at the same time reducing its own military capabilities.

IMPLICATIONS FOR THE WEST

THIS ARTICLE DOES not argue that civilization identities will replace all other identities, that nation states will disappear, that each civilization will become a single coherent political entity, that groups within a civilization will not conflict with and even fight each other. This paper does set forth the hypotheses that differences between civilizations are real and important; civilization-consciousness is increasing; conflict between civilizations will supplant ideological and other forms of conflict as the dominant global form of conflict; international relations, historically a game played out within Western civilization, will increasingly be de-Westernized and become a game in which non-Western civilizations are actors and not simply objects; successful political, security and economic international institutions are more likely to develop within civilizations than across civilizations; conflicts between groups in different civilizations will be more frequent, more sustained and more violent than conflicts between groups in the same civilization; violent conflicts between groups in different civilizations are the most likely and most dangerous source of escalation that could lead to global wars; the paramount axis of world politics will be the relations between "the West and the Rest"; the elites in some torn non-Western countries will try to make their countries part of the West, but in most cases face major obstacles to accomplishing this; a central focus of conflict for the immediate future will be between the West and several Islamic-Confucian states.

This is not to advocate the desirability of conflicts between civilizations. It is to set forth descriptive hypotheses as to what the future may be like. If these are plausible hypotheses, however, it is necessary to consider their implications for Western policy. These implications should be divided between short-term advantage and long-term accommodation. In the short term it is clearly in the interest of the West to promote greater cooperation and unity within its own civilization, particularly between its European and North American components; to incorporate into the West societies in Eastern Europe and Latin America whose cultures are close to those of the West; to promote and maintain cooperative relations with Russia and Japan; to prevent escalation of local inter-civilization conflicts into major inter-civilization wars; to limit the expansion of the military strength of Confucian and Islamic states; to moderate the reduction of Western military capabilities and maintain military superiority in East and Southwest Asia; to exploit differences and conflicts among Confucian and Islamic states; to support in other civilizations groups sympathetic to Western values and interests; to strengthen international institutions that reflect and legitimate Western interests and values and to promote the involvement of non-Western states in those institutions.

In the longer term other measures would be called for. Western civilization is both Western and modern. Non-Western civilizations have attempted to become modern without becoming Western. To date only Japan has fully succeeded in this quest. Non-Western civilizations will continue to attempt to acquire the wealth, technology, skills, machines and weapons that are part of being modern. They will also attempt to reconcile this modernity with their traditional culture and values. Their economic and military strength relative to the West will increase. Hence the West will increasingly have to accommodate these non-Western modern civilizations whose power approaches that of the West but whose values and interests differ significantly from those of the West. This will require the West to maintain the economic and military power necessary to protect its interests in relation to these civilizations. It will also, however, require the West to develop a more profound understanding of the basic religious and philosophical assumptions underlying other civilizations and the ways in which people in those civilizations see their interests. It will require an effort to identify elements of commonality between Western and other civilizations. For the relevant future, there will be no universal civilization, but instead a world of different civilizations, each of which will have to learn to coexist with the others.

The Summoning

'But They Said, We Will Not Hearken'

JEREMIAH 6:17

Fouad Ajami

In Joseph Conrad's *Youth*, a novella published at the turn of the century, Marlowe, the narrator, remembers when he first encountered "the East":

> And then, before I could open my lips, the East spoke to me, but it was in a Western voice. A torrent of words was poured into the enigmatical, the fateful silence; outlandish, angry words mixed with words and even whole sentences of good English, less strange but even more surprising. The voice swore and cursed violently; it riddled the solemn peace of the bay by a volley of abuse. It began by calling me Pig, and from that went crescendo into unmentionable adjectives—in English.

The young Marlowe knew that even the most remote civilization had been made and remade by the West, and taught new ways.

Not so Samuel P. Huntington. In a curious essay, "The Clash of Civilizations," Huntington has found his civilizations whole and intact, watertight under an eternal sky. Buried alive, as it were, during the years of the Cold War, these civilizations (Islamic, Slavic-Orthodox, Western, Confucian, Japanese, Hindu, etc.) rose as soon as the stone was rolled off, dusted themselves off, and proceeded to claim the loyalty of their adherents. For this student of history and culture, civilizations

---

FOUAD AJAMI is Majid Khadduri Professor of Middle Eastern Studies at the School of Advanced International Studies, The Johns Hopkins University.

Reprinted by permission from *Foreign Affairs*, 72:4 (September/October 1993).

have always seemed messy creatures. Furrows run across whole civilizations, across individuals themselves—that was modernity's verdict. But Huntington looks past all that. The crooked and meandering alleyways of the world are straightened out. With a sharp pencil and a steady hand Huntington marks out where one civilization ends and the wilderness of "the other" begins.

More surprising still is Huntington's attitude toward states, and their place in his scheme of things. From one of the most influential and brilliant students of the state and its national interest there now comes an essay that misses the slyness of states, the unsentimental and cold-blooded nature of so much of what they do as they pick their way through chaos. Despite the obligatory passage that states will remain "the most powerful actors in world affairs," states are written off, their place given over to clashing civilizations. In Huntington's words, "The next world war, if there is one, will be a war between civilizations"

THE POWER OF MODERNITY

Huntington's meditation is occasioned by his concern about the state of the West, its power and the terms of its engagement with "the rest."[1] "He who gives, dominates," the great historian Fernand Braudel observed of the traffic of civilizations. In making itself over the centuries, the West helped make the others as well. We have come to the end of this trail, Huntington is sure. He is impressed by the "de-Westernization" of societies, their "indigenization" and apparent willingness to go their own way. In his view of things such phenomena as the "Hinduization" of India and Islamic fundamentalism are ascendant. To these detours into "tradition" Huntington has assigned great force and power.

But Huntington is wrong. He has underestimated the tenacity of modernity and secularism in places that acquired these ways against great odds, always perilously close to the abyss, the darkness never far.

[1]The West itself is unexamined in Huntington's essay. No fissures run through it. No multiculturalists are heard from. It is orderly within its ramparts. What doubts Huntington has about the will within the walls, he has kept within himself. He has assumed that his call to unity will be answered, for outside flutter the banners of the Saracens and the Confucians.

India will not become a Hindu state. The inheritance of Indian secularism will hold. The vast middle class will defend it, keep the order intact to maintain India's—and its own—place in the modern world of nations. There exists in that anarchic polity an instinctive dread of playing with fires that might consume it. Hindu chauvinism may coarsen the public life of the country, but the state and the middle class that sustains it know that a detour into religious fanaticism is a fling with ruin. A resourceful middle class partakes of global culture and norms. A century has passed since the Indian bourgeoisie, through its political vehicle the Indian National Congress, set out to claim for itself and India a place among nations. Out of that long struggle to overturn British rule and the parallel struggle against "communalism," the advocates of the national idea built a large and durable state. They will not cede all this for a political kingdom of Hindu purity.

We have been hearing from the traditionalists, but we should not exaggerate their power, for traditions are often most insistent and loud when they rupture, when people no longer really believe and when age-old customs lose their ability to keep men and women at home. The phenomenon we have dubbed as Islamic fundamentalism is less a sign of resurgence than of panic and bewilderment and guilt that the border with "the other" has been crossed. Those young urban poor, half-educated in the cities of the Arab world, and their Sorbonne-educated lay preachers, can they be evidence of a genuine return to tradition? They crash Europe's and America's gates in search of liberty and work, and they rail against the sins of the West. It is easy to understand Huntington's frustration with this kind of complexity, with the strange mixture of attraction and repulsion that the West breeds, and his need to simplify matters, to mark out the borders of civilizations.

Tradition-mongering is no proof, though, that these civilizations outside the West are intact, or that their thrashing about is an indication of their vitality, or that they present a conventional threat of arms. Even so thorough and far-reaching an attack against Western hegemony as Iran's theocratic revolution could yet fail to wean that society from the culture of the West. That country's cruel revolution was born of the realization of the "armed Imam" that his people were being seduced by America's ways. The gates had been thrown wide open in the 1970's, and the high walls Ayatollah Khomeini built around his polity were a response to that cultural seduction. Swamped, Iran was "rescued" by men claiming authenticity as their banner. One extreme led to another.

"We prayed for the rain of mercy and received floods," was the way Mehdi Bazargan, the decent modernist who was Khomeini's first prime minister, put it. But the millennium has been brought down to earth, and the dream of a pan-Islamic revolt in Iran's image has vanished into the wind. The terror and the shabbiness have caught up with the utopia. Sudan could emulate the Iranian "revolutionary example." But this will only mean the further pauperization and ruin of a desperate land. There is no rehabilitation of the Iranian example.

A battle rages in Algeria, a society of the Mediterranean, close to Europe—a wine-producing country for that matter—and in Egypt between the secular powers that be and an Islamic alternative. But we should not rush to print with obituaries of these states. In Algeria the nomenklatura of the National Liberation Front failed and triggered a revolt of the young, the underclass and the excluded. The revolt raised an Islamic banner. Caught between a regime they despised and a reign of virtue they feared, the professionals and the women and the modernists of the middle class threw their support to the forces of "order." They hailed the army's crackdown on the Islamicists; they allowed the interruption of a democratic process sure to bring the Islamicists to power; they accepted the "liberties" protected by the repression, the devil you know rather than the one you don't.

The Algerian themes repeat in the Egyptian case, although Egypt's dilemma over its Islamicist opposition is not as acute. The Islamicists continue to hound the state, but they cannot bring it down. There is no likelihood that the Egyptian state—now riddled with enough complacency and corruption to try the celebrated patience and good humor of the Egyptians—will go under. This is an old and skeptical country. It knows better than to trust its fate to enforcers of radical religious dogma. These are not deep and secure structures of order that the national middle classes have put in place. But they will not be blown away overnight.

Nor will Turkey lose its way, turn its back on Europe and chase after some imperial temptation in the scorched domains of Central

Asia. Huntington sells that country's modernity and secularism short when he writes that the Turks—rejecting Mecca and rejected by Brussels—are likely to head to Tashkent in search of a Pan-Turkic role. There is no journey to that imperial past. Ataturk severed that link with fury, pointed his country westward, embraced the civilization of Europe and did it without qualms or second thoughts. It is on Frankfurt and Bonn—and Washington—not on Baku and Tashkent that the attention of the Turks is fixed. The inheritors of Ataturk's legacy are too shrewd to go chasing after imperial glory, gathering about them the scattered domains of the Turkish peoples. After their European possessions were lost, the Turks clung to Thrace and to all that this link to Europe represents.

Huntington would have nations battle for civilizational ties and fidelities when they would rather scramble for their market shares, learn how to compete in a merciless world economy, provide jobs, move out of poverty. For their part, the "management gurus" and those who believe that the interests have vanquished the passions in today's world tell us that men want Sony, not soil.[2] There is a good deal of truth in what they say, a terrible exhaustion with utopias, a reluctance to set out on expeditions of principle or belief. It is hard to think of Russia, ravaged as it is by inflation, taking up the grand cause of a "second Byzantium," the bearer of the orthodox-Slavic torch.

And where is the Confucian world Huntington speaks of? In the busy and booming lands of the Pacific Rim, so much of politics and ideology has been sublimated into finance that the nations of East Asia have turned into veritable workshops. The civilization of Cathay is dead; the Indonesian archipelago is deaf to the call of the religious radicals in Tehran as it tries to catch up with Malaysia and Singapore. A different wind blows in the lands of the Pacific. In that world economics, not politics, is in command. The world is far less antiseptic than Lee Kuan Yew, the sage of Singapore, would want it to be. A nemesis could lie in wait for all the prosperity that the 1980's brought to the Pacific. But the lands of the Pacific Rim—protected, to be sure,

---

[2]Kenichi Ohmae, "Global Consumers Want Sony, Not Soil," *New Perspectives Quarterly*, Fall 1991.

by an American security umbrella—are not ready for a great falling out among the nations. And were troubles to visit that world they would erupt within its boundaries, not across civilizational lines.

The things and ways that the West took to "the rest"—those whole sentences of good English that Marlowe heard a century ago—have become the ways of the world. The secular idea, the state system and the balance of power, pop culture jumping tariff walls and barriers, the state as an instrument of welfare, all these have been internalized in the remotest places. We have stirred up the very storms into which we now ride.

THE WEAKNESS OF TRADITION

Nations "cheat": they juggle identities and interests. Their ways meander. One would think that the traffic of arms from North Korea and China to Libya and Iran and Syria shows this—that states will consort with any civilization, however alien, as long as the price is right and the goods are ready. Huntington turns this routine act of selfishness into a sinister "Confucian-Islamic connection." There are better explanations: the commerce of renegades, plain piracy, an "underground economy" that picks up the slack left by the great arms suppliers (the United States, Russia, Britain and France).

Contrast the way Huntington sees things with Braudel's depiction of the traffic between Christendom and Islam across the Mediterranean in the sixteenth century—and this was in a religious age, after the fall of Constantinople to the Turks and of Granada to the Spanish: "Men passed to and fro, indifferent to frontiers, states and creeds. They were more aware of the necessities for shipping and trade, the hazards of war and piracy, the opportunities for complicity or betrayal provided by circumstances."[3]

Those kinds of "complicities" and ambiguities are missing in Huntington's analysis. Civilizations are crammed into the nooks and crannies—and checkpoints—of the Balkans. Huntington goes where only the brave would venture, into that belt of mixed populations

---

[3]Ferdinand Braudel, *The Mediterranean and the Mediterranean World in the Age of Philip II*, Vol. II, New York: Harper & Row, 1976, p. 759.

stretching from the Adriatic to the Baltic. Countless nationalisms make their home there, all aggrieved, all possessed of memories of a fabled past and equally ready for the demagogues vowing to straighten a messy map. In the thicket of these pan-movements he finds the line that marked "the eastern boundary of Western Christianity in the year 1500." The scramble for turf between Croatian nationalism and its Serbian counterpart, their "joint venture" in carving up Bosnia, are made into a fight of the inheritors of Rome, Byzantium and Islam.

But why should we fall for this kind of determinism? "An outsider who travels the highway between Zagreb and Belgrade is struck not by the decisive historical fault line which falls across the lush Slavonian plain but by the opposite. Serbs and Croats speak the same language, give or take a few hundred words, have shared the same village way of life for centuries."[4] The cruel genius of Slobodan Milosevic and Franjo Tudjman, men on horseback familiar in lands and situations of distress, was to make their bids for power into grand civilizational undertakings—the ramparts of the Enlightenment defended against Islam or, in Tudjman's case, against the heirs of the Slavic-Orthodox faith. Differences had to be magnified. Once Tito, an equal opportunity oppressor, had passed from the scene, the balancing act among the nationalities was bound to come apart. Serbia had had a measure of hegemony in the old system. But of the world that loomed over the horizon—privatization and economic reform—the Serbs were less confident. The citizens of Sarajevo and the Croats and the Slovenes had a head start on the rural Serbs. And so the Serbs hacked at the new order of things with desperate abandon.

Some Muslim volunteers came to Bosnia, driven by faith and zeal. Huntington sees in these few stragglers the sweeping power of "civilizational rallying," proof of the hold of what he calls the "kin-country syndrome." This is delusion, No Muslim cavalry was ever going to ride to the rescue. The Iranians may have railed about holy warfare, but the Chetniks went on with their work. The work of order and mercy would have had to be done by the United States if the cruel utopia of the Serbs was to be contested.

---

[4]Michael Ignatieff, "The Balkan Tragedy," *New York Review of Books*, May 13, 1993.

It should have taken no powers of prophecy to foretell where the fight in the Balkans would end. The abandonment of Bosnia was of a piece with the ways of the world. No one wanted to die for Srebrenica. The Europeans averted their gaze, as has been their habit. The Americans hesitated for a moment as the urge to stay out of the Balkans did battle with the scenes of horror. Then "prudence" won out. Milosevic and Tudjman may need civilizational legends, but there is no need to invest their projects of conquest with this kind of meaning.

In his urge to find that relentless war across Islam's "bloody borders," Huntington buys Saddam Hussein's interpretation of the Gulf War. It was, for Saddam and Huntington, a civilizational battle. But the Gulf War's verdict was entirely different. For if there was a campaign that laid bare the interests of states, the lengths to which they will go to restore a tolerable balance of power in a place that matters, this was it. A local despot had risen close to the wealth of the Persian Gulf, and a Great Power from afar had come to the rescue. The posse assembled by the Americans had Saudi, Turkish, Egyptian, Syrian, French, British and other riders.

True enough, when Saddam Hussein's dream of hegemony was shattered, the avowed secularist who had devastated the *ulama*, the men of religion in his country, fell back on Ayatollah Khomeini's language of fire and brimstone and borrowed the symbolism and battle cry of his old Iranian nemesis. But few, if any, were fooled by this sudden conversion to the faith. They knew the predator for what he was: he had a Christian foreign minister (Tariq Aziz); he had warred against the Iranian revolution for nearly a decade and had prided himself on the secularism of his regime. Prudent men of the social and political order, the *ulama* got out of the way and gave their state the room it needed to check the predator at the Saudi/Kuwaiti border.[5] They knew this was one of those moments when purity bows to necessity. Ten days after Saddam swept into Kuwait, Saudi Arabia's most authoritative religious body, the Council of Higher Ulama, issued a *fatwa*, or a ruling opinion,

---

[5]Huntington quotes one Safar al Hawali, a religious radical at Umm al Qura Univeristy in Mecca, to the effect that the campaign against Iraq was another Western campaign against Islam. But this can't do as evidence. Safar al Hawali was a crank. Among the *ulama* class and the religious scholars in Saudi Arabia he was, for all practical purposes, a loner.

supporting the presence of Arab and Islamic and "other friendly forces." All means of defense, the ulama ruled, were legitimate to guarantee the people "the safety of their religion, their wealth, and their honor and their blood, to protect what they enjoy of safety and stability." At some remove, in Egypt, that country's leading religious figure, the Shaykh of Al Ashar, Shaykh Jadd al Haqq , denounced Saddam as a tyrant and brushed aside his Islamic pretensions as a cover for tyranny.

Nor can the chief Iranian religious leader Ayatollah Ali Khamenei's rhetoric against the Americans during the Gulf War be taken as evidence of Iran's disposition toward that campaign. Crafty men, Iran's rulers sat out that war. They stood to emerge as the principal beneficiaries of Iraq's defeat. The American-led campaign against Iraq held out the promise of tilting the regional balance in their favor. No tears were shed in Iran for what befell Saddam Hussein's regime.

It is the mixed gift of living in hard places that men and women know how to distinguish between what they hear and what there is: no illusions were thus entertained in vast stretches of the Arab Muslim world about Saddam, or about the campaign to thwart him for that matter. The fight in the gulf was seen for what it was: a bid for primacy met by an imperial expedition that laid it to waste. A circle was closed in the gulf: where once the order in the region "east of Suez" had been the work of the British, it was now provided by Pax Americana. The new power standing sentry in the gulf belonged to the civilization of the West, as did the prior one. But the American presence had the anxious consent of the Arab lands of the Persian Gulf. The stranger coming in to check the kinsmen.

The world of Islam divides and subdivides. The battle lines in the Caucasus, too, are not coextensive with civilizational fault lines. The lines follow the interests of states. Where Huntington sees a civilizational duel between Armenia and Azerbaijan, the Iranian state has cast religious zeal and fidelity to the wind. Indeed, in that battle the Iranians have tilted toward Christian Armenia.

THE WRIT OF STATES

We have been delivered into a new world, to be sure. But it is not a world where the writ of civilizations runs. Civilizations and civilizational fidelities remain. There is to them an astonishing measure of permanence. But let us be clear: civilizations do not control states, states control civilizations. States avert their gaze from blood ties when they need to; they see brotherhood and faith and kin when it is in their interest to do so.

We remain in a world of self-help. The solitude of states continues; the disorder in the contemporary world has rendered that solitude more pronounced. No way has yet been found to reconcile France to Pax Americana's hegemony, or to convince it to trust its security or cede its judgment to the preeminent Western power. And no Azeri has come up with a way the lands of Islam could be rallied to the fight over Nagorno Karabakh. The sky has not fallen in Kuala Lumpur or in Tunis over the setbacks of Azerbaijan in its fight with Armenia.

The lesson bequeathed us by Thucydides in his celebrated dialogue between the Melians and the Athenians remains. The Melians, it will be recalled, were a colony of the Lacedaemonians. Besieged by Athens, they held out and were sure that the Lacedaemonians were "bound, if only for very shame, to come to the aid of their kindred." The Melians never wavered in their confidence in their "civilizational" allies: "Our common blood insures our fidelity."[6] We know what became of the Melians. Their allies did not turn up, their island was sacked, their world laid to waste.

---

[6]Thucydides, *The Peloponnesian War*, New York: The Modern American Library, 1951, pp. 334–335.

Where Are the Great Powers?

At Home with the Kids

Edward N. Luttwak

During the Cold War as before it, local and regional conflicts were often instigated or at least encouraged and materially supported by rival great powers. Now, by contrast, the absence of functioning great powers is the cause of the world's inability to cope with all manner of violent disorders. The result is that not only groups of secessionists and aggressive small powers, such as Serbia, but even mere armed bands can now impose their will or simply rampage, unchecked by any greater force from without. Today there is neither the danger of great power wars nor the relative tranquillity once imposed by each great power within its own sphere of influence.

By the traditional definition, great powers were states strong enough to successfully wage war without calling on allies. But that distinction is now outdated, because the issue today is not whether war can be made with or without allies, but whether war can be made at all. Historically, there have been tacit preconditions to great power status: a readiness to use force whenever it was advantageous to do so and an acceptance of the resulting combat casualties with equanimity, as long as the number was not disproportionate.

In the past, those preconditions were too blatantly obvious and too easily satisfied to deserve a mention by either practitioners or theoreticians. Great powers normally relied on intimidation rather than combat, but only because a willingness to use force was assumed. Moreover, they would use force undeterred by the prospect of the ensuing casualties, within limits of course.

NOT-SO-GREAT BEHAVIOR

The Somalia debacle, precipitated by the loss of 18 U.S. soldiers, and the Haiti fiasco, caused by the fear that a handful of U.S. troops might be killed while defeating that country's military dictatorship, sufficiently exposed the current unreality of the great power concept. In

EDWARD N. LUTTWAK is a Senior Fellow at the Center for Strategic and International Studies in Washington, D.C. He is the author of *The Endangered American Dream.*

pride or shame, Americans might dispute any wider conclusion from those events. They would like to reserve for themselves the special sensitivity that forces policy to change completely because 18 professional soldiers are killed (soldiers, one might add, who come from a country in which gun-related deaths were last clocked at one every 14 minutes). But in fact the virtue or malady, as the case may be, is far from exclusively American.

Most recently, Britain and France (not to mention that other putative great power, Germany) flatly refused to risk their ground troops in combat to resist aggression in the former Yugoslavia. Overcoming the fear of reprisals against their own troops, it was only with great reluctance, after almost two years of horrific outrages, that the two countries finally consented to the carefully circumscribed threat of NATO air strikes issued in February 1994. To be sure, neither Britain nor France nor any other European power has any vital interests at stake in the former Yugoslavia. But that is the very essence of the matter: the great powers of history would have viewed the disintegration of Yugoslavia not as a noxious problem to be avoided but as an opportunity to be exploited. Using the need to protect populations under attack as their propaganda excuse and with the restoration of law and order as their ostensible motive, they would have intervened to establish zones of influence for themselves, just as the genuine great powers did in their time (even distant Russia disputed the Austro-Hungarian annexation of Bosnia-Herzegovina in 1908). Thus the power vacuum would have been filled, to the disappointment of local small power ambitions, and to the great advantage of local populations and peace.

As for why nothing of the kind happened in the former Yugoslavia in the face of atrocities not seen since the Second World War, the reason is not in dispute: no European government was any more willing than the U.S. government to risk its soldiers in combat. Of Japan, literally nothing need be said on this score.

The refusal to tolerate combat casualties is not confined to democracies. The Soviet Union was still an intact totalitarian dictatorship when it engaged in the classic great power venture of Afghanistan, only to find that even its tightly regimented society would not tolerate the resulting casualties. At the time, outside observers were distinctly puzzled by the minimal Soviet theater strategy in Afghanistan. After an abortive effort to establish territorial control, the Soviet strategy defended only the largest towns and the ring road that connected them, otherwise conceding almost the entire country to guerrillas. Likewise, knowledgeable observers were astonished by the inordinately prudent tactics of Soviet ground forces. Except for a few commando units, they mostly remained confined inside their fortified garrisons, often failing to sally out even when guerrillas were known to be nearby. At the time, the explanation most commonly offered was the reluctance of Soviet commanders to rely on their poorly trained conscript troops. But there is a better explanation: the Soviet headquarters was under constant and intense pressure from Moscow to avoid casualties at all costs because of the outraged reactions of families and friends.

This example also allows us to eliminate another superficial explanation for the novel refusal to accept even modest numbers of combat casualties: the impact of television coverage. The Soviet Union never allowed its population to see any television images of war like those shown in the United States, and still the reaction of Soviet society to the casualties of the Afghan war was essentially identical to the American reaction to the Vietnam War. Although in both cases cumulative casualties over the span of many years did not reach the casualty figures of one day of battle in past wars, they were nevertheless deeply traumatic.

THE WAR OF ALL MOTHERS

There is a more fundamental explanation that remains valid in cases with or without democratic governance, with or without uncontrolled war reportage by television: the demographic character of modern, postindustrial societies. The populations of the great powers of history were commonly comprised of families of four, five or six children; families of one, two or three were rarer than families of seven, eight or nine. On the other hand, infant mortality rates were also high. When it was normal to lose one or more children to disease, the loss of one more youngster in war had a different meaning than it has for today's families, which have two or three children, all of whom are expected to survive, and each of whom represents a larger share of the family's emotional economy.

As any number of historical studies have shown, death itself was a much more normal part of the familial experience when it was not confined mostly to the very old. To lose a young family member for any reason was no doubt always tragic, yet a death in combat was not the extraordinary and fundamentally unacceptable event that it has now become. Parents who commonly approved of their sons' and daughters' decisions to join the armed forces, thereby choosing a career dedicated to combat and its preparation just as a fireman's career is dedicated to the fighting of fires, now often react with astonishment and anger when their children are actually sent into potential combat situations. And they are apt to view their wounding or death as an outrageous scandal, rather than as an occupational hazard.

The Italians, perhaps more postindustrial than most in this sense, with Europe's lowest birthrate, have a word for these reactions: *mammismo*, which might be translated as "motherism." These attitudes have great political resonance nowadays, powerfully constraining the use of force. The Soviet experience in Afghanistan proves that the constraint can become operative even without a mass media eager to publicize private grief, members of Congress ready to complain at the instance of relatives, or pointed questions being asked in a parliament.

Present attitudes toward combat losses that derive from the new family demography are powerful because they are not confined to the relatives and friends of servicemen on active duty. They are shared throughout society—and were shared even within the Soviet elite, it turns out—generating an extreme reluctance to impose a possible sacrifice that has become so much greater than it was when national populations were perhaps much smaller but families were much larger.

What of the Gulf War, then, or for that matter Britain's war to reconquer the Falklands? Do they not suggest a much simpler explanation: that attitudes depend on the perceived importance of the undertaking, the objective value of what is at stake, or—more realistically—the sheer ability of political leaders to justify the necessity of combat? After all, even during World War II, soldiers greatly resented assignments to what were described as secondary fronts, quickly dubbing any theater that was less than highly publicized as "forgotten." The less immediately compelling the justification, the more likely combat and its casualties are to be opposed. It might therefore seem that the new 2.2-children-per-family demographics and the resulting *mammismo* are irrelevant, that what counts is only what has always counted, namely the importance of the interests at stake, the political orchestration of the event and plain leadership.

Those contentions undoubtedly have some merit, but much less than meets the eye. In the first place, if lives can only be placed at risk in situations already dramatically prominent on the national scene, hence on a larger rather than a smaller scale, and only in final extremities, that in itself already rules out the most efficient use of force—early and on a small scale to prevent escalation.

CONSTRICTED VISIONS

In the past, there was no question of limiting the use of force to situations in which genuinely vital interests, that is, survival interests, were at stake. To struggle for mere survival was the unhappy predicament of threatened small powers, which had to fight purely to defend themselves and could not hope to achieve anything more with their modest strength. Great powers were different; they could only remain great if they were seen as willing and able to use force to acquire and protect even non-vital interests, including distant possessions or minor additions to their spheres of influence. To lose a few hundred soldiers in some minor probing operation or a few thousand in a small war or expeditionary venture were routine events for the great powers of history.

Great powers are in the business of threatening, rather than being threatened. A great power cannot be that unless it asserts all sorts of claims that far exceed the needs of its own immediate security, including the protection of allies and clients as well as other less-than-vital interests. It must therefore risk combat for purposes that may be fairly recondite, perhaps in little-known distant lands, but definitely in situations in which it is not compelled to fight but rather deliberately chooses to do so. And that is the choice now denied by the fear of casualties.

Even now, exceptional strivings by exceptionally determined leaders skilled in the art of political leadership can widen a great power's freedom of action, overcoming at least in part the effects of the new family demographics. That was obviously the case in the Persian Gulf intervention and the Falklands reconquest; both would have been impossible undertakings had it not been for the exceptional leadership of President George Bush and Prime Minister Margaret Thatcher, respectively. Their leadership was the decisive factor, not the undoubted significance of keeping Iraq from controlling Saudi and Kuwaiti oil, or the equally undoubted insignificance of the Falklands for any practical purpose whatsoever (another illustration of the irrelevance of the "objective" value of whatever is at stake).

Leadership is important, but that consideration cuts both ways, because the routine functioning of a great power cannot depend on the fortuitous presence of exceptional leadership. It will be recalled, moreover, that a very low opinion of Argentine military strength (indeed, a gross underestimate of Argentine air power) and the resulting belief that casualties would be very low were crucial to Britain's commitment to war in the Falklands. Likewise, the imperative of minimizing casualties was the leitmotiv of the entire Persian Gulf intervention, from the initial deployment, which was originally presented as purely defensive, to the sudden decision to call off the ground war. (To be sure, there were other considerations as well, notably the fear that Iran would become the next threat if Iraq's army were utterly destroyed.) In any case, it seems clear that the freedom of action gained by successful leadership was still very narrow; it is not hard to guess what would have happened to President Bush and his administration if the casualties of the Persian Gulf venture had reached the levels of any one day of serious fighting in either world war.

NATIONS OF FAMILIES

If the significance of the new family demographics is accepted, it follows that no advanced low-birth-rate countries can play the role of a classic great power anymore, not the United States or Russia, not Britain, France or, least of all, Germany or Japan. They may still possess the physical attributes of military strength or the economic base to develop such strength even on a great scale, but their societies are so allergic to casualties that they are effectively debellicized, or nearly so.

Aside from self-defense and exceptional cases à la the Persian Gulf War, only such conflict as can take place without soldiers is likely to be tolerated. Much can be done by air power, with few lives at risk, especially if bureaucratic resistance to the use of air power alone can be overcome. Sea power too can be useful at times, and robotic weapons will be used increasingly. But Bosnia, Somalia and Haiti remind us that the typical great power business of restoring order still requires ground forces. In the end, the infantry, albeit mechanized, is still indispensable, although now mostly withheld by the fear of casualties. It is true of course that high-birth-rate countries can still fight wars by choice, and several have in recent years. But even those very few among them that have competent armed forces lack other key great power attributes, including any significant strategic reach.

In the absence of functioning great powers, the entire character of world politics has changed. Under the old *machtpolitik* rules, for example, the United States should have been eager to extend its military influence to the Russian border by granting full NATO membership to Poland and other former Warsaw Pact countries. Instead the United States opposed NATO's expansion. In the central arena of world affairs, only the commercial and industrial policies that I have elsewhere labeled "geo-economic" still have a recognizably conflictual flavor.

Unless the world is content to cohabit with chronic disorder and widespread violence, a synthetic version of law-and-order interventionism by great powers will have to be invented. The remedies we already have are certainly inadequate. To keep the armed forces of the United States as powerful as possible—the preferred military option, of course—is ineffectual when intimidation will not do it, yet the United States refuses to fight. And U.S. ability to intimidate cannot but decline as the word spreads.

IMPROBABLE STAND-INS

Two rather improbable schemes are therefore left. Both satisfy the essential requirement of circumventing the intolerance of casualties. Both could be organized quite efficiently, given the will to do so. Yet both would be furiously opposed by the military establishment, and both undeniably have unpleasant moral connotations.

One scheme would be to copy the Ghurka model, recruiting troops in some suitable region abroad, if not in Nepal itself. They would be mercenaries, of course, but they would be of high quality, and a common ethnic origin would assure their basic cohesion. In practice, U.S. Ghurkas would provide the infantry units, with native U.S. forces providing the more technical forms of combat support involving smaller risks and fewer casualties.

The alternative is to copy the foreign legion model, with units that combine U.S. officers and nonnative volunteers who have renounced their national allegiance, perhaps attracted by the offer of U.S. citizenship after a given term of service. Under both schemes, political responsibility for any casualties would be much reduced, even if not eliminated. The United States, by the way, raised ethnic mercenary units in Indochina with rather good results, and it recruited individual foreign volunteers for Europe-based special forces. So neither scheme is as outlandish or unprecedented as it may seem. Still, one would not want to bet that they would be seriously considered, let alone adopted.

If no remedy can be found for the passing of the great powers and the conspicuous inability of the United States itself to play that role, both the United States and the world had better become habituated to the consequences. Violent disorders unchecked by effective great power interventions have both immediate and delayed effects, including disrupted export markets, refugees and new sources of international crime and terrorism. But Americans will also have to learn not to see, hear or feel much that would otherwise offend their moral sensitivities. Richer inhabitants of the poorest countries learn from childhood how to step politely over the quadruple-amputee beggar in their path without ever actually looking at him, and how not to see the starving mother and child, the waif and the abandoned elderly who try to beg from them as they walk into a restaurant or bank. Blindness can be learned, and Americans will have to learn how to passively ignore avoidable tragedies and horrific atrocities. The experience of Bosnia-Herzegovina shows that Americans have already made much progress in that direction.

FOREIGN AFFAIRS

JULY/AUGUST 1999

Redefining the National Interest

Joseph S. Nye, Jr.

Volume 78 • Number 4

Redefining the National Interest

Joseph S. Nye, Jr.

CONFUSION AFTER KOSOVO

NATO'S MILITARY intervention in Kosovo dramatically raises a larger problem: how should the United States define its interests in today's world? After the collapse of the Soviet Union, what are the limits of America's concerns abroad? Can one define interests conventionally in the information age? The "national interest" is a slippery concept, used to describe as well as prescribe foreign policy. Hence the considerable debate about it. Some scholars have even regretted the waning of the very idea of a "national" interest today. Writing in these pages, Samuel P. Huntington argued recently that "without a sure sense of national identity, Americans have become unable to define their national interests, and as a result subnational commercial interests and transnational and nonnational ethnic interests have come to dominate foreign policy."

For almost five decades, the containment of Soviet power provided a North Star to guide American foreign policy. From a longer historical perspective, however, the Cold War was the anomalous period, and even it involved some bitter disputes over where our interests lay—during the Vietnam War, for example. Before World War II, confusion was more often the rule. For example, ethnic differences colored appraisals of whether the United States should enter World War I. Peter

---

JOSEPH S. NYE, JR., is Dean of Harvard's Kennedy School of Government and served as Assistant Secretary of Defense for International Security Affairs in 1994 and 1995.

[22]

Trubowitz's recent study of American definitions of national interests in the 1890s, 1930s, and 1980s concludes that "there is no single national interest. Analysts who assume that America has a discernible national interest whose defense should determine its relations with other nations are unable to explain the persistent failure to achieve domestic consensus on international objectives."

With all that said, it would be a mistake to discard the term. As the Commission on America's National Interests declared in 1996, "national interests are the fundamental building blocks in any discussion of foreign policy. . . . In fact, the concept is used regularly and widely by administration officials, members of Congress, and citizens at large." The commission goes on to identify five vital interests that most agree would justify the unilateral use of force. Not everyone would agree with this particular list. Economic and humanitarian interests are also widely thought important. Many experts argue that vital strategic concerns are more widely shared than other interests, and deserve priority because were we to fail to protect them, more Americans would be affected and in more profound ways. Leaders and experts are right to point out dangers to the public and to try to persuade it. Yet even "objective" threats are not always obvious. The connection between a particular event (Iraq's invasion of Kuwait or Serbia's rejection of the Rambouillet agreement) and an American interest may involve a long causal chain. Different people see different risks and dangers. And priorities vary: reasonable people can disagree, for example, about how much insurance to buy against remote threats and whether to do so before pursuing other values (such as human rights). In a democracy, such political struggles over the exact definition of national interests—and how to pursue them—are both inevitable and healthy. Foreign-policy experts can help clarify causation and tradeoffs in particular cases, but experts alone cannot decide. Nor should they. The national interest is too important to leave solely to the geopoliticians. Elected officials must play the key role.

In a democracy, the national interest is simply the set of shared priorities regarding relations with the rest of the world. It is broader than strategic interests, though they are part of it. It can include values such as human rights and democracy, if the public feels that those values are so important to its identity that it is willing to pay a price to promote them. The American people clearly think that their interests include certain values and their promotion abroad—such as opposition to ethnic cleansing in the Balkans. A democratic definition of the national interest does not accept the distinction between a morality-based and an interest-based foreign policy. Moral values are simply intangible interests. Leaders and experts may point out the costs of indulging these values. But if an informed public disagrees, experts cannot deny the legitimacy of public opinion. Polls show that the American people are neither isolationist nor eager to serve as the world's police. But finding a middle course is proving difficult and complex.

THE IMPACT OF THE INFORMATION AGE

STRATEGISTS ADVISE that interests should be defined in relation to power—but how would one describe the distribution of power in the information age? Some think the end of the bipolar world left multipolarity in its stead. But that is not a very good description of a world in which one country, the United States, is so much more powerful than all the others. On the other hand, unipolarity is not a very good description either, because it exaggerates the degree to and ease with which the United States is able to get what it wants—witness Kosovo.

Instead, power today is distributed like a three-dimensional chess game. The top, military board is unipolar, with the United States far outstripping all other states. The middle, economic board is multipolar, with the United States, Europe, and Japan accounting for two-thirds of world production. But the bottom—representing transnational relations that cross borders and lie outside the control of governments—has a more dispersed structure of power. This complexity makes policymaking today more difficult. It means playing on several boards at the same time. Moreover, although it is important not to ignore the continuing importance of military force for some purposes, it is equally important not to be misled into thinking that American power can always get its way in nonmilitary matters. The United States is a preponderant, but not a dominant, power.

Another distinction to keep in mind is that between "hard power" (a country's economic and military ability to buy and coerce) and "soft power" (the ability to attract through cultural and ideological appeal). It is important that half a million foreign students want to study in the United States each year, that Europeans and Asians want to watch American films and TV, and that American liberties are attractive in many parts of the world. Our values are significant sources of soft power. Both hard and soft power remain vital, but in the information age soft power is becoming more compelling than ever before.

Massive flows of cheap information have expanded the number of contacts across national borders. In a deregulated world, global markets and nongovernmental actors play a larger role. States are more easily penetrated today and less like the classic realist model of solid billiard balls bouncing off each other. As a result, political leaders are finding it more difficult to maintain a coherent set of priorities in foreign policy, and more difficult to articulate a single national interest.

Yet the United States, with its democratic society, is well placed to benefit from the rapidly developing information age. Although greater pluralism may diminish the coherence of government policies, our institutions are attractive and the openness of our society enhances credibility—a crucial resource in an information age. Thus the United States is well placed to make use of soft power. At the same time, the soft power that comes from being a "city on the hill" does not provide the coercive capability that hard power does. Alone, it does not support a very venturesome foreign policy.

Hence different aspects of the information age mean different things for America's national interests. On the one hand, a good case can be made that the information revolution will have long-term benefits for democracies. Democratic societies can create credible information because they are not threatened by it. Authoritarian states will have more trouble. Governments can limit their citizens' access to the Internet and global markets, but they pay a high price if they do so. Singapore and China, for example, are currently wrestling with these problems. Moreover, transparency is becoming a key asset for countries seeking investments. Governments that want rapid development will have to give up some of the barriers to information flows.

On the other hand, some aspects of the information age are less benign. The free flow of broadcast information in open societies has always had an impact on public opinion and the formulation of foreign policy. But now the flow has increased in volume and shortened news cycles have reduced the time for deliberation. By focusing on certain conflicts and human rights problems, the media pressure politicians to respond to some foreign problems and not others—for example, Somalia rather than southern Sudan in 1992. The so-called CNN effect makes it hard to keep items that might otherwise warrant a lower priority off the top of the public agenda. Now, with the added interactivity of groups on the Internet, it will be harder than ever to maintain a consistent agenda.

Also problematic is the effect of transnational information flows on the stability of national communities. The Canadian media guru Marshall McLuhan once prophesied that communications technologies would turn the world into a global village. Instead of a single cosmopolitan community, however, they may have produced a congeries of global villages, each with all the parochial prejudices that the word implies, but with a greater awareness of global inequality. Transnational economic forces are disrupting traditional lifestyles, and this increases economic integration and communal disintegration at the same time. This is particularly true in the post-Soviet states and the old European-built empires of Africa. Political entrepreneurs use inexpensive information channels to mobilize the discontented on sub-national tribal levels: some to the cause of repressive nationalism, and some to transnational ethnic and religious communities. This in turn leads to increased demands for self-determination, increased violence, and other violations of human rights—all in the presence of television cameras and the Internet.

AMERICAN POWER AND PRIORITIES

WILLIAM PERRY and Ashton Carter have recently argued that we should rethink the way we understand risks to U.S. security. At the top of their new hierarchy they put "A list" threats like that the Soviet Union once presented to our survival. The "B list" features imminent threats to U.S. interests—but not to our survival—such as North Korea or Iraq. The "C list" includes important "contingencies that indirectly affect U.S. security but do not directly threaten U.S. interests":

"the Kosovos, Bosnias, Somalias, Rwandas, and Haitis."

What is striking is how the "C list" has come to dominate today's foreign policy agenda. Carter and Perry speculate that this is because of the disappearance of "A list" threats since the end of the Cold War. But another reason is that "C list" issues dominate media attention in the information age. Dramatic visual portrayals of immediate human conflict and suffering are far easier to convey to the public than "A list" abstractions like the possibility of a "Weimar Russia," the rise of a hegemonic China and the importance of our alliance with Japan, or the potential collapse of the international system of trade and investment. Yet if these larger, more abstract strategic issues were to turn out badly, they would have a far greater impact on the lives of most Americans.

How should America set priorities in the information age?

How should Americans set priorities in such a world? We should start by understanding our power. On one hand, for reasons given above, American power is now less fungible and effective than it might first appear. On the other, the United States is likely to remain preponderant well into the next century. For a variety of reasons, the information revolution is likely to enhance rather than diminish American power.

As a wealthy status quo power, the United States has an interest in maintaining international order. Behind the abstractions about rising interdependence are changes that make it more difficult to isolate the United States from the effects of events in the rest of the world. More concretely, there are two simple reasons why Americans have a national interest in preventing disorder beyond our borders. First, events and actors out there can hurt us; and second, Americans want to influence distant governments and organizations on a variety of issues such as the proliferation of weapons of mass destruction, terrorism, drugs, shared resources, and the environment.

To do so, the United States cannot merely set a good example—it needs hard-power resources. Maintaining these will require an investment that Americans have recently been unwilling to make—witness the decline in the foreign affairs budget and the reluctance to take casualties. It is difficult to be a superpower on the cheap. Second, the United

AP/WIDE WORLD PHOTOS

What should be our foreign policy priority? Russian soldiers . . .

States has to recognize a basic proposition of public-goods theory: if the largest beneficiary of a public good (such as international order) does not provide disproportionate resources toward its maintenance, the smaller beneficiaries are unlikely to do so. This puts a different twist on Secretary of State Madeleine K. Albright's phrase that the United States is "the indispensable nation," and one less palatable to the public and to Congress.

Third, we should make sure that top priority is given to those aspects of the international system that, if not attended to properly, would have profound effects on the basic international order and therefore on the lives and welfare of Americans. Some analysts have suggested that we can learn something from the lesson of the United Kingdom in the nineteenth century, when it was also a preponderant but not dominating power. Three public goods that Britain attended to were maintaining the balance of power among the major states, promoting an open international economic system, and maintaining open international commons such as the freedom of the seas. All

AP/WIDE WORLD PHOTOS

... or Kosovar refugees?

three translate relatively well to the current American case. In terms of the distribution of power, we need to continue to "shape the environment" (in the words of the Pentagon's *Quadrennial Defense Review*), and that is why we keep 100,000 troops based in Europe, another 100,000 in Asia, and some 20,000 near the Persian Gulf. Our role as a stabilizer and a reassurance against the rise of hostile hegemons in important regions has to remain a top priority, an "A list" issue.

Meanwhile, promoting an open international economic system is good not just for America's economic growth but for other countries' as well. In the long term, economic growth is likely to foster stable democratic middle-class societies around the world. To keep the global system open, the United States must resist protectionism at home and strengthen international monitoring institutions such as the World Trade Organization, the International Monetary Fund, and the Bank for International Settlements. In regard to international commons, the United States, like nineteenth-century Britain, has an interest in freedom of the seas, but also in the environment, in the preservation of endangered species, and in the uses of outer space and of the new cyberspace.

Beyond the nineteenth-century analogy, in today's world the United States has a general interest in developing and maintaining the international laws and institutions that deal not just with trade and the environment, but with arms proliferation, peacekeeping, human rights, and other concerns. Those who denigrate the importance of law and institutions forget that the United States is a status quo power. They also ignore the extent to which legitimacy is a power reality. True realists would not make such a mistake.

Finally, as a preponderant power, the United States can provide an important public good by acting as a mediator and convener. By helping to organize coalitions of the willing and by using its good offices to mediate conflicts in places like Northern Ireland, the Middle East, or the Aegean Sea, the United States can help to shape the world in ways that are beneficial to us as well as to other nations.

THE C LIST

IF WE did not live in the information age, the foregoing strategy for prioritizing America's national interests might suffice. But the reality is that nonvital crises like Somalia, Bosnia, Haiti, and Kosovo continue to force their way to the foreground because of their ability to command massive media attention. Such crises raise moral concerns that the American people consistently include in their list of foreign policy interests. Policy experts may deplore such sympathies, but they are a democratic reality.

Some might object that a strategy based on "A list" issues does not take account of the ongoing erosion of Westphalian national sovereignty that is occurring today. It is true that old-fashioned state sovereignty is eroding—both de facto, through the penetration of national borders by transnational forces, and de jure, as seen in the imposition of sanctions against South Africa for apartheid, the development of an International Criminal Court, and the bombing of Yugoslavia over its policies in Kosovo. But the erosion of sovereignty is a long-term trend of decades and centuries, and it is a mixed blessing rather a clear good. Although the erosion may help advance human rights in repressive regimes by exposing them to international attention, it also portends considerable disorder. Recall that the seventeenth-century Peace of Westphalia created a system of sovereign states to curtail vicious civil wars over religion. Although it is true that sovereignty stands in the way of national self-determination, such self-determination is not the unequivocal moral good it first appears. In a world where there are some two hundred states but many thousands of often overlapping entities that might eventually make a claim to nationhood, blind promotion of self-determination would have highly problematic consequences.

A human rights policy is not a foreign policy; it is an important part of a foreign policy.

So what do we do about the humanitarian concerns and strong moral preferences that Americans want to see expressed in their foreign policy? Americans have rarely accepted pure realpolitik as a guiding principle, and human rights and the alleviation of humanitarian disasters have long been important aspects of our foreign policy. But foreign policy involves trying to accomplish varied objectives in a complex and recalcitrant world. This entails tradeoffs. A human rights policy is not itself a foreign policy; it is an important *part* of a foreign policy. During the Cold War, this balancing act often meant tolerating human rights abuses by regimes that were crucial to balancing Soviet power—for example, in South Korea before its transition to democracy. Similar problems persist in the current period—witness our policy toward Saudi Arabia, or our efforts to balance human rights in China with our long-term strategic objectives.

In the information age, humanitarian concerns dominate attention to a greater degree than before, often at the cost of diverting attention from "A list" strategic issues. Since pictures are more powerful than words, arguments about tradeoffs become emotional and difficult. Of course, acting on humanitarian values is often appropriate. Few Americans can look at television pictures of starving people or miserable refugees and not say that their country should do something about them. And the United States often does respond to such catastrophes. Sometimes this is quite easily done, such as hurricane relief to Central America or the early stages of famine relief in Somalia. But apparently simple cases like Somalia can turn out to be extremely difficult to resolve, and others, like Kosovo, are difficult from the start.

The problem with such hard cases is that the humanitarian interest that instigates the action often turns out to be a mile wide and an inch deep. The American public's impulse to help starving Somalis (whose food supply was being interrupted by various warlords) vanished in the face of televised pictures of dead U.S. soldiers being dragged through the streets of Mogadishu. Such transience is sometimes attributed to popular reluctance to accept casualties. But that is too simple. Americans went into the Gulf War expecting and willing to accept some ten thousand casualties. As this suggests, Americans are reluctant to accept casualties only in cases where their *only* foreign policy goals are unreciprocated humanitarian interests. Ironically, when opinion turns against such cases, this may not only divert attention and limit willingness to support "A list" interests but may also undermine support for action in other, more serious humanitarian crises. One of the direct effects of the Somalia disaster was America's failure (along with other countries) to support and reinforce the United Nations peacekeeping force in Rwanda that could have limited a true genocide in 1994.

One effect of Somalia was America's failure to prevent true genocide in Rwanda in 1994.

There are no easy answers for such cases. We could not simply turn off the television or unplug our computers even if we wanted to. The "C list" cannot simply be ignored. But there are certain rules of prudence that may help the integration of such issues into the larger strategy for advancing the national interest. First, there are many degrees of humanitarian concern and many degrees of intervention to reflect them, such as condemnation, sanctions targeted on individuals, broad sanctions, and various uses of force. We should save violent options for the most egregious cases. When we do use force, it is worth remembering some principles of the "just war" doctrine: having a just cause in the eyes of others; discrimination in means so as to not unduly punish the innocent; proportionality of means to ends; and a high probability of good consequences (rather than wishful thinking).

We should generally avoid the use of force except in cases where our humanitarian interests are reinforced by the existence of other strong national interests. This was the case in the Gulf War, where the United States was concerned not only with the aggression against Kuwait, but also with energy supplies and regional allies. This was not the case in Somalia. In the former Yugoslavia (Bosnia and Kosovo), our interests combine both humanitarian values and the strategic concerns of European allies and NATO. We should try to involve other regional actors, preferably in the lead role when possible. In Africa after 1995, the United States offered to help with training, intelligence, logistics, and transportation if African countries provided the troops for a peacekeeping force. There were few takers. If African states are unwilling to do their part, we should be wary of going it alone. In Europe, we should welcome the idea of combined joint task forces that would be separable but not separate from NATO and encourage the Europeans to take the lead on such issues.

We should also be clearer about what are true cases of genocide. The American people have a real humanitarian interest in not letting another Holocaust occur. Yet we did just that in Rwanda in 1994. We therefore need to do more to organize prevention and response to real cases of genocide. Unfortunately, the Genocide Convention is written so loosely and the word is so abused for political purposes that there is danger of the term becoming trivialized. But a strict historical interpretation of the crime, based on the precedents of the Holocaust and Rwanda, can help to avoid such pitfalls.

Finally, Americans should be very wary about intervention in civil wars over self-determination. The principle is dangerously ambiguous; atrocities are often committed by activists on both sides and the precedents can have disastrous consequences.

How could these rules of prudence have helped in the case of Kosovo? At an earlier stage, they would have produced more caution. In December 1992, President Bush issued a vague threat that Serbia should not attack ethnic Albanians in its Kosovo province while he remained silent on Bosnia. A year later, the Clinton administration reiterated the warning. The United States was saved from having to back up these threats by the Kosovar Albanians' pacifist leader, Ibrahim Rugova, who espoused a Gandhian response to Serbian oppression. After 1996, the rise of the militantly pro-independence

Kosovo Liberation Army undermined Rugova's leadership. According to journalist Chris Hedges, the radicals of the KLA, who combine "hints of fascism on one side and whiffs of communism on the other," have been labeled a terrorist organization by U.S. government officials. A KLA victory might well have involved atrocities and ethnic cleansing of the Serb minority in Kosovo. The KLA's refusal to sign the Rambouillet agreement in the first round of talks in February let the NATO alliance off the moral hook and should have been used as an opportunity to step back. Instead, the United States "fixed the problem" by pretending to believe the KLA's promise to accept autonomy within Yugoslavia. The United States then threatened to bomb Serbia. Milošević called the American bluff and initiated his planned ethnic cleansing of Kosovo.

At that point, new facts on the ground raised Kosovo from the "C list" to the "B list" of U.S. foreign policy concerns. The scale and ferocity of Milošević's ethnic cleansing could not be ignored. European allies such as the United Kingdom, France, and even Germany joined the United States in calling for NATO action. If the United States had then pulled the rug out from under its pro-interventionist allies, it would have produced a NATO crisis on the scale of Suez in 1956. The humanitarian impact had grown immensely and was now reinforced by a strategic interest in the future of the American alliance with Europe. Skeptics argue that one should never pursue "sunk costs." By this argument, if Kosovo was not worth intervention before, it is not worth it now. But history is path-dependent, since choices, once made, eliminate certain options and create others. In calculating the costs and benefits of future actions, policymakers must realistically assess the current situation, not the past. It does no good to lament the more prudent paths not taken at an earlier stage.

Kosovo illustrates how a "C list" issue can migrate to the "B list" of national interests that merit the use of force. Kosovo itself is not a vital American interest, and it only touches tangentially on an "A list" issue (the credibility of the NATO alliance). The "A list" also includes the future of Russia and of international laws and institutions such as the United Nations. NATO, Russia, and the United Nations must all figure in how we resolve the Kosovo crisis. And the rules of prudence must still be applied as we insist on the return of the refugees and the withdrawal of Serbian forces. If moral outrage or unilateralist temptations blind Americans to their other "A list" priorities, the United States may dangerously overreach itself and turn a just cause into a counterproductive crusade.

Prudence alone cannot determine the national interest in the information age. But better consequences will flow if American values and goals are related to American power, and interests are rationally pursued within prudent limits. Determining the national interest has always been contentious throughout U.S. history. That is to be expected in a healthy democracy. But the debate about the American national interest in the information age should pay more attention to the peculiar nature of American power today; it should establish strategic priorities accordingly; and it should develop prudential rules that allow the United States to meld its strategic, economic, and humanitarian interests into an effective foreign policy.

Promoting the National Interest

Condoleezza Rice

LIFE AFTER THE COLD WAR

THE UNITED STATES has found it exceedingly difficult to define its "national interest" in the absence of Soviet power. That we do not know how to think about what follows the U.S.-Soviet confrontation is clear from the continued references to the "post–Cold War period." Yet such periods of transition are important, because they offer strategic opportunities. During these fluid times, one can affect the shape of the world to come.

The enormity of the moment is obvious. The Soviet Union was more than just a traditional global competitor; it strove to lead a universal socialist alternative to markets and democracy. The Soviet Union quarantined itself and many often-unwitting captives and clients from the rigors of international capitalism. In the end, it sowed the seeds of its own destruction, becoming in isolation an economic and technological dinosaur.

But this is only part of the story. The Soviet Union's collapse coincided with another great revolution. Dramatic changes in information technology and the growth of "knowledge-based" industries altered

CONDOLEEZZA RICE is Senior Fellow at the Hoover Institution and Professor of Political Science at Stanford University. She is also foreign policy adviser to Republican presidential candidate George W. Bush.

Editors' Note: Democratic views will be published in forthcoming issues.

the very basis of economic dynamism, accelerating already noticeable trends in economic interaction that often circumvented and ignored state boundaries. As competition for capital investment has intensified, states have faced difficult choices about their internal economic, political, and social structures. As the prototype of this "new economy," the United States has seen its economic influence grow—and with it, its diplomatic influence. America has emerged as both the principal benefactor of these simultaneous revolutions and their beneficiary.

The process of outlining a new foreign policy must begin by recognizing that the United States is in a remarkable position. Powerful secular trends are moving the world toward economic openness and—more unevenly—democracy and individual liberty. Some states have one foot on the train and the other off. Some states still hope to find a way to decouple democracy and economic progress. Some hold on to old hatreds as diversions from the modernizing task at hand. But the United States and its allies are on the right side of history.

In such an environment, American policies must help further these favorable trends by maintaining a disciplined and consistent foreign policy that separates the important from the trivial. The Clinton administration has assiduously avoided implementing such an agenda. Instead, every issue has been taken on its own terms—crisis by crisis, day by day. It takes courage to set priorities because doing so is an admission that American foreign policy cannot be all things to all people—or rather, to all interest groups. The Clinton administration's approach has its advantages: If priorities and intent are not clear, they cannot be criticized. But there is a high price to pay for this approach. In a democracy as pluralistic as ours, the absence of an articulated "national interest" either produces a fertile ground for those wishing to withdraw from the world or creates a vacuum to be filled by parochial groups and transitory pressures.

THE ALTERNATIVE

AMERICAN FOREIGN POLICY in a Republican administration should refocus the United States on the national interest and the pursuit of key priorities. These tasks are

- to ensure that America's military can deter war, project power, and fight in defense of its interests if deterrence fails;

• to promote economic growth and political openness by extending free trade and a stable international monetary system to all committed to these principles, including in the western hemisphere, which has too often been neglected as a vital area of U.S. national interest;

• to renew strong and intimate relationships with allies who share American values and can thus share the burden of promoting peace, prosperity, and freedom;

• to focus U.S. energies on comprehensive relationships with the big powers, particularly Russia and China, that can and will mold the character of the international political system; and

• to deal decisively with the threat of rogue regimes and hostile powers, which is increasingly taking the forms of the potential for terrorism and the development of weapons of mass destruction (WMD).

INTERESTS AND IDEALS

POWER MATTERS, both the exercise of power by the United States and the ability of others to exercise it. Yet many in the United States are (and have always been) uncomfortable with the notions of power politics, great powers, and power balances. In an extreme form, this discomfort leads to a reflexive appeal instead to notions of international law and norms, and the belief that the support of many states—or even better, of institutions like the United Nations—is essential to the legitimate exercise of power. The "national interest" is replaced with "humanitarian interests" or the interests of "the international community." The belief that the United States is exercising power legitimately only when it is doing so on behalf of someone or something else was deeply rooted in Wilsonian thought, and there are strong echoes of it in the Clinton administration. To be sure, there is nothing wrong with doing something that benefits all humanity, but that is, in a sense, a second-order effect. America's pursuit of the national interest will create conditions that promote freedom, markets, and peace. Its pursuit of national interests after World War II led to a more prosperous and democratic world. This can happen again.

So multilateral agreements and institutions should not be ends in themselves. U.S. interests are served by having strong alliances and can be promoted within the U.N. and other multilateral organizations, as

well as through well-crafted international agreements. But the Clinton administration has often been so anxious to find multilateral solutions to problems that it has signed agreements that are not in America's interest. The Kyoto treaty is a case in point: whatever the facts on global warming, a treaty that does not include China and exempts "developing" countries from tough standards while penalizing American industry cannot possibly be in America's national interest.

Similarly, the arguments about U.S. ratification of the Comprehensive Test Ban Treaty are instructive. Since 1992, the United States has refrained unilaterally from testing nuclear weapons. It is an example to the rest of the world yet does not tie its own hands "in perpetuity" if testing becomes necessary again. But in pursuit of a "norm" against the acquisition of nuclear weapons, the United States signed a treaty that was not verifiable, did not deal with the threat of the development of nuclear weapons by rogue states, and threatened the reliability of the nuclear stockpile. Legitimate congressional concerns about the substance of the treaty were ignored during negotiations. When faced with the defeat of a bad treaty, the administration attacked the motives of its opponents—incredibly branding long-standing internationalists like Senators Richard Lugar (R-Ind.) and John Warner (R-Va.) as isolationists.

Certainly, Republican presidents have not been immune to the practice of pursuing symbolic agreements of questionable value. According to the Senate Foreign Relations Committee, some 52 conventions, agreements, and treaties still await ratification; some even date back to 1949. But the Clinton administration's attachment to largely symbolic agreements and its pursuit of, at best, illusory "norms" of international behavior have become an epidemic. That is not leadership. Neither is it isolationist to suggest that the United States has a special role in the world and should not adhere to every international convention and agreement that someone thinks to propose.

Even those comfortable with notions of the "national interest" are still queasy with a focus on power relationships and great-power politics. The reality is that a few big powers can radically affect international peace, stability, and prosperity. These states are capable of disruption on a grand scale, and their fits of anger or acts of beneficence affect hundreds of millions of people. By reason of size, geographic position, economic potential, and military strength, they are capable of influencing American welfare for good or ill. Moreover, that kind of power is usually accompanied by a sense of entitlement to play a decisive role in international politics. Great powers do not just mind their own business.

Great powers do not just mind their own business.

Some worry that this view of the world ignores the role of values, particularly human rights and the promotion of democracy. In fact, there are those who would draw a sharp line between power politics and a principled foreign policy based on values. This polarized view—you are either a realist or devoted to norms and values—may be just fine in academic debate, but it is a disaster for American foreign policy. American values are universal. People want to say what they think, worship as they wish, and elect those who govern them; the triumph of these values is most assuredly easier when the international balance of power favors those who believe in them. But sometimes that favorable balance of power takes time to achieve, both internationally and within a society. And in the meantime, it is simply not possible to ignore and isolate other powerful states that do not share those values.

The Cold War is a good example. Few would deny that the collapse of the Soviet Union profoundly transformed the picture of democracy and human rights in eastern and central Europe and the former Soviet territories. Nothing improved human rights as much as the collapse of Soviet power. Throughout the Cold War, the United States pursued a policy that promoted political liberty, using every instrument from the Voice of America to direct presidential intervention on behalf of dissidents. But it lost sight neither of the importance of the geopolitical relationship with Moscow nor of the absolute necessity of retaining robust American military power to deter an all-out military confrontation.

In the 1970s, the Soviet Union was at the height of its power—which it was more than willing to use. Given its weak economic and technological base, the victories of that period turned out to be Pyrrhic. President Reagan's challenge to Soviet power was both resolute and well timed. It included intense substantive engagements with Moscow across the entire range of issues captured in the "four-part agenda" (arms control, human rights, economic issues, and regional conflicts). The Bush administration then focused greater attention on rolling back Soviet power in central and eastern Europe. As the Soviet Union's might waned, it could no longer defend its interests and gave up peacefully (thankfully) to the West—a tremendous victory for Western power and also for human liberty.

SETTING PRIORITIES

THE UNITED STATES has many sources of power in the pursuit of its goals. The global economy demands economic liberalization, greater openness and transparency, and at the very least, access to information technology. International economic policies that leverage the advantages of the American economy and expand free trade are the decisive tools in shaping international politics. They permit us to reach out to states as varied as South Africa and India and to engage our neighbors in the western hemisphere in a shared interest in economic prosperity. The growth of entrepreneurial classes throughout the world is an asset in the promotion of human rights and individual liberty, and it should be understood and used as such. Yet peace is the first and most important condition for continued prosperity and freedom. America's military power must be secure because the United States is the only guarantor of global peace and stability. The current neglect of America's armed forces threatens its ability to maintain peace.

The Bush administration had been able to reduce defense spending somewhat at the end of the Cold War in 1991. But the Clinton administration witlessly accelerated and deepened these cuts. The results were devastating: military readiness declined, training suffered, military pay slipped 15 percent below civilian equivalents, morale plummeted, and the services cannibalized existing equipment to keep airplanes flying, ships afloat, and tanks moving. The increased difficulty in recruiting people to the armed forces or retaining them is hardly surprising.

Moreover, the administration began deploying American forces abroad at a furious pace—an average of once every nine weeks. As it cut defense spending to its lowest point as a percentage of GDP since Pearl Harbor, the administration deployed the armed forces more often than at any time in the last 50 years. Some of the deployments themselves were questionable, such as in Haiti. But more than anything it was simply unwise to multiply missions in the face of a continuing budget reduction. Means and mission were not matched, and (predictably) the already thinly stretched armed forces came close to a breaking point. When all these trends became so obvious and embarrassing that they could no longer be ignored, the administration finally requested increased defense spending. But the "death spiral," as the administration's own undersecretary of defense called it—robbing procurement and research and development simply to operate the armed forces—was already well under way. That the administration did nothing, choosing instead to live off the fruits of Reagan's military buildup, constitutes an extraordinary neglect of the fiduciary responsibilities of the commander in chief.

Now the next president will be confronted with a prolonged job of repair. Military readiness will have to take center stage, particularly those aspects that affect the living conditions of the troops—military pay, housing—and also training. New weapons will have to be procured in order to give the military the capacity to carry out today's missions. But even in its current state, the American military still enjoys a commanding technological lead and therefore has a battlefield advantage over any competitor. Thus the next president should refocus the Pentagon's priorities on building the military of the 21st century rather than continuing to build on the structure of the Cold War. U.S. technological advantages should be leveraged to build forces that are lighter and more lethal, more mobile and agile, and capable of firing accurately from long distances. In order to do this, Washington must reallocate resources, perhaps in some cases skipping a generation of technology to make leaps rather than incremental improvements in its forces.

The other major concern is a loss of focus on the mission of the armed forces. What does it mean to deter, fight, and win wars and defend the national interest? First, the American military must be able to meet decisively the emergence of any hostile military power in the Asia-Pacific region, the Middle East, the Persian Gulf, and Europe—areas in which not only our interests but also those of our key allies are at stake. America's military is the only one capable of this deterrence function, and it must not be stretched or diverted into areas that weaken these broader responsibilities. It is the role that the United States played when Saddam Hussein threatened the Persian Gulf, and it is the power needed to deter trouble on the Korean Peninsula or across the Taiwan Strait. In the latter cases, the goal is to make it inconceivable for North Korea or China to use force because American military power is a compelling factor in their equations.

If it is worth fighting for, you had better be prepared to win.

Some small-scale conflicts clearly have an impact on American strategic interests. Such was the case with Kosovo, which was in the backyard of America's most important strategic alliance: NATO. In fact, Yugoslav President Slobodan Milošević's rejection of peaceful coexistence with the Kosovar Albanians threatened to rock the area's fragile ethnic balance. Eastern Europe is a patchwork of ethnic minorities. For the most part, Hungarians and Romanians, Bulgarians and Turks, and even Ukrainians and Russians have found a way since 1991 of preventing their differences from exploding. Milošević has been the exception, and the United States had an overriding strategic interest in stopping him. There was, of course, a humanitarian disaster looming as well, but in the absence of concerns based on the interests of the alliance, the case for intervention would have been more tenuous.

The Kosovo war was conducted incompetently, in part because the administration's political goals kept shifting and in part because it was not, at the start, committed to the decisive use of military force. That President Clinton was surprised at Milošević's tenacity is, well, surprising. If there is any lesson from history, it is that small powers with everything to lose are often more stubborn than big powers, for whom the conflict is merely one among many problems. The lesson, too, is that if it is worth fighting for, you had better be prepared to win. Also, there must be a political game plan that will permit the withdrawal of our forces—something that is still completely absent in Kosovo.

But what if our values are attacked in areas that are not arguably of strategic concern? Should the United States not try to save lives in the absence of an overriding strategic rationale? The next American president should be in a position to intervene when he believes, and can make the case, that the United States is duty-bound to do so. "Humanitarian intervention" cannot be ruled out a priori. But a decision to intervene in the absence of strategic concerns should be understood for what it is. Humanitarian problems are rarely only humanitarian problems; the taking of life or withholding of food is almost always a political act. If the United States is not prepared to address the underlying political conflict and to know whose side it is on, the military may end up separating warring parties for an indefinite period. Sometimes one party (or both) can come to see the United States as the enemy. Because the military cannot, by definition, do anything decisive in these "humanitarian" crises, the chances of misreading the situation and ending up in very different circumstances are very high. This was essentially the problem of "mission creep" in Somalia.

The president must remember that the military is a special instrument. It is lethal, and it is meant to be. It is not a civilian police force. It is not a political referee. And it is most certainly not designed to build a civilian society. Military force is best used to support clear political goals, whether limited, such as expelling Saddam from Kuwait, or comprehensive, such as demanding the unconditional surrender of Japan and Germany during World War II. It is one thing to have a limited political goal and to fight decisively for it; it is quite another to apply military force incrementally, hoping to find a political solution somewhere along the way. A president entering these situations must ask whether decisive force is possible and is likely to be effective and must know how and when to get out. These are difficult criteria to meet, so U.S. intervention in these "humanitarian" crises should be, at best, exceedingly rare.

This does not mean that the United States must ignore humanitarian and civil conflicts around the world. But the military cannot be involved everywhere. Often, these tasks might be better carried out by regional actors, as modeled by the Australian-led intervention in East Timor. The U.S. might be able to lend financial, logistical, and intelligence support. Sometimes tough, competent diplomacy in the beginning can prevent the need for military force later. Using the American armed forces as the world's "911" will degrade capabilities, bog soldiers down in peacekeeping roles, and fuel concern among other great powers that the United States has decided to enforce notions of "limited sovereignty" worldwide in the name of humanitarianism. This overly broad definition of America's national interest is bound to backfire as others arrogate the same authority to themselves. Or we will find ourselves looking to the United Nations to sanction the use of American military power in these cases, implying that we will do so even when our vital interests are involved, which would also be a mistake.

DEALING WITH THE POWERFUL

ANOTHER CRUCIAL TASK for the United States is to focus on relations with other powerful states. Although the United States is fortunate to count among its friends several great powers, it is important not to take them for granted—so that there is a firm foundation when it comes time to rely on them. The challenges of China and North Korea require coordination and cooperation with Japan and South Korea. The signals that we send to our real partners are important. Never again should an American president go to Beijing for nine days and refuse to stop in Tokyo or Seoul.

There is work to do with the Europeans, too, on defining what holds the transatlantic alliance together in the absence of the Soviet threat. NATO is badly in need of attention in the wake of Kosovo and with the looming question of its further enlargement in 2002 and beyond. The door to NATO for the remaining states of eastern and central Europe should remain open, as many are actively preparing to meet the criteria for membership. But the parallel track of NATO's own evolution, its attention to the definition of its mission, and its ability to digest and then defend new members has been neglected. Moreover, the United States has an interest in shaping the European defense identity—welcoming a greater European military capability as long as it is within the context of NATO. NATO has a very full agenda. Membership in NATO will mean nothing to anyone if the organization is no longer militarily capable and if it is unclear about its mission.

For America and our allies, the most daunting task is to find the right balance in our policy toward Russia and China. Both are equally important to the future of international peace, but the challenges they pose are very different. China is a rising power; in economic terms, that should be good news, because in order to maintain its economic dynamism, China must be more integrated into the international economy. This will require increased openness and transparency and the growth of private industry. The political struggle in Beijing is over how to maintain the Communist Party's monopoly on power. Some see economic reform, growth, and a better life for the Chinese people as the key. Others see the inherent contradiction in loosening economic control and maintaining the party's political dominance. As China's economic problems multiply due to slowing growth rates, failing banks, inert state enterprises, and rising unemployment, this struggle will intensify.

Trade can open China's economy— and its politics, too.

It is in America's interest to strengthen the hands of those who seek economic integration because this will probably lead to sustained and organized pressures for political liberalization. There are no guarantees, but in scores of cases from Chile to Spain to Taiwan, the link between democracy and economic liberalization has proven powerful over the long run. Trade and economic interaction are, in fact, good—not only for America's economic growth but for its political aims as well. Human rights concerns should not move to the sidelines in the meantime. Rather, the American president should press the Chinese leadership for change. But it is wise to remember that our influence through moral arguments and commitment is still limited in the face of Beijing's pervasive political control. The big trends toward the spread of information, the access of young Chinese to American values through educational exchanges and training, and the growth of an entrepreneurial class that does not owe its livelihood to the state are, in the end, likely to have a more powerful effect on life in China.

Although some argue that the way to support human rights is to refuse trade with China, this punishes precisely those who are most likely to change the system. Put bluntly, Li Peng and the Chinese conservatives want to continue to run the economy by state fiat. Of course, there should be tight export controls on the transfer of militarily sensitive technology to China. But trade in general can open up the Chinese economy and, ultimately, its politics too. This view requires faith in the power of markets and economic freedom to drive political change, but it is a faith confirmed by experiences around the globe.

Even if there is an argument for economic interaction with Beijing, China is still a potential threat to stability in the Asia-Pacific region. Its military power is currently no match for that of the United States. But that condition is not necessarily permanent. What we do know is that China is a great power with unresolved vital interests, particularly concerning Taiwan and the South China Sea. China resents the role of the United States in the Asia-Pacific region. This means that China is not a "status quo" power but one that would like to alter Asia's balance of power in its own favor. That alone makes it a strategic competitor, not the "strategic partner" the Clinton administration once called it. Add to this China's record of cooperation with Iran and Pakistan in the proliferation of ballistic-missile technology, and the security problem is obvious. China will do what it can to enhance its position, whether by stealing nuclear secrets or by trying to intimidate Taiwan.

China's success in controlling the balance of power depends in large part on America's reaction to the challenge. The United States must deepen its cooperation with Japan and South Korea and maintain its commitment to a robust military presence in the region. It should pay closer attention to India's role in the regional balance. There is a strong tendency conceptually to connect India with Pakistan and to think only of Kashmir or the nuclear competition between the two states. But India is an element in China's calculation, and it should be in America's, too. India is not a great power yet, but it has the potential to emerge as one.

The United States also has a deep interest in the security of Taiwan. It is a model of democratic and market-oriented development, and it invests significantly in the mainland's economy. The longstanding U.S. commitment to a "one-China" policy that leaves to a future date the resolution of the relationship between Taipei and Beijing is wise. But that policy requires that neither side challenge the status quo and that Beijing, as the more powerful actor, renounce the use of force. U.S. resolve anchors this policy. The Clinton administration tilted toward Beijing, when, for instance, it used China's formulation of the "three no's" during the president's trip there. Taiwan has been looking for attention and reassurance ever since. If the United States is resolute, peace can be maintained in the Taiwan Strait until a political settlement on democratic terms is available.

Some things take time. U.S. policy toward China requires nuance and balance. It is important to promote China's internal transition through economic interaction while containing Chinese power and security ambitions. Cooperation should be pursued, but we should never be afraid to confront Beijing when our interests collide.

RUSSIAN WEAKNESS

RUSSIA PRESENTS a different challenge. It still has many of the attributes of a great power: a large population, vast territory, and military potential. But its economic weakness and problems of national identity threaten to overwhelm it. Moscow is determined to assert itself in the world and often does so in ways that are at once haphazard and threatening to American interests. The picture is complicated by Russia's own internal transition—one that the United States wants to see succeed. The old Soviet system has broken down, and some of the basic elements of democratic development are in place. People are free to say what they think, vote for whom they please, and (for the most part) worship freely. But the democratic fragments are not institutionalized—with the exception of the Communist Party, political parties are weak—and the balance of political power is so strongly in favor of the president that he often rules simply by decree. Of course, few pay attention to Boris Yelstin's decrees, and the Russian government has been mired in inaction and stagnation for at least three years. Russia's economic troubles and its high-level corruption have been widely discussed in recent months; Russia's economy is not becoming a market but is mutating into something else. Widespread barter, banks that are not banks, billions of rubles stashed abroad and in mattresses at home, and bizarre privatization schemes that have enriched the so-called reformers give Moscow's economy a medieval tinge.

The problem for U.S. policy is that the Clinton administration's embrace of Yeltsin and those who were thought to be reformers around him has failed. Yeltsin is Russia's president and clearly the

United States had to deal with the head of state. But support for democracy and economic reform became support for Yeltsin. His agenda became the American agenda. The United States certified that reform was taking place where it was not, continuing to disburse money from the International Monetary Fund in the absence of any evidence of serious change. The curious privatization methods were hailed as economic liberalization; the looting of the country's assets by powerful people either went unnoticed or was ignored. The realities in Russia simply did not accord with the administration's script about Russian economic reform. The United States should not be faulted for trying to help. But, as the Russian reformer Grigori Yavlinsky has said, the United States should have "told the truth" about what was happening.

Now we have a dual credibility problem—with Russians and with Americans. There are signs of life in the Russian economy. The financial crash of August 1998 forced import substitution, and domestic production has increased as the resilient Russian people have taken matters into their own hands. Rising oil prices have helped as well. But these are short-term fixes. There is no longer a consensus in America or Europe on what to do next with Russia. Frustrated expectations and "Russia fatigue" are direct consequences of the "happy talk" in which the Clinton administration engaged.

Russia's economic future is now in the hands of the Russians. The country is not without assets, including its natural resources and an educated population. It is up to Russia to make structural reforms, particularly concerning the rule of law and the tax codes, so that investors—foreign and domestic—will provide the capital needed for economic growth. That opportunity will arise once there is a new government in Moscow after last December's Duma elections and next June's presidential election. But the cultural changes ultimately needed to sustain a functioning civil society and a market-based economy may take a generation. Western openness to Russia's people, particularly its youth, in exchange programs and contact with the private sector and educational opportunities can help that process. It is also important to engage the leadership of Russia's diverse regions, where economic and social policies are increasingly pursued independently of Moscow.

In the meantime, U.S. policy must concentrate on the important security agenda with Russia. First, it must recognize that American security is threatened less by Russia's strength than by its weakness and incoherence. This suggests immediate attention to the safety and security of Moscow's nuclear forces and stockpile. The Nunn-Lugar program should be funded fully and pursued aggressively. (Because American contractors do most of the work, the risk of the diversion of funds is low.) Second, Washington must begin a comprehensive discussion with Moscow on the changing nuclear threat. Much has been made by Russian military officials about their increased reliance on nuclear weapons in the face of their declining conventional readiness. The Russian deterrent is more than adequate against the U.S. nuclear arsenal, and vice versa. But that fact need no longer be enshrined in a treaty that is almost 30 years old and is a relic of a profoundly adversarial relationship between the United States and the Soviet Union. The Anti-Ballistic Missile Treaty was intended to prevent the development of national missile defenses in the Cold War security environment. Today, the principal concerns are nuclear threats from the Iraqs and North Koreas of the world and the possibility of unauthorized releases as nuclear weapons spread.

American security is threatened less by Russia's strength than by its weakness and incoherence.

Moscow, in fact, lives closer to those threats than Washington does. It ought to be possible to engage the Russians in a discussion of the changed threat environment, their possible responses, and the relationship of strategic offensive-force reductions to the deployment of defenses. The United States should make clear that it prefers to move cooperatively toward a new offense-defense mix, but that it is prepared to do so unilaterally. Moscow should understand, too, that any possibilities for sharing technology or information in these areas would depend heavily on its record—problematic to date—on the proliferation of ballistic-missile and other technologies related to WMD. It would be foolish in the extreme to share defenses with Moscow if it either leaks or deliberately transfers weapons technologies to the very states against which America is defending.

Finally, the United States needs to recognize that Russia is a great power, and that we will always have interests that conflict as well as coincide. The war in Chechnya, located in the oil-rich Caucasus, is particularly dangerous. Prime Minister Vladimir Putin has used the war to stir nationalism at home while fueling his own political fortunes. The Russian military has been uncharacteristically blunt and vocal in asserting its duty to defend the integrity of the Russian Federation—an unwelcome development in civil-military relations. The long-term effect on Russia's political culture should not be underestimated. And the war has affected relations between Russia and its neighbors in the Caucasus, as the Kremlin hurls charges of harboring and abetting Chechen terrorists against states as diverse as Saudi Arabia, Georgia, and Azerbaijan. The war is a reminder of the vulnerability of the small, new states around Russia and of America's interest in their independence. If they can become stronger, they will be less tempting to Russia. But much depends on the ability of these states to reform their economies and political systems—a process, to date, whose success is mixed at best.

COPING WITH ROGUE REGIMES

As HISTORY MARCHES toward markets and democracy, some states have been left by the side of the road. Iraq is the prototype. Saddam Hussein's regime is isolated, his conventional military power has been severely weakened, his people live in poverty and terror, and he has no useful place in international politics. He is therefore determined to develop WMD. Nothing will change until Saddam is gone, so the United States must mobilize whatever resources it can, including support from his opposition, to remove him.

The regime of Kim Jong Il is so opaque that it is difficult to know its motivations, other than that they are malign. But North Korea also lives outside of the international system. Like East Germany, North Korea is the evil twin of a successful regime just across its border. It must fear its eventual demise from the sheer power and pull of South Korea. Pyongyang, too, has little to gain and everything to lose from engagement in the international economy. The development of WMD thus provides the destructive way out for Kim Jong Il.

President Kim Dae Jung of South Korea is attempting to find a peaceful resolution with the north through engagement. Any U.S. policy toward the north should depend heavily on coordination with

Seoul and Tokyo. In that context, the 1994 framework agreement that attempted to bribe North Korea into forsaking nuclear weapons cannot easily be set aside. Still, there is a trap inherent in this approach: sooner or later Pyongyang will threaten to test a missile one too many times, and the United States will not respond with further benefits. Then what will Kim Jong Il do? The possibility for miscalculation is very high.

One thing is clear: the United States must approach regimes like North Korea resolutely and decisively. The Clinton administration has failed here, sometimes threatening to use force and then backing down, as it often has with Iraq. These regimes are living on borrowed time, so there need be no sense of panic about them. Rather, the first line of defense should be a clear and classical statement of deterrence—if they do acquire WMD, their weapons will be unusable because any attempt to use them will bring national obliteration. Second, we should accelerate efforts to defend against these weapons. This is the most important reason to deploy national and theater missile defenses as soon as possible, to focus attention on U.S. homeland defenses against chemical and biological agents, and to expand intelligence capabilities against terrorism of all kinds.

Finally, there is the Iranian regime. Iran's motivation is not to disrupt simply the development of an international system based on markets and democracy, but to replace it with an alternative: fundamentalist Islam. Fortunately, the Iranians do not have the kind of reach and power that the Soviet Union enjoyed in trying to promote its socialist alternative. But Iran's tactics have posed real problems for U.S. security. It has tried to destabilize moderate Arab states such as Saudi Arabia, though its relations with the Saudis have improved recently. Iran has also supported terrorism against America and Western interests and attempted to develop and transfer sensitive military technologies.

Iran presents special difficulties in the Middle East, a region of core interest to the United States and to our key ally Israel. Iranian weaponry increasingly threatens Israel directly. As important as Israel's efforts to reach peace with its Arab neighbors are to the future of the Middle East, they are not the whole story of stability in the region. Israel has a real security problem, so defense cooperation with the United States—particularly in the area of ballistic missile defense—is critical. That in turn will help Israel protect itself both through agreements and through enhanced military power.

Still, it is important to note that there are trends in Iran that bear watching. Mohammad Khatami's election as president has given some hope of a new course for a country that once hosted a great and thriving civilization—though there are questions about how much authority he exercises. Moreover, Khatami's more moderate domestic views may not translate into more acceptable behavior abroad. All in all, changes in U.S. policy toward Iran would require changes in Iranian behavior.

BUILDING A CONSENSUS FOR THE NATIONAL INTEREST

AMERICA IS BLESSED with an extraordinary opportunity. It has had no territorial ambitions for nearly a century. Its national interest has been defined instead by a desire to foster the spread of freedom, prosperity, and peace. Both the will of the people and the demands of modern economies accord with that vision of the future. But even America's advantages offer no guarantees of success. It is up to America's presidential leadership and policy to bridge the gap between tomorrow's possibilities and today's realities.

The president must speak to the American people about national priorities and intentions and work with Congress to focus foreign policy around the national interest. The problem today is not an absence of bipartisan spirit in Congress or the American people's disinterest. It is the existence of a vacuum. In the absence of a compelling vision, parochial interests are filling the void.

Foreign policy in a Republican administration will most certainly be internationalist; the leading contenders in the party's presidential race have strong credentials in that regard. But it will also proceed from the firm ground of the national interest, not from the interests of an illusory international community. America can exercise power without arrogance and pursue its interests without hectoring and bluster. When it does so in concert with those who share its core values, the world becomes more prosperous, democratic, and peaceful. That has been America's special role in the past, and it should be again as we enter the next century.

The Strategy of Terrorism

David Fromkin

The grim events at the Athens airport on August 5, 1973, were in a sense symbolic. Dreadfully real to those who were involved, the occurrences of that day also transcended their own reality, somewhat as myths do, epitomizing an entire aspect of contemporary existence in one specific drama.

When the hand grenades were hurled into the departure lounge and the machine gunners simultaneously mowed down the passengers waiting to embark for New York City, it seemed incomprehensible that so harmless a group should be attacked. The merest glance at their hand-luggage, filled with snorkels and cameras, would have shown that they had spent their time in such peaceful pursuits as swimming, sunbathing, and snapping photos of the Parthenon.

The raid had been undertaken on behalf of an Arab Palestine. Yet the airport passengers had done the Arabs no harm. Their journey had only been to Greece. Palestine had nothing to do with them; it was another country, across the sea, and its problems were not of their making. Moreover, Athens was a capital friendly to the Arab cause—as was Paris, the scene of more recent airline attacks.

Similar incidents have occurred with terrible frequency throughout the 1960's and 1970's. The generations that have come to maturity in Europe and America since the end of the Second World War have asked only to bask in the sunshine of a summertime world; but increasingly they have been forced instead to live in the fearful shadow of other people's deadly quarrels. Gangs of politically motivated gunmen have disrupted everyday life, intruding

---

and forcing their parochial feuds upon the unwilling attention of everybody else.

True, other ages have suffered from crime and outrage, but what we are experiencing today goes beyond such things. Too small to impose their will by military force, terrorist bands nonetheless are capable nowadays of causing enough damage to intimidate and blackmail the governments of the world. Only modern technology makes this possible—the bazooka, the plastic bomb, the submachine gun, and perhaps, over the horizon, the nuclear mini-bomb. The transformation has enabled terrorism to enter the political arena on a new scale, and to express ideological goals of an organized sort rather than mere crime, madness, or emotional derangement as in the past.

Political terrorism is a distinctive disorder of the modern world. It originated as a term and, arguably, as a practice, less than two centuries ago and has come into the spotlight of global conflict in our lifetime. Whereas both organized and irregular (or guerrilla) warfare began with the human race, political terrorism emerged as a concept only in 1793. As a political strategy, it is both new and original; and if I am correct, its nature has not yet fully been appreciated.

Of course nobody can remain unaware of the upsurge of global terrorism that has occurred in recent years. But the novelty of it has not been perceived. Force usually generates fear, and fear is usually an additional weapon. But terrorism employs the weapon of fear in a special and complicated sort of way.

II

The disassociation of fear from force in the context of organized politics emerged first in the Reign of Terror, the episode (1793–1794) during the history of revolutionary France from which the English and French words for terrorism derive. The terrorists in question were, of course, Robespierre and his satellites, St. Just and Couthon. Sitting as a faction in the Committee of Public Safety, their accusations of treason sent victims to the guillotine in droves. By the mere threat of accusation against their fellow Committee members, they used the entire Committee, thus united, in order to dominate the National Convention and the other public bodies of the French Republic.

Robespierre was overthrown when his system was used against him. His mistake was in letting Joseph Fouché know that he was the next intended victim; and Fouché, the wily intriguer who later became Napoleon's minister of police, made the best possible use of his few remaining days. He persuaded the feuding, rival politicians of his day that they had to unite against the triumvirs or else face execution one by one; fear of the regime should cause them not to serve it, but to overthrow it. On 8 Thermidor (July 26, 1794) Robespierre made another mistake when he told the Convention that he had prepared a new list of traitors in their midst—and then refused to tell them whose names were on the list. Fouché's warnings were confirmed, and his counsel was heeded. When Robespierre entered the National Convention late in the stormy summer morning of 9 Thermidor, he found a mob of delegates united by the determination to murder him before he could murder them; and that was the end of him.

Robespierre had coerced a nation of 27 million people into accepting his dictatorship. His followers sent many thousands either to jail or to their deaths; one scholar's estimate is 40,000 deaths and 300,000 arrests. Yet when retribution came and Robespierre and his group of supporters were executed, it turned out that in all there were only 22 of them.

Of course it is not meant to suggest that this is the whole story of the French Terror. Yet what emerges most strongly from any account of these events is the dramatic disparity between the objective weakness of the Robespierre faction, whose numbers were few and whose military resources were limited, and their immense subjective power, which allowed them to kill, imprison, or control so many. There was no need to fear the triumvirs other than the fact that other people feared them and therefore would execute their orders. Their power was unreal; it was an illusionist's trick. No citadels had to be stormed, no armies had to be crushed, in order to overthrow them. If the public ignored what they said, then the terrorists went back to being political nobodies. Their dictatorship vanished in an instant when Robespierre and his colleagues were prevented from reaching the speakers' platform on 9 Thermidor.

In the end, the terrorists overreached themselves, and men saw through them and stood up to them. Then—and only then—it became clear that France had never had anything to fear from them other than fear itself.

III

Perhaps the closest parallel to Robespierre's method was that followed by the late Senator Joseph McCarthy in 1950–54. Like Robespierre, McCarthy claimed to have lists of traitors whose names he would not immediately reveal, and many did his will in order to avoid being accused by him of treason or of lack of patriotism. And, like Robespierre's, his power stopped when he went too far and Joseph Welch, his Fouché, stood up to him on television. But McCarthy never seized supreme power in the country, nor did his accusations send people to the guillotine. In that sense it can be said that Robespierre has had no successors.

Since his time, in fact, political terrorism has become especially notorious in a different cause from that in which Robespierre used it. It has been used to destroy governments rather than to sustain them. This changed the way in which many people thought of it as a political strategy and how they viewed its adherents. As revolutionaries, terrorists have come to seem romantic figures to many. Their life of dangers and disguises, risks and betrayals, conspiracies and secret societies, exerted a powerful fascination. As torn and tormented characters, they provided authors with the stuff of which complex and interesting novels can be made.

Though the terrorists seemed romantic, until recently they also seemed ineffective. Until the Irish Treaty of 1921, they scored no significant political successes. The most famous of the terrorist groups up to that time was the Terrorist Brigade of the Russian Socialists-Revolutionists; and not merely did they fail to change the Tsarist government in the ways in which they desired, they also failed to pick up the pieces when it was overthrown by others. Plekhanov, Lenin, Trotsky and the other Russian disciples of Marx had seen more clearly in placing their emphasis on mass organization rather than on individual terrorism. The Bolsheviks came to power by winning the metropolitan workmen, the sailors of the Baltic fleet, and the soldiers to their side. Organization proved to be the key to victory. It was not individual gunmen but armed masses who seized power in Russia. Revolution, like war, is the strategy of the strong; terrorism is the strategy of the weak.

It is an uncertain and indirect strategy that employs the weapon of fear in a special sort of way in which to make governments react. Is fear an effective method? Is fright any kind of weapon at all? What can terrorists hope to accomplish by sowing fear? How can it help their side to vanquish its opponents? Clearly it can do so in many ways. Fright can paralyze the will, befuddle the mind, and exhaust the strength of an adversary. Moreover, it can persuade an opponent that a particular political point of view is taken with such deadly seriousness by its few adherents that it should be accommodated, rather than suffering casualties year after year in a campaign to suppress it.

All of these elements came together, for example, in the struggle that led to the independence of southern Ireland. It is difficult to disentangle the role of terrorism in this achievement from the other elements that were involved, for the Irish also had put in motion what was, in effect, a guerrilla warfare campaign. Moreover, the Liberal members of the coalition that then governed the United Kingdom had a political commitment that went back more than a quarter of a century to the cause of Irish Home Rule. Yet there can be little doubt that terrorism played a major role in causing Britain to tire of the struggle.

Terrorism can also make heroes out of gunmen, and thereby rally popular support to their cause. The problem this creates for them is that when the time comes to make the compromises necessary in order to negotiate the terms of their victory, the glamour wanes, and with it, the political support. Michael Collins was a romantic figure who captured the imagination of all Ireland as long as he was an outlaw; but when he sat down to make peace, he was seen by many in a much different light. As he signed the Irish Treaty of 1921 on Britain's behalf, Lord Birkenhead remarked to Collins, "I may have signed my political death-warrant tonight"; to which Collins replied, "I may have signed my actual death-warrant." Eight months later Michael Collins lay dead on an Irish roadway with a bullet through his head.

Just as it can make gangsters into heroes, terrorist provocations can also make policemen into villains. The Black-and-Tans who fought the Irish revolutionists were, in an objective sense, so successful at repression that Michael Collins told an English official afterwards, in regard to the July 1921 peace negotiations: "You had us dead beat. We could not have lasted another three weeks." Yet Black-and-Tan methods made the cause of repression so odious that Britain was induced to choose another course of action.

Brutality is an induced governmental response that can boomerang. It is this ability to use the strength of repression against itself, in many different ways, that has enabled terrorist strategies to succeed in many situations that have, rightly or wrongly, been described as colonialist in the modern world.

IV

Sophisticated approaches have been developed along these lines. One of these was explained to me and to others at a meeting in New York City sometime in 1945 by one of the founders of the Irgun Zvai Leumi, a tiny group of Jewish militants in what was then the British-mandated territory of Palestine. His organization had no more than 1,000 or 1,500 members, and it was at odds with the Palestinian Jewish community almost as much as it was with the mandatory regime. Yet he proposed to combat Great Britain, then a global power whose armed forces in the Second World War numbered in the millions, and to expel Great Britain from Palestine.

How could such a thousand-to-one struggle be won? To do so, as he explained it, his organization would attack property interests. After giving advance warning to evacuate them, his small band of followers would blow up buildings. This, he said, would lead the British to overreact by garrisoning the country with an immense army drawn from stations in other parts of the world. But postwar Britain could not afford financially to maintain so great an army either there or anywhere else for any extended period of time. Britain urgently needed to demobilize its armed forces. The strain would tell; and eventually economic pressure would drive the Attlee-Bevin government either to withdraw from Palestine or else to try some reckless and possibly losing gamble in an effort to retrieve the situation.

It can be argued that such is in fact what happened. Of course Britain might have withdrawn anyway, at some other time or for some other reason. But that is really beside the point, for the Irgun wanted independence then and there, in order to open up the country to refugees from Hitler's Europe. They got what they wanted when they wanted it by doing it in their own way.

There were two flaws in the Irgun strategy. It would have failed had the British not reacted to the destruction of buildings as they were expected to do. If instead they had done nothing at all, maintained only a modest military garrison, and sent for no reinforcements, all that would have happened would have been that a few more buildings would have been blown up and the owners would have collected the insurance money and would have rebuilt them; and the Irgun would have proved a failure.

In the second place, the plan of attacking property without hurting people proved to be unrealistic. Accidents inevitably occur when violence is unleashed. Almost a hundred persons were killed when the Irgun blew up the King David Hotel in Jerusalem. According to the plan, they should have been evacuated before the blast, but in actual life people misunderstand, or their telephone line is busy, or somebody forgets to give them the message in time. Moreover, terrorism generates its own momentum, and before long the killing becomes deliberate. The bloodshed caused by the Irgun isolated it politically and alienated the rest of the Palestinian Jewish community. The British failed to perceive or exploit this situation. But Ben-Gurion did; in 1948 he made use of it to crush the Irgun, for the Israeli army might have been unwilling to carry out orders to attack those unloading the Irgun ship the *Altalena*, if the Irgun had not used up its political credit before then by the taking of too many lives.

Yet despite its flaws, the strategy was sufficiently ingenious so that the Irgun played a big part in getting the British to withdraw. Its ingenuity lay in using an opponent's own strength against him. It was a sort of jujitsu. First the adversary was made to be afraid, and then, predictably, he would react to his fear by increasing the bulk of his strength, and then the sheer weight of that bulk would drag him down. Another way of saying this is that the Irgun, seeing that it was too small to defeat Great Britain, decided, as an alternative approach, that Britain was big enough to defeat itself.

V

In the 1950's, the nationalist rebel group in Algeria developed yet another method of using the strength of an occupying power against itself. Their method was to induce that strength to be used as a form of persuasion.

For, in Algeria, the whole question was one of persuasion. The problem initially faced by the miniscule band of Algerian nationalists that called itself the National Liberation Front (or, in its French initials, FLN) was that Algeria at that time had little sense of national identity. Its population was not homogeneous; and the Berbers, the Arabs, and the settlers of European descent were peoples quite different from one another. The name and separate existence of Algeria were only of recent origin. For most of recorded history, Algeria had been no more than the middle part of North Africa, with no distinct history of its own. Legally it was merely the southern part of France. The French had treated Morocco and Tunisia as protectorates, with separate identities, but not Algeria, which was absorbed into France herself. With sarcasm, Frenchmen used to reply to Americans who urged independence for Algeria by saying that, on the same basis, the United States should set Wisconsin free or give back independence to South Carolina.

It was a jibe that went to the heart of the matter. Colonial empires were coming to an end in the 1950's and 1960's. If Algeria was a nation, then inevitably it would be set free to govern itself. Only if it were genuinely a part of France could it continue to be ruled from Paris. All depended, therefore, on whether the indigenous population could be convinced by the French government that Algeria was not a separate country, or upon whether they could be persuaded by the FLN to change their minds so as to think of themselves as a nation.

The FLN strategy of terrorism addressed itself to this central and decisive issue. By itself, as has been said, terror can accomplish nothing in terms of political goals; it can only aim at obtaining a response that will achieve those goals for it. What the FLN did was to goad the French into reacting in such a way as to demonstrate the unreality of the claim that there was no distinct Algerian nation. Unlike the Irgun, the FLN did not set out to campaign merely against property; it attacked people. It used random violence, planting bombs in market places and in other crowded locations. The instinctive French reaction was to treat all persons of non-European origin as suspects; but, as Raymond Aron was to write, "As suspects, all the Muslims felt excluded from the existing community," Their feeling was confirmed when, in the middle 1950's, the authorities further reacted by transferring the French army units composed of Muslim Algerian troops out of Algeria and into mainland France, and replacing them in Algeria by European troops. By such actions they showed in the most unmistakable way that they regarded no Algerians as Frenchmen except for the European settlers. They spoke of we and us, and of they and them, and did not realize that their doing so meant the end of Algérie Française.

Thus the French conceded the issue of the war at its very outset. They threw away the potential support of Muslim Algeria because they were skeptical of the possibility that it could be obtained. From that moment the conclusion of the conflict was foregone. Once the sympathies of the population had shifted to its side, the FLN was able to outgrow mere terrorism and to organize a campaign of guerrilla warfare. It also was enabled to appeal to world sympathies on behalf of a people fighting for its freedom. From the French point of view all had become hopeless; for no amount of force can keep an unwilling population indefinitely in subjection. Even though the FLN had written the script, the French, with suicidal logic, went ahead to play the role for which they had been cast.

The FLN success was therefore a special case. It required a particular kind of opponent. It could not be duplicated in other circumstances and conditions.

VI

Revolutionist-terrorists of the last decade have failed to perceive the special characteristics of the colonialist situation that facilitated success for Irish, Irgun, and Algerian terrorists. They have tried to apply the strategy of terrorism in situations that are essentially different. This has been true, for example, of extremist groups seeking to overthrow liberal-pluralistic regimes during the 1960's. Their theory has been that their terrorist attacks would force hitherto liberal regimes to become repressive, a change which in turn would alienate the masses, thus setting the stage for revolution. But it has not worked out that way in practice. In the United States, for example, terrorist bomb attacks have not led to any change at all in the form of government, much less to a transformation of America into a police state. On the other hand, in Uruguay, once the model democracy of Latin America, the terror of the Tupamaro bands has led to a military dictatorship that brutally destroyed the Tupamaros, but that does not seem, at least as yet, to have led to the predicted reaction by the masses in favor of revolutionary action.

Other revolutionary groups have taken a somewhat different approach. They have argued that liberal democracies are already police states. Thus, the object of revolutionary terrorist action should be to reveal this hidden reality to the population at large. Unthinking reaction by the authorities to terrorist provocation would accomplish the desired result. Thus the aim of terrorism would be to trick the government into taking off its mask.

In open societies such as Great Britain and the United States, the liberal democratic features have proved to be a face and not a mask: there is nothing to take off, and the strategy failed because its factual premise proved to be untrue.

In closed societies, the strategy has been to show that authoritarian regimes are actually impotent despite their outward show of virility. In such circumstances, supposedly, by demonstrating that the public authorities are powerless to enforce law and order, a campaign of terror can cause a government to collapse; but the flaw in the theory is that the terrorists usually are not strong enough to take its place. Either some more broadly based group will seize power, or else, as in Argentina, private groups will take the law into their own hands and retaliate in kind against murder and extortion, so that society relapses into a semi-anarchic state of reprisals and blood feuds, where terrorists are buried with their victims.

VII

It is against this background that Arab Palestinian terrorism has seized the attention of the contemporary world. It is aimed at Israel;

it is aimed at the Arabs who live within Israel; and it is aimed at the world outside. It is, in other words, a mixed strategy. Each of its mixed aspects has to be considered separately. All that Arab terrorism can accomplish in the land that has been promised to so many is to frighten and to threaten the Arab inhabitants of Israel in order to keep them from cooperating with the Israeli authorities. Israel itself, however, cannot be terrorized into disappearing of its own accord; yet removing Israel from the map has long been the proclaimed goal of the Arab terrorist movement.

Terrorism can be employed more successfully in colonialist situations than in Palestine because a colonial power suffers the disadvantage of fighting the battle away from its own base, and also because a colonial power, having a country of its own to which it can withdraw, is under no compulsion to fight to the bitter end. The Israelis, though termed colonialist by the Arabs, are fighting on home territory, and they have no other country to which they can withdraw; they fight with their backs to the sea. They can be goaded into a self-defeating reaction, but unless they permit that to happen, nothing can be done to their domestic public opinion that is likely to destroy them. The Arab terrorists therefore have turned elsewhere, and have attacked the arteries of world transportation in hopes that a world indifferent to the merits of the Arab-Israeli dispute will turn against the Israelis in order to end the annoyance of a disrupted airline service.

In doing so they have strayed across a frontier and into the eerie world of Mr. McLuhan, and they have transformed terrorism into a form of mass communication—but communication aimed at the whole world and not, as in the case of Algeria, mostly at the indigenous population. Theirs is a campaign that needs publicity in order to succeed, and therefore they have come to operate within the ambit of contemporary public relations and communications arts: the world of cinema, camp fashion, and pop art, in which deadlines and prime-time are the chief realities and in which shock value is the chief virtue. If audiences throughout the world react with horror, and turn against the political cause in whose name so many innocent people have been harmed and killed, the strategy will have backfired. So far they have not done so and it has not done so.

It is a corruption of the human spirit for which all political sides are responsible. The left-wing journalist Paul Johnson wrote an article some months back arguing that left-wing movements are as much at fault as anybody else for accepting the murder of the innocent as a legitimate means for the pursuit of political ends. He quoted the sixteenth-century humanist Castellio, "who was lucky to escape burning by both Catholics and Protestants, and who pointed out in his tract for toleration, *Whether Heretics Are To Be Persecuted?*, that no certitude of righteousness justifies violence: 'To kill a man is not to defend a doctrine, it is to kill a man'." Appalled at the welcome accorded by the United Nations to the leader of the Arab terrorists, Johnson wrote that, "Step by step, almost imperceptibly, without anyone being aware that a fatal watershed has been crossed, mankind has descended into the age of terror."

VIII

If this is an age of terror, then it has become all the more important for us to understand exactly what it is that terrorism means. Terrorism, as has been seen, is the weapon of those who are prepared to use violence but who believe that they would lose any contest of sheer strength. All too little understood, the uniqueness of the strategy lies in this: that it achieves its goal not through its acts but through the response to its acts. In any other such strategy, the violence is the beginning and its consequences are the end of it. For terrorism, however, the consequences of the violence are themselves merely a first step and form a stepping stone toward objectives that are more remote. Whereas military and revolutionary actions aim at a physical result, terrorist actions aim at a psychological result.

But even that psychological result is not the final goal. Terrorism is violence used in order to create fear; but it is aimed at creating fear in order that the fear, in turn, will lead somebody else—not the terrorist—to embark on some quite different program of action that will accomplish whatever it is that the terrorist really desires. Unlike the soldier, the guerrilla fighter, or the revolutionist, the terrorist therefore is always in the paradoxical position of undertaking actions the immediate physical consequences of which are not particularly desired by him. An ordinary murderer will kill somebody because he wants the person to be dead, but a terrorist will shoot somebody even though it is a matter of complete indifference to him whether that person lives or dies. He would do so, for example, in order to provoke a brutal police repression that he believes will lead to political conditions propitious to revolutionary agitation and organization aimed at overthrowing the government. The act of murder is the same in both cases, but its purpose is different, and each act plays a different role in the strategies of violence.

Only an understanding of the purpose for which such an act is undertaken can enable us to know the nature of the act. When Julius Caesar was murdered in the Roman Senate, it was an assassination of the traditional sort, intended to eliminate a specific figure from the political scene; but had he been killed there by the representative of a subversive sect, intent on plunging his dagger into the first Roman leader he encountered in order to provoke a certain political response from the Senate, it would instead have been an act of political terrorism.

It is because an action of the same sort may be undertaken by two different groups with two quite different ends in view that terrorism is so often confused with guerrilla warfare, for terrorists and guerrillas often seem to be doing the same sorts of things. Both of them, for example, often sabotage transportation facilities. When T. E. Lawrence led his classic guerrilla warfare campaign against Turkish rule in Arabia, he systematically dynamited railway tracks and bridges. Lawrence's strategy was later explained by Winston Churchill as follows: "The Turkish armies operating against Egypt depended upon the desert railway. This slender steel track ran through hundreds of miles of blistering desert. If it were permanently cut the Turkish armies must perish." And Lawrence therefore rode on camel-back across the sands to destroy the enemy army by blowing up its transportation facilities. In recent years those who say that they wish to destroy the state of Israel have also blown up transportation facilities in the Arab desert; in this case, jet airplanes belonging to civil aviation companies. Yet if thereby they were to permanently cut the airline networks of TWA or BOAC they would not cause the Israeli army to perish. Indeed the fate of such civil aviation companies is a matter of indifference to the terrorists. Lawrence the guerrilla leader attacked a railway because he wanted to destroy it, whereas Arab terrorists attack an airline even though they do not want to destroy it.

The distinction is of more than academic importance. The French lost their empire over Algeria when they mistook terrorism for guerrilla warfare. They thought that when the FLN planted a bomb in a public bus, it was in order to blow up the bus; whereas the real FLN purpose in planting the bomb was not to blow up the bus, but to lure authorities into reacting by arresting all the non-Europeans in the area as suspects.

The terrorist is like a magician who tricks you into watching his right hand while his left hand, unnoticed, makes the switch. It is understandable that the French authorities in Algeria became totally obsessed by the need to stamp out criminal attacks, but it was fatal to their policy to do so, for the violent attacks were merely a subsidiary issue. The tiny FLN band of outlaws could have blown up every bus in all of Algeria and never won a convert to their cause of independence. Failing to understand the strategy of terrorism, the French did not see that it was not the FLN's move, but rather the French countermove, that would determine whether the FLN succeeded or failed.

It may be the case that the current Israeli policy of attacking Arab terrorist bases in southern Lebanon is another example of concentrating too much attention on preventing terrorist actions and too little attention on foiling terrorist purposes. The Israeli policy is certainly understandable on many grounds, and valid arguments can be adduced in its support; but the weakening of an essentially benevolent Lebanese government, as well as the further estrangement of world opinion, are results of the Israeli raids into Lebanon that may outweigh the value of using that particular approach to the problem of combating terrorism.

For the Israelis, threatened by enemies outside of their society, the problem is an enormously difficult one. For societies threatened only by enemies from within, it is considerably less so. The very wickedness of terrorism makes it a vulnerable strategy in such a society. Other strategies sometimes kill the innocent by mistake. Terrorism kills the innocent deliberately; for not even the terrorist necessarily believes that the particular person who happens to become his victim deserves to be killed or injured. It is horrifying not merely because of the deed that is done but also because at first the deed seems pointless. If you want to make war on the United States on behalf of Puerto Rican independence, why blow up a historic tavern in New York's financial district? What has Fraunces Tavern got to do with Puerto Rico? Why not attack the alleged forces of occupation in Puerto Rico instead? If you opposed by force and violence the continuation of U.S. aid to South Vietnam, why threaten to destroy the Smithsonian Institution? What had its plant collections and its ichthyological specimens to do with American policy in Southeast Asia? The destruction seems so purposeless that it is a natural reaction to turn on those who perpetrate it in hatred and in anger.

The tragedies that befall great public figures can sometimes seem to have been deserved; but when a man on the street is killed at random on behalf of a cause with which he had nothing to do, it is a different matter and provokes a different reaction. In a homogeneous society, at any rate, it leads to a reaction against the terrorism, and it renders it vulnerable to a campaign that politically isolates it in order to physically destroy it, for the nature of the attacks tends to demonstrate that terrorists are enemies of the people rather than merely of the government. It is for this reason that Che Guevara, as a theoretician and practitioner of guerrilla warfare, warned against the strategy of terrorism, arguing that it hinders "contact with the masses and makes impossible unification for actions that will be necessary at a critical moment."

Even in the international arena, terrorist movements are vulnerable when their actions alienate support. This was tacitly recognized by the Palestine Liberation Organization (PLO) when on January 29, 1975, it announced that henceforth it had decided to treat hijacking of airplanes, ships, or trains as crimes and would impose death penalties on hijackers if their actions led to the loss of life. Whether the PLO will indeed abandon its campaign of terror against international transportation remains to be seen. Yet the declaration of its intention to do so is in itself significant, for it suggests a realization that a point has arrived when a public identification with terrorist activity will harm rather than help. This is because terrorism is so much more evil than other strategies of violence that public opinion sometimes can be rallied against it.

Indeed, in view of its inherent weakness, it is remarkable how many political successes have been scored by the strategy of terrorism in the last few decades. Its success seems to be due in large part to a miscomprehension of the strategy by its opponents. They have neglected the more important of the two levels on which terrorism operates. They have failed to focus on the crucial issue of how the manner in which they, as opponents, respond affects the political goals of the terrorists. Discussion instead has centered on the criminal justice aspects of the question: prevention and punishment.

Much has been written, for example, about the technological defenses that have been developed or could be developed against terrorism in order to prevent it from occurring. This can be a highly useful line of approach, as the successful use of electronic surveillance devices at airports seems to have demonstrated. It may even be advisable to require that any new technologies that are developed from time to time should incorporate some sort of internal defense against attack, much as environmentalists argue that pollution control devices should be incorporated in equipment and its cost charged to the manufacturers. Yet no technology is perfect, and there will always be somebody who will manage to slip by any defenses that can be created.

Prevention of terrorism in non-technological ways scarcely merits discussion. Perhaps one day the social sciences will teach us how to drain the swamps of misery in which hatred and fanaticism breed, but at the moment that day seems far distant. The hollow formalism of the law offers, if anything, even less help. Ingenious schemes for new international tribunals and procedures have been proposed, and they completely miss the point. The manifest unwillingness of many governments to use existing legal remedies against terrorism shows that the real problem is the lack of a will and not the lack of a way. For example, it was only when an attack was staged at the Paris airport that the French Minister of the Interior, in January of 1975, proposed to negotiate an international convention to provide for the punishment of terrorist acts. It is not any kind of genuine solution, in any event, but it will be interesting to see if Michel Poniatowski perseveres in even so ritualistic a response as this after the fleeting memory of injured national pride fades from view. There are all too many who object to terrorism only when they are its victims.

Far more effective than the reaction of M. Poniatowski was that of the French press. There were suggestions in the newspapers that the pro-Arab policy of the French government should be reversed because it had failed to prevent the attack at Orly airport. Within days the Palestine Liberation Organization strongly condemned the attack. It also announced that it had taken measures to punish persons who engaged in the hijacking of airplanes, boats or trains. What the French journalists had correctly intuited was that the locus of the struggle was not at the Orly airport: it was at the Elysée Palace and at the Quai d'Orsay.

The overriding questions are not legal or technological; they are philosophical and political. Terrorism is the indirect strategy that wins or loses only in terms of how you respond to it. The decision as to how accommodating or how uncompromising you should be in your response to it involves questions that fall primarily within the domain of political philosophy.

XI

Those who are the targets of terrorism—and who are prepared to defend themselves by doing whatever is necessary in order to beat it—start with a major advantage. The advantage is that success or failure depends upon them alone. Terrorism wins only if you respond to it in the way that the terrorists want you to; which means that its fate is in your hands and not in theirs. If you choose not to respond at all, or else to respond in a way different from that which they desire, they will fail to achieve their objectives.

The important point is that the choice is yours. That is the ultimate weakness of terrorism as a strategy. It means that, though terrorism cannot always be prevented, it can always be defeated. You can always refuse to do what they want you to do.

Whether to pay the price of defeating terrorism is increasingly going to be a major question in our time. The answer is relatively easy in most kidnapping and ransom situations: experience has shown that blackmailers and extortionists usually are encouraged to try it again if you give in to their demands the first time. So, if you can do so, you should accept the consequences, however terrible, of standing firm in order to avoid an infinite sequence of painful events.

But the price of doing so is constantly rising, as technology increases the range and magnitude of horrible possibilities. Terrorist outrages, when they occur, are bound to become more deadly. Increasingly, we will be under pressure to abridge our laws and liberties in order to suppress the terrorists. It is a pressure that should be resisted.

In our personal lives we sometimes have to choose between these alternatives: whether to live a good life or whether to live a long life. Political society in the years to come is likely to face a similar choice. An open society such as ours is especially vulnerable to terrorist violence, which seems to threaten us with ever more dreadful and drastic fates. Have we the stoicism to endure nonetheless? Will we be tempted to abandon our political and moral values? Will we be willing to go on paying an ever higher price in order to defeat the terrorists by refusing to respond in the way they want us to?

Of course it would make things easier if terrorism simply would go away. It seems unlikely to do so. The weapons are at hand, and they probably will be used, for terrorism will never cease until the day when the Old Man of the Mountain loses his last disciple. The old man was grand master of the sect called the Assassions (hashish-ins) because of the hashish which he gave them. The old man, according to Marco Polo, used to drug his young disciples and transport them while they were asleep to his secret pleasure garden, persuading them when they awoke in it that it was paradise itself. Drugging them again, he would transport them back to the everyday world while they slept. Never afterward did they doubt that their Master could and would reward them with eternal paradise after death if they did his killing for him while they were alive. And so they did do his killing for him.

If anything, the modern world seems to breed more and more votaries of this peculiar sect. They seem to thrive and multiply everywhere in the world, bomb or machine gun in hand, motivated by political fantasies and hallucinations, fully convinced that their slaughter of the innocent will somehow usher in a political millennium for mankind. "*Voici le temps des* ASSASSINS," as Rimbaud wrote in the dawn of the industrial age; and we do indeed live in the time of the Assassins.

FOREIGN AFFAIRS

NOVEMBER / DECEMBER 2005

Iraq: Learning the Lessons of Vietnam

Melvin R. Laird

Volume 84 • Number 6

Iraq: Learning the Lessons of Vietnam

Melvin R. Laird

SETTING THE RECORD STRAIGHT

RICHARD NIXON was elected in 1968 on the assumption that he had a plan to end the Vietnam War. He didn't have any such plan, and my job as his first secretary of defense was to remedy that—quickly. The only stated plan was wording I had suggested for the 1968 Republican platform, saying it was time to de-Americanize the war. Today, nearly 37 years after Nixon took office as president and I left Congress to join his cabinet, getting out of a war is still dicier than getting into one, as President George W. Bush can attest.

There were two things in my office that first day that gave my mission clarity. The first was a multivolume set of binders in my closet safe that contained a top-secret history of the creeping U.S. entry into the war that had occurred on the watch of my predecessor, Robert McNamara. The report didn't remain a secret for long: it was soon leaked to *The New York Times*, which nicknamed it "the Pentagon Papers." I always referred to the study as "the McNamara Papers," to give credit where credit belonged. I didn't read the full report when I moved into the office. I had already spent seven years on the Defense Subcommittee of the House Appropriations Committee listening to McNamara justify the escalation of the war. How we got into

MELVIN R. LAIRD was Secretary of Defense from 1969 to 1973, Counselor to the President for Domestic Affairs from 1973 to 1974, and a member of the House of Representatives from 1952 to 1969. He currently serves as Senior Counselor for National and International Affairs at the Reader's Digest Association.

[22]

CORBIS

Drawing down: General Creighton Abrams and the author, An Hoi, Vietnam, 1970

Vietnam was no longer my concern. (Although, in retrospect, those papers offered a textbook example of how *not* to commit American military might.)

The second item was another secret document, this one shorter and infinitely more troubling. It was a one-year-old request from General William Westmoreland to raise the U.S. troop commitment in Vietnam from 500,000 to 700,000. At the time he had made the request, Westmoreland was the commander of U.S. forces there. As soon as the idea had reached the ears of President Lyndon Johnson, Westmoreland's days in Saigon were numbered. Johnson bumped him upstairs to be army chief of staff, so that the Pentagon bureaucracy could dilute his more-is-better philosophy during the coming presidential campaign.

The memo had remained in limbo in the defense secretary's desk, neither approved nor rejected. As my symbolic first act in office, it gave me great satisfaction to turn down that request formally. It was the beginning of a four-year withdrawal from Vietnam that, in retrospect, became the textbook description of how the U.S. military should decamp.

Others who were not there may differ with this description. But they have been misinformed by more than 30 years of spin about the Vietnam War. The resulting legacy of that misinformation has left the United States timorous about war, deeply averse to intervening in even a just cause, and dubious of its ability to get out of a war once it is in one. All one need whisper is "another Vietnam," and palms begin to sweat. I have kept silent for those 30 years because I never believed that the old guard should meddle in the business of new administrations, especially during a time of war. But the renewed vilification of our role in Vietnam in light of the war in Iraq has prompted me to speak out.

Some who should know better have made our current intervention in Iraq the most recent in a string of bogeymen peeking out from under the bed, spawned by the nightmares of Vietnam that still haunt us. The ranks of the misinformed include seasoned politicians, reporters, and even veterans who earned their stripes in Vietnam but who have since used that war as their bully pulpit to mold an isolationist American foreign policy. This camp of doomsayers includes Senator Edward Kennedy, who has called Iraq "George Bush's Vietnam." Those who wallow in such Vietnam angst would have us be not only reticent to help the rest of the world, but ashamed of our ability to do so and doubtful of the value of spreading democracy and of the superiority of freedom itself. They join their voices with those who claim that the current war is "all about oil," as though the loss of that oil were not enough of a global security threat to merit any U.S. military intervention and especially not "another Vietnam."

The Vietnam War that I saw, first from my seat in Congress and then as secretary of defense, cannot be wrapped in a tidy package and tagged "bad idea." It was far more complex than that: a mixture of good and evil from which there are many valuable lessons to be learned. Yet the only lesson that seems to have endured is the one that begins and ends with "Don't go there." The war in Iraq is not "another Vietnam." But it could become one if we continue to use Vietnam as a sound bite while ignoring its true lessons.

I acknowledge and respect the raw emotions of those who fought in Vietnam, those who lost loved ones, and those who protested, and I also respect the sacrifice of those who died following orders of people such as myself, half a world away. Those raw emotions are once again being felt as our young men and women die in Iraq and Afghanistan. I cannot speak for the dead or the angry. My voice is that of a policymaker, one who once decided which causes were worth fighting for, how long the fight should last, and when it was time to go home. The president, as our commander-in-chief, has the overall responsibility for making these life-or-death decisions, in consultation with Congress. The secretary of defense must be supportive of those decisions, or else he must leave.

It is time for a reasonable look at both Vietnam and Iraq—and at what the former can teach us about the latter. My perspective comes from military service in the Pacific in World War II (I still carry shrapnel in my body from a kamikaze attack on my destroyer, the U.S.S. *Maddox*), nine terms in the U.S. House of Representatives, and four years as secretary of defense to Nixon.

Today, we deserve a view of history that is based on facts rather than emotional distortions and the party line of tired politicians who play on emotions. Mine is not a rosy view of the Vietnam War. I didn't miss the fact that it was an ugly, mismanaged, tragic episode in U.S. history, with devastating loss of life for all sides. But there are those in our nation who would prefer to pick at that scab rather than let it heal. They wait for opportunities to trot out the Vietnam demons whenever another armed intervention is threatened. For them, Vietnam is an insurance policy that pretends to guarantee peace at home as long as we never again venture abroad. Certain misconceptions about that conflict, therefore, need to be exposed and abandoned in order to restore confidence in the United States' nation-building ability.

STAYING THE COURSE

THE TRUTH about Vietnam that revisionist historians conveniently forget is that the United States had not lost when we withdrew in 1973. In fact, we grabbed defeat from the jaws of victory two years later when Congress cut off the funding for South Vietnam that had allowed it to continue to fight on its own. Over the four years of Nixon's first term, I had cautiously engineered the withdrawal of the majority of our forces while building up South Vietnam's ability to defend itself. My colleague and friend Henry Kissinger, meanwhile, had negotiated a viable agreement between North and South Vietnam, which was signed in January 1973. It allowed for the United States to withdraw completely its few remaining troops and for the United States and the Soviet Union to continue funding their respective allies in the war at a specified level. Each superpower was permitted to pay for replacement arms and equipment. Documents released from North Vietnamese historical files in recent years have proved that the Soviets violated the treaty from the moment the ink was dry, continuing to send more than $1 billion a year to Hanoi. The United States barely stuck to the allowed amount of military aid for two years, and that was a mere fraction of the Soviet contribution.

Yet during those two years, South Vietnam held its own courageously and respectably against a better-bankrolled enemy. Peace talks continued between the North and the South until the day in 1975 when Congress cut off U.S. funding. The Communists walked out of the talks and never returned. Without U.S. funding, South Vietnam was quickly overrun. We saved a mere $297 million a year and in the process doomed South Vietnam, which had been ably fighting the war without our troops since 1973.

I believed then and still believe today that given enough outside resources, South Vietnam was capable of defending itself, just as I believe Iraq can do the same now. From the Tet offensive in 1968 up to the fall of Saigon in 1975, South Vietnam never lost a major battle. The Tet offensive itself was a victory for South Vietnam and devastated the North Vietnamese army, which lost 289,000 men in 1968 alone. Yet the overriding media portrayal of the Tet offensive and the war thereafter was that of defeat for the United States and the Saigon government. Just so, the overriding media portrayal of the Iraq war is one of failure and futility.

Vietnam gave the United States the reputation for not supporting its allies. The shame of Vietnam is not that we were there in the first place, but that we betrayed our ally in the end. It was Congress that turned its back on the promises of the Paris accord. The president, the secretary of state, and the secretary of defense must share the blame. In the end, they did not stand up for the commitments our nation had made to South Vietnam. Any president or cabinet officer who is turned down by Congress when he asks for funding for a matter of national security or defense simply has not tried hard enough. There is no excuse for that failure. In my four years at the Pentagon, when public support for the Vietnam War was at its nadir, Congress never turned down any requests for the war effort or Defense Department programs. These were tense moments, but I got the votes and the appropriations. A defense secretary's relationship with Congress is second only to his relationship with the men and women in uniform. Both must be able to trust him, and both must know that he respects them. If not, Congress will not fund, and the soldiers, sailors, and air personnel will not follow.

Donald Rumsfeld has been my friend for more than 40 years. Gerald Ford and I went to Evanston to support him in his first congressional race, and I urged President Bush to appoint him secretary of defense. But his overconfident and self-assured style on every issue, while initially endearing him to the media, did not play well with Congress during his first term. My friends in Congress tell me Rumsfeld has modified his style of late, wisely becoming more collegial. Several secretaries during my service on the Appropriations Committee, running all the way from the tenure of Charlie Wilson to that of Clark Clifford, made the mistake of thinking they must appear much smarter than the elected officials to whom they reported. It doesn't always work.

If Rumsfeld wants something from those who are elected to make decisions for the American people, then he must continue to show more deference to Congress. To do otherwise will endanger public support and the funding stream for the Iraq war and its future requirements. A sour relationship on Capitol Hill could doom the whole effort. The importance of this solidarity between Congress and the administration did not escape Saddam Hussein, nor has it escaped the insurgents. In the days leading up to the U.S. invasion of Iraq, television stations there showed 1975 footage of U.S. embassy support personnel escaping to helicopters from the roof of the U.S. embassy in Saigon. It was Saddam's message to his people that the United States does not keep its commitments and that we are only as good as the word of our current president. We failed to deliver the logistical support to our allies in South Vietnam during the post-Watergate period because of a breakdown of leadership in Washington. The failure of one administration to keep the promises of another had a devastating effect on the North-South negotiations.

There are no guarantees of continuity in a partisan democracy. We are making commitments as to the future of Iraq on an almost daily basis. These commitments must be understood now so they can be honored later. Every skirmish on the home front that betrays a lack of solidarity on Iraq gives the insurgents more hope and ultimately endangers the men and women we have sent to Iraq to fight in this war for us. We are now committed to a favorable outcome in Iraq, but it must be understood that this will require long-term assistance or our efforts will be in vain.

VIETNAMIZATION AS THE MODEL

ALONG WITH our abandonment of our allies, another great tragedy of Vietnam was the Americanization of the war. This threatens to be the tragedy of Iraq also. John F. Kennedy committed a few hundred military advisers to Saigon. Johnson saw Southeast Asia as the place to stop the spread of communism, and he spared no expense or personnel. By the time Nixon and I inherited the war in 1969, there were more than half a million U.S. troops in South Vietnam and 1.2 million more U.S. soldiers, sailors, and air personnel supporting the war from aircraft carriers and military bases in surrounding nations and at sea. The war needed to be turned back to the people who cared about it, the Vietnamese. They needed U.S. money and training but not more American blood. I called our program "Vietnamization," and in spite of the naysayers, I have not ceased to believe that it worked.

Nixon was reelected in 1972 based in large part on our progress toward ending U.S. direct involvement in the war, ending the draft, and establishing the all-volunteer military service. His opponent that year, George McGovern, made the war the primary issue of the campaign, claiming that Democrats—the party in power that had escalated the war to an intolerable level—would be the best folks to get us out. McGovern lost because the American people didn't agree with him.

We need to put our resources and unwavering public support behind a program of "Iraqization" so that we can get out of Iraq and leave the

Iraqis in a position to protect themselves. The Iraq war should have been focused on Iraqization even before the first shot was fired. The focus is there now, and Americans should not lose heart.

We came belatedly to Vietnamization; nonetheless, there are certain principles we followed in Vietnam that would be helpful in Iraq. The most important is that the administration must adhere to a standard of competence for the Iraqi security forces, and when that standard is met, U.S. troops should be withdrawn in corresponding numbers. That is the way it worked in Vietnam, from the first withdrawal of 50,000 troops in 1969 to the last prisoner of war off the plane in January of 1973. Likewise, in Iraq, the United States should not let too many more weeks pass before it shows its confidence in the training of the Iraqi armed forces by withdrawing a few thousand U.S. troops from the country. We owe it to the restive people back home to let them know there is an exit strategy, and, more important, we owe it to the Iraqi people. The readiness of the Iraqi forces need not be 100 percent, nor must the new democracy be perfect before we begin our withdrawal. The immediate need is to show our confidence that Iraqis can take care of Iraq on their own terms. Our presence is what feeds the insurgency, and our gradual withdrawal would feed the confidence and the ability of average Iraqis to stand up to the insurgency.

I gave President Nixon the same advice about Vietnam from our first day in office. As secretary of defense, I took the initiative in the spring of 1969 to change our mission statement for Vietnam from one of applying maximum pressure against the enemy to one of giving maximum assistance to South Vietnam to fight its own battles. Then, the opponents of our withdrawal were the South Vietnamese government, which we had turned into a dependent, and some in our own military who harbored delusions of total victory in Southeast Asia using American might. Even if such a victory had been possible, it was wrong to Americanize the war from the beginning, and by that point the patience of the American people had run out.

Even with the tide of public opinion running against the war, withdrawal was not an easy sell inside the Nixon administration. Our first round of withdrawals was announced after a conference between Nixon and South Vietnamese President Nguyen Van Thieu on Midway

Island in June 1969. I had already softened the blow for Thieu by visiting him in Saigon in March, at which point I told him the spigot was being turned off. He wanted more U.S. soldiers, as did almost everyone in the U.S. chain of command, from the chair of the Joint Chiefs of Staff on down. For each round of troop withdrawals from Vietnam, the Joint Chiefs suggested a miserly number based on what they thought they still needed to win the war. I bumped those numbers up, always in counsel with General Creighton Abrams, then the commander of U.S. forces in Vietnam. Even Nixon, who had promised to end the war, accepted each troop-withdrawal request from me grudgingly. It took four years to bring home half a million troops. At times, it seemed my only ally was General Abrams. He understood what the others did not: that the American people's patience for the war had worn thin.

Bush is not laboring under similar handicaps in his military. His commanders share his goal of letting Iraq take care of itself as soon as its fledgling democracy is ready. And for the moment, there is still patience at home for a commonsensical, phased drawdown. In fact, the voices expressing the most patience about a sensible withdrawal and the most support for the progress of Iraqi soldiers are coming from within the U.S. military. These people are also the most eager to see the mission succeed and the most willing to see it through to the end. It is they who are at high risk and who are the ones being asked to serve not one but multiple combat tours. They are dedicated and committed to a mission that ranges from the toughest combat to the most elementary chores of nation building. We should listen to them, and trust them.

In those four years of Vietnamization, I never once publicly promised a troop number for withdrawal that I couldn't deliver. President Bush should move ahead with the same certainty. I also did not announce what our quantitative standards for readiness among the South Vietnamese troops were, just as Bush should not make public his specific standards for determining when Iraqi troops are ready to go it alone. In a report to Congress in July 2005, the Pentagon hinted that those measurable standards are in place. However, it would be a mistake for the president to rely solely on the numbers. Instead, his top commander in the field should have the final say on how many U.S. troops can come home, commensurate with the readiness of Iraqi forces. If Bush does not trust his commander's judgment, as I trusted General Abrams, Bush should replace him with someone he does trust. That trust must be conveyed to the American people, too, if they are to be patient with an orderly withdrawal of our troops.

THE PRETEXT FOR WAR

IN THIS business of trust, President Bush got off to a bad start. Nixon had the same problem. Both the Vietnam War and the Iraq war were launched based on intelligence failures and possibly outright deception. The issue was much more egregious in the case of Vietnam, where the intelligence lapses were born of our failure to understand what motivated Ho Chi Minh in the 1950s. Had we understood the depth of his nationalism, we might have been able to derail his communism early on.

The infamous pretext for leaping headlong into the Vietnam War was the Gulf of Tonkin incident. My old destroyer, the U.S.S. *Maddox*, was patrolling the Gulf of Tonkin 25 miles off the coast of North Vietnam on August 2, 1964, when it was attacked by three North Vietnamese torpedo boats. That solitary attack would have been written off as an aberration, but two days later the U.S.S. *Maddox*, joined then by the U.S.S. *Turner Joy*, reported that it was under attack again. From all I was able to determine when I read the dispatches five years later as secretary of defense, there was no second attack. There was confusion, hysteria, and miscommunication on a dark night. President Johnson and Defense Secretary McNamara either dissembled or misinterpreted the faulty intelligence, and McNamara hotfooted it over to Capitol Hill with a declaration that was short of war but that resulted in a war anyway. I, along with 501 colleagues in the House and Senate, voted for the Tonkin Gulf resolution, which was Johnson's ticket to escalate our role in Vietnam. Until then, the United States had been part bystander, part covert combatant, and part adviser.

In Iraq, the intelligence blunder concerned Saddam's nonexistent weapons of mass destruction, which in the end may or may not have been Bush's real motivation for going to war. My view is that it was better to find that Saddam had not progressed as far as we thought in his

WMD development than to discover belatedly that he had. Whatever the truth about WMD in Iraq, it cannot be said that the United States slipped gradually, covertly, or carelessly into Iraq, as we did into Vietnam.

MARKETING THE MISSION

THE MISTAKE on the question of WMD in Iraq has led many to complain that the United States was drawn into the war under false pretenses, that what began as self-defense has morphed into nation building. Welcome to the reality of war. It is neither predictable nor tidy. This generation of Americans was spoiled by the quick-and-clean Operation Desert Storm, in 1991, when the first President Bush adhered to the mission, freed Kuwait, and brought home the troops. How would Iraq look today if George H.W. Bush had changed that mission on the fly and ordered a march to Baghdad and the overthrow of Saddam? The truth is, wars are fluid things and missions change. This is more the rule than the exception. It was true in Vietnam, and it is true in Iraq today.

The early U.S. objective in Southeast Asia was to stop the spread of communism. With changes in the relationship between the Soviet Union and China and the 1965 suppression of the communist movement in Indonesia, the threat of a communist empire diminished. Unwilling to abandon South Vietnam, the United States changed its mission to self-determination for Vietnam.

The current President Bush was persuaded that we would find WMD in Iraq and did what he felt he had to do with the information he was given. When we did not find the smoking gun, it would have been unconscionable to pack up our tanks and go home. Thus, there is now a new mission, to transform Iraq, and it is not a bad plan. Bush sees Iraq as the frontline in the war on terror—not because terrorists dominate there, but because of the opportunity to displace militant extremists' Islamist rule throughout the region. Bush's greatest strength is that terrorists believe he is in this fight to the end. I have no patience for those who can't see that big picture and who continue to view Iraq as a failed attempt to find WMD. Now, because Iraq has been set on a new course, Bush has an opportunity to reshape the region. "Nation building" is not an epithet or a slogan. After the attacks of September 11, 2001, it is our duty.

Unfortunately, Bush has done an uneven job of selling his message, particularly since he was relieved of the pressure of reelection. Nixon lost his leadership leverage because of Watergate and thus lost ground in the battle for public support. By contrast, I believe the American people would still want to follow Bush if they had a clear understanding of what was at stake. Recent polls showing a waning of support for the war are a sign to the president that he needs to level with the American people. When troops are dying, the commander-in-chief cannot be coy, vague, or secretive. We learned that in Vietnam, too.

Bush is losing the public relations war by making the same strategic mistakes we made in Vietnam. General Abrams frequently spoke to me about his frustration with the war that the U.S. media portrayed at home and how it contrasted with the war he was seeing up close. His sense of defeat in his own public relations war, with its 500-plus reporters based in Saigon, comes through in the hundreds of meetings held in his office in Saigon—meetings that were taped for the record. (Transcripts of those tapes are ably assembled and analyzed by Lewis Sorley in his recent book, *Vietnam Chronicles: The Abrams Tapes, 1968–1972*.)

In Vietnam, correspondents roamed the country almost at will, and their work brought home to the United States the first televised war. Until that war, families back home worried about the welfare of their soldiers but could not see the danger. Had the mothers and fathers of U.S. soldiers serving in World War II seen a real-time CNN report of D-day in the style of *Saving Private Ryan*, they might not have thought Europe was worth saving. Operation Desert Storm married 24-hour cable news and war for the first time. The embedding of journalists with combat units in Iraq 12 years later was a solid idea, but it has meant that casualties are captured on tape and then replayed on newscasts thousands of times. The deaths of ten civilians in a suicide bombing are replayed and analyzed and thus become the psychological equivalent of 10,000 deaths. The danger to one U.S. soldier captured on tape becomes a threat to everyone's son or father or daughter or mother.

I have made too many phone calls to grieving families to ever downplay the loss of even one life. But I have also been in combat, and it looks different from the inside, from the viewpoint of those who volunteered and trained to fight for just causes. For a soldier, ducking a sniper's bullet in downtown Baghdad is all in a day's work, no matter how alarming it looks on television. The soldier will shrug it off and walk the same streets the next day if he believes in his mission. The key for Bush is to communicate that same sense of mission to the people back home. His west Texas cowboy approach—shoot first and answer questions later, or do the job first and let the results speak for themselves—is not working. With his propensity to wrap up a package and present it as a fait accompli, Bush declared, "Mission accomplished!" at the end of the major combat phase of the Iraq war. That was a well-earned high-five for the military, but it soon became obvious that the mission had only just begun.

The president must articulate a simple message and mission. Just as the spread of communism was very real in the 1960s, so the spread of radical fundamentalist Islam is very real today. It was a creeping fear until September 11, 2001, when it showed itself capable of threatening us. Iraq was a logical place to fight back, with its secular government and modern infrastructure and a populace that was ready to overthrow its dictator. Our troops are not fighting there only to preserve the right of Iraqis to vote. They are fighting to preserve modern culture, Western democracy, the global economy, and all else that is threatened by the spread of barbarism in the name of religion. That is the message and the mission. It is not politically correct, nor is it comforting. But it is the truth, and sometimes the truth needs good marketing.

Condoleezza Rice is one person in the administration who understands and has consistently and clearly stated this message. When she was national security adviser, the media seemed determined to sideline her repeated theme, perhaps because she was perceived as a mere water bearer for the president. As secretary of state, she is in a better position to speak independently. The administration should do its best to keep the microphone in her hands.

BUILDING A LEGITIMATE GOVERNMENT

As was the case in Vietnam, the task in Iraq involves building a new society from the ground up. Two Vietnam experts, Jeffrey Record and W. Andrew Terrill, recently produced an exhaustive comparison of the Vietnam and Iraq wars for the Army War College. They note that in both wars, the United States sought to establish a legitimate indigenous government. In Iraq, the goal is a democratic government, whereas in Vietnam the United States would have settled for any regime that advanced our Cold War agenda.

Those who call the new Iraqi government Washington's "puppet" don't know what a real puppet government is. The Iraqis are as eager to be on their own as we are to have them succeed. In Vietnam, an American, Ambassador Philip Habib, wrote the constitution in 1967. Elections were choreographed by the United States to empower corrupt, selfish men who were no more than dictators in the garb of statesmen.

Little wonder that the passionate nationalists in the North came off as the group with something to offer. I do not personally believe the Saigon government was fated to fall apart someday through lack of integrity, and apparently the Soviet Union didn't think so either or it would not have pursued the war. But it is true that the U.S. administrations at the time severely underestimated the need for a legitimate government in South Vietnam and instead assumed that a shadow government and military force could win the day. In Iraq, a legitimate government, not window-dressing, must be the primary goal. The factious process of writing the Iraqi constitution has been painful to watch, and the varying factions must be kept on track. But the process is healthy and, more important, homegrown.

In hindsight, we can look at the Vietnam War as a success story—albeit a costly one—in nation building, even though the democracy we sought halfheartedly to build failed. Three decades ago, Asia really was threatened by the spread of communism. The Korean War was a fresh memory. In Malaysia, Singapore, Indonesia, the Philippines, and even India, communist movements were gaining a foothold. They failed in large part because the United States drew a line at Vietnam that distracted and sucked resources away from its Cold War nemesis, the Soviet Union. Similarly, the effect of our stand in Iraq is already being felt around the Middle East. Opposition parties are demanding to be heard. Veiled women are insisting on a voice. Syrian troops have left Lebanon. Egypt has held an election. Iran is being pressured by the United States and Europe alike on its development of nuclear weapons. The voices for change are building in Saudi Arabia. The movement even has a name: Kifaya—"Enough!" The parasites who have made themselves fat by promoting ignorance, fear, and repression in the region are squirming. These are baby steps, but that is where running begins.

INSURGENTS AS ENEMIES

INSURGENTS WERE and are the enemy in both wars, and insurgencies fail without outside funding. In Vietnam, the insurgents were heavily funded and well equipped by the Soviet Union. They followed a powerful and charismatic leader, Ho Chi Minh, who nurtured their passionate nationalist goals. In Iraq, the insurgency is fragmented, with no identifiable central leadership and no unifying theology, strategy, or vision other than to get the United States out of the region. If that goal were accomplished now, they would turn on each other, as they already have done in numerous skirmishes. Although they do rely on outside funding, their benefactors are fickle and without deep pockets.

There is no way of counting the precise number of insurgents in the Iraq war, but it appears to be in the thousands, which in comparative terms is paltry. Communist forces in Vietnam numbered well over 1 million in 1973. North Vietnam, over the course of the war, lost 1.1 million soldiers and 2 million civilians, and yet they were willing to fight on and we were not. Why? Record and Terrill say the key to understanding any war in which a weaker side prevails over a stronger one is the concept of the "asymmetry of stakes." Victory meant everything to North Vietnam and nothing to the average American. We had few economic interests in Vietnam. Our national security interest—preventing the domino scenario, in which the entire world would fall under the sway of communism if we lost Southeast Asia—didn't have enough currency to carry the day.

It is a very different story in Iraq, where the Bush administration hopes to implant democracy side by side with Islam. The stakes could not be higher for the continued existence of our own democracy and, yes, for the significant matter of oil. We are not the only nation dependent on Persian Gulf oil. We share that dependency with every industrialized nation on the planet. Picture those oil reserves in the hands of religious extremists whose idea of utopia is to knock the world economy and culture back more than a millennium to the dawn of Islam.

Bush's belief that he can replace repression with democracy is not some neoconservative fantasy. Our support of democracy dates from the founding of our nation. Democracies are simply better for the planet. Witness the courage of the Iraqi people who shocked the world and defied all the pessimists by showing up to vote in January 2005, even with guns pointed at their heads. The enemies of freedom in Iraq know what a powerful message that was to the rest of the Arab world, otherwise they would not have responded by escalating the violence.

Although Vietnam may have been a success story when it came to defeating an insurgency, the domestic insurgency—conducted by the Vietcong—was unfortunately only one front in the war, the larger front being the conventional military forces of North Vietnam. The Vietcong were largely suppressed by a combination of persuasion and force. A similar combination of deadly force against the Iraqi insurgency's leaders and incentives to co-opt their followers may work in Iraq, where the insurgency is the only enemy.

Vietnam, however, should be a cautionary tale when fighting guerrilla style, whether it be in the streets or in the jungle. Back then, frightened and untrained U.S. troops were ill equipped to govern their baser instincts and fears. Countless innocent civilians were killed in the indiscriminate hunt for Vietcong among the South Vietnamese peasantry. Some of the worst historical memories of the Vietnam War stem from those atrocities. Our volunteer troops in Iraq are better trained and supervised, yet the potential remains for a slaughter of innocents. Reports have already surfaced of skittish American soldiers shooting Iraqi civilians in acts that can only be attributed to poor training and discipline.

To stop abuses and mistakes by the rank and file, whether in the prisons or on the streets, heads must roll at much higher levels than they have thus far. I well remember the unexpected public support for Lieutenant William Calley, accused in the massacre of civilians in the village of My Lai. The massacre did not occur on my watch, but Calley's trial did, and Americans flooded the White House with letters of protest when it appeared that Calley would be the scapegoat while his superiors walked free. The best way to keep foot soldiers honest is to make sure their commanders know that they themselves will be held responsible for any breach of honor.

For me, the alleged prison scandals reported to have occurred in Iraq, in Afghanistan, and at Guantánamo Bay have been a disturbing reminder of the mistreatment of our own POWs by North Vietnam. The conditions in our current prison camps are nowhere near as horrific as they were at the "Hanoi Hilton," but that is no reason to pat ourselves on the back. The minute we begin to deport prisoners to other nations where they can legally be tortured, when we hold people without charges or trial, when we move prisoners around to avoid the prying inspections of the Red Cross, when prisoners die inexplicably on our watch, we are on a slippery slope toward the inhumanity that we deplore. In Vietnam, I made sure we always took the high ground with regard to the treatment of enemy prisoners. I opened our prison camps wide to international inspectors, so that we could demand the same from Hanoi. In Iraq, there are no American POWs being held in camps by the insurgents. There are only murder victims whose decapitated bodies are left for us to find. But that does not give us license to be brutal in return.

LIMITED WARFARE

OUR COMMANDERS in Iraq have another advantage over those in Vietnam: President Bush seems unlikely to be whipsawed by public opinion, but will take the war to wherever the enemy rears its head. In Vietnam, we waged a ground war in the South and did not permit our troops to cross into North Vietnam. The air war over the North and in Laos and Cambodia was waged in fits and starts, in secret and in the open, covered by lies and subterfuge, manipulated more by opinion polls than by military exigencies. In the early years, the services squabbled with one another. Even the State Department was allowed to veto air strikes. President Johnson stayed up late calling the plays while generals were sidelined.

In all, 2.8 million Americans served in and around Vietnam during the war, yet less than ten percent of them were in-line infantry units, the men we think of as our Vietnam veterans. Men were drafted and given a few weeks of training before being attached to a unit of strangers. With few exceptions, our all-volunteer military in Iraq is motivated, well trained, well equipped, and in cohesive units. This is not to say that any of these troops want to be there. They don't. Yet they are far more motivated to fight this war than were the average conscripts in Vietnam.

They are also part of a much smarter military, thanks in large part to the lessons of Vietnam. In 1986, the Goldwater-Nichols Department of Defense Reorganization Act, with input from some veterans of my team at the Pentagon, cleaned up many of the command problems that hindered us in Vietnam and for a decade thereafter. The old system encouraged the Joint Chiefs of Staff to be anything but joint. They protected their fiefdoms and withheld cooperation from one another. The Goldwater-Nichols act centralized authority in the chair of the Joint Chiefs as the primary adviser to the president and the secretary of defense. The separate services are now responsible for training their people for war, but the area commanders who run the wars control all the assets. Today's soldiers, sailors, and air personnel can also be more secure knowing that the people who make life-or-death decisions represent a better balance between military expertise and the will of the people as expressed through their elected officials.

Such confidence is critical to sustaining an all-volunteer military. As the secretary of defense who ended the draft in 1972, I see no need to return to conscription, even now that the prospect of combat has somewhat dampened the enthusiasm for military service. As long as servicepeople—current and future—know where their president is leading them, the enlistments will follow.

As it did in Vietnam, in Iraq the enemy has sought to weaken the United States' will by dragging out the hostilities. In Vietnam, that strategy was reflected in a bottomless well of men, sophisticated arms, and energy the enemy threw into the fight. Similarly in Iraq, the insurgents have pinpointed the weakness of the American public's will and hope to exploit it on a much smaller scale, with the weapon of choice being the improvised explosive device, strapped to one person, loaded into a car or hidden at a curb, and with the resulting carnage then played over and over again on the satellite feed. But one lesson learned from Vietnam that is not widely recognized is that fear of casualties is *not* the prime motivator of the American people during a war. American soldiers will step up to the plate, and the American public will tolerate loss of life, if the conflict has worthy, achievable goals that are clearly espoused by the administration and if their leadership deals honestly with them.

Such was not the case in Vietnam. When President Nixon ordered the secret bombing of Cambodia, I protested vigorously. I did not oppose the bombing itself, as I believed the United States should fight the war as it needed to be fought—wherever the enemy was hiding—or not fight it at all. What I opposed was the deception. Behind closed doors, my opinion was so well known that when the secret was exposed, as I knew it would be, I was immediately and wrongly pinpointed as being the leak. The president approved Kissinger's order to the FBI to tap my military assistant's home phone, hoping to catch the two of us in a plot to leak secrets. Americans will not be lied to, and they will not tolerate secrets nor be sidelined in a war debate. As with the Vietnam War, if necessary they will take to the streets to be heard.

AT WHAT COST?

THE GREATEST cost of war is human suffering. But every war has its monetary price tag, too, even if it is rarely felt in real time. As with Vietnam, the Iraq war is revealing chinks in our fiscal armor. Only after the Vietnam War ended did its drain on the U.S. economy become apparent. During the war, our military readiness to fight other conflicts was precarious. Billions of dollars were drained away from other missions to support the war. It became a juggling act to support our forces around the world. I reduced our contingent in Korea by 29,000 men, and I persuaded Japan to begin paying the bills for its post–World War II defense by our troops. In retrospect, those two steps were positive results from the financial drain that the Vietnam War caused. But there were plenty of other places where the belt-tightening suffocated good programs. The Army Reserve and National Guard units fell into disrepair. President Johnson chose to draft the unwilling, rather than use trained reservists and National Guard soldiers and air personnel. As unpopular as the draft was, it was still an easier sell for Johnson than deploying whole National Guard and Reserve units out of the communities in middle America. So the second-string troops stayed home and saw their budgets cannibalized. Their training was third-rate and their equipment secondhand. Now, in our post-Vietnam wisdom, we have embraced the "total force" concept. After two decades of retooling, most National Guard units and reservists were better prepared to respond when called up for Operation Desert Storm.

Yet, because of pandering to the butter-not-guns crowd, we still do not spend enough of our total budget on national defense. The annual U.S. GDP is in excess of $11.5 trillion. The percentage of GDP going to the Defense Department amounts to 3.74 percent. In 1953, during the Korean War, it was 14 percent. In 1968, during the Vietnam War, it was nearly 10 percent—an amount that sapped domestic programs and ended up demoralizing President Johnson because he could not maintain his Great Society social programs. Now our spending priorities have shifted to social programs, with 6.8 percent of GDP, for example, going to Social Security and Medicare. That is more than twice what it was during the Vietnam War.

It will not be easy or popular to reverse the downward trend in defense spending. But the realities of the global threat of terrorism and the outside possibility of conventional warfare with an enemy such as China or North Korea demand that we take off the blinders. To increase defense spending to 4 percent of GDP would be adequate, but it is especially important to increase the share of the pie spent on the U.S. Army. It now gets 24 percent of the total Defense Department budget, but given the new realities of modern warfare, it should receive at least 28 percent. The army is currently strung along through the budget year with special appropriations, and that is no way to run a military service.

Reserve and National Guard units are understaffed and have been abused by deployments that have taken individuals out of their units to serve as de facto army regulars, many in specialties for which they have not been trained, a practice that eats at the morale of reservists. Nearly 80 percent of the airlift capacity for this war and about 48 percent of the troops have come from Reserve and National Guard units. The high percentages are due, in part, to the specialized missions of those troops: transporting cargo, policing, rebuilding infrastructure, translating, conducting government affairs—in short, the stuff of building a new nation. We have realized too late that our regular army forces have not been as well trained as they should have been for the new reality of an urban insurgent enemy. Nor was the military hierarchy paying serious attention to the hints that their mission in the twenty-first century would be nation building.

Secretary Rumsfeld is trying to reshape the army to be more mobile with fewer soldiers, in "units of action" built on the Special Forces model. But he is not being honest with himself or with Congress and the American people about how much money will be needed to make the transformation. Those specialized units will be more suited for urban guerrilla warfare, but light and lean is not the only way to maintain our military. Although guerrilla warfare looks like the wave of the future, we still face the specter of conventional divisional and corps warfare against other enemies. Both capabilities are expensive, but the downward trend of defense budgets does not recognize that. Except for bumps up in the Ronald Reagan years and during the Gulf War, the defense budget has been on a downward slide when viewed in constant dollars. We are coasting on the investments in research, development, and equipment made during earlier years.

SHORING UP OUR ALLIES

OUR PATTERN of fighting our battles alone or with a marginal "coalition of the willing" contributes to the downward spiral in resources and money. Ironically, Nixon had the answer back in 1969. At the heart of the Nixon Doctrine, announced that first year of his presidency, was the belief that the United States could not go it alone. As he said in his foreign policy report to Congress on February 18, 1970, the United States will participate in the defense and development of allies and friends, but "America cannot—and will not—conceive *all* the plans, design *all* the programs, execute *all* the decisions and undertake *all* the defense of the free nations of the world. We will help where it makes a real difference and is considered in our interest" (emphasis in the original).

Three decades later, we have fallen into a pattern of neglecting our treaty alliances, such as NATO, and endangering the aid we can give our allies by throwing our resources into fights that our allies refuse to join. Vietnam was just such a fight, and Iraq is, too. If our treaty alliances were adequately tended to and shored up—and here I include the UN—we would not have so much trouble persuading others to join us when our cause is just. Still, as the only superpower, there will be times when we must go it alone.

President Bush does not have the luxury of waiting for the international community to validate his policies in Iraq. But we do have the lessons of Vietnam. In Vietnam, the voices of the "cut-and-run" crowd ultimately prevailed, and our allies were betrayed after all of our work to set them on their feet. Those same voices would now have us cut and run from Iraq, assuring the failure of the fledgling democracy there and damning the rest of the Islamic world to chaos fomented by extremists. Those who look only at the rosy side of what defeat did to help South Vietnam get to where it is today see a growing economy there and a warming of relations with the West. They forget the immediate costs of the United States' betrayal. Two million refugees were driven out of the country, 65,000 more were executed, and 250,000 were sent to "reeducation camps." Given the nature of the insurgents in Iraq and the catastrophic goals of militant Islam, we can expect no better there.

As one who orchestrated the end of our military role in Vietnam and then saw what had been a workable plan fall apart, I agree that we cannot allow "another Vietnam." For if we fail now, a new standard will have been set. The lessons of Vietnam will be forgotten, and our next global mission will be saddled with the fear of its becoming "another Iraq."

Seeing Baghdad, Thinking Saigon

Stephen Biddle

THE GRAND DELUSION

CONTENTIOUS AS the current debate over Iraq is, all sides seem to make the crucial assumption that to succeed there the United States must fight the Vietnam War again—but this time the right way. The Bush administration is relying on an updated playbook from the Nixon administration. Pro-war commentators argue that Washington should switch to a defensive approach to counterinsurgency, which they feel might have worked wonders a generation ago. According to the antiwar movement, the struggle is already over, because, as it did in Vietnam, Washington has lost hearts and minds in Iraq, and so the United States should withdraw.

But if the debate in Washington is Vietnam redux, the war in Iraq is not. The current struggle is not a Maoist "people's war" of national liberation; it is a communal civil war with very different dynamics. Although it is being fought at low intensity for now, it could easily escalate if Americans and Iraqis make the wrong choices.

Unfortunately, many of the policies dominating the debate are ill adapted to the war being fought. Turning over the responsibility for fighting the insurgents to local forces, in particular, is likely to make matters worse. Such a policy might have made sense in Vietnam, but in Iraq it threatens to exacerbate the communal tensions that underlie the conflict and undermine the power-sharing negotiations needed to end it. Washington must stop shifting the responsibility for the

---

STEPHEN BIDDLE is a Senior Fellow in Defense Policy at the Council on Foreign Relations and the author of *Military Power*.

---

country's security to others and instead threaten to manipulate the military balance of power among Sunnis, Shiites, and Kurds in order to force them to come to a durable compromise. Only once an agreement is reached should Washington consider devolving significant military power and authority to local forces.

NOT AGAIN

AS IT IS in 2006, in 1969 Washington's strategy was built around winning hearts and minds while handing off more and more of the fighting to indigenous forces. From the outset of the Vietnam War, efforts to coax the Vietnamese people away from the communists and into supporting the Washington-backed government in Saigon were a crucial part of U.S. policy. "The task," President Lyndon Johnson said in 1965, "is nothing less than to enrich the hope and existence of more than a hundred million people." The United States transferred $2.9 billion in economic aid to South Vietnam between 1961 and 1968 alone. In 1967, allied forces distributed more than half a million cakes of soap and instructed more than 200,000 people in personal hygiene. By then, thanks to U.S. pressure, elections at all levels of government had taken place throughout South Vietnam. The plan was to undermine the Vietcong by improving the lives of the South Vietnamese through economic development and political reform.

Of course, the counterinsurgency was about more than winning hearts and minds; it was also about fighting. At first, following Congress' decision in 1965 to commit large-scale U.S. ground forces, Americans did much of South Vietnam's defensive work. But in 1969, the Nixon administration changed course and decided to transfer responsibility for ground combat to the South Vietnamese. "We have adopted a plan which we have worked out in cooperation with the South Vietnamese for the complete withdrawal of all U.S. combat ground forces and their replacement by South Vietnamese forces on an orderly scheduled timetable," Richard Nixon declared. "This withdrawal will be made from strength and not from weakness. As South Vietnamese forces become stronger, the rate of American withdrawal can become greater." The strategy, which became known as "Vietnamization," led to the complete withdrawal of U.S.

ground forces from Vietnam by 1973. After that, South Vietnamese troops who had been trained and equipped by the Americans conducted all ground operations.

U.S. strategy in Iraq today is remarkably similar. To win the war, President George W. Bush has advocated following three parallel tracks—one for politics, one for economics, and one for security. The first two involve using democratic reform and economic reconstruction to persuade Iraqis to side with the new government in Baghdad and oppose the insurgents. The goal of the Bush administration's third track is the creation of an Iraqi national military and an Iraqi police force that can shoulder the burden of counterinsurgency on their own—a project many call "Iraqization," after its counterpart from Vietnam. The details of how to implement today's policy may differ from those for the policy in the 1960s, but the two plans' intents are effectively indistinguishable. Even the rhetoric surrounding the two plans is strikingly similar. Bush's claim that "as the Iraqi security forces stand up, coalition forces can stand down" parallels Nixon's hope that "as South Vietnamese forces become stronger, the rate of American withdrawal can become greater."

Meanwhile, commentators such as Andrew Krepinevich argue essentially that Washington is not refighting Vietnam properly ("How to Win in Iraq," September/October 2005). Krepinevich sees the current U.S. strategy as a repeat of the failed search-and-destroy missions of early Vietnam and wants Washington to adopt instead the approach of territorial defense used in late Vietnam. Former Secretary of Defense Melvin Laird argues that Vietnamization was working fine until Congress pulled the plug on support for South Vietnam in 1975, and so he advocates recycling the strategy and following through with it ("Iraq: Learning the Lessons of Vietnam," November/December 2005). Journalists scorn U.S. officers who insist on overusing firepower—a mistake made in Vietnam—and lionize those who try to bring good governance to Iraq by holding local council elections, fixing sewers, and getting the trash picked up—the good lessons of Vietnam. Advocates of outright withdrawal think the United States has already lost the hearts and minds of Iraqis and should therefore cut its losses now, earlier than it did last time around.

A CATEGORY MISTAKE

UNFORTUNATELY, the parallel does not hold. A Maoist people's war is, at bottom, a struggle for good governance between a class-based insurgency claiming to represent the interests of the oppressed public and a ruling regime portrayed by the insurgents as defending entrenched privilege. Using a mix of coercion and inducements, the insurgents and the regime compete for the allegiance of a common pool of citizens, who could, in principle, take either side. A key requirement for the insurgents' success, arguably, is an ideological program—people's wars are wars of ideas as much as they are killing competitions—and nationalism is often at the heart of this program. Insurgents frame their resistance as an expression of the people's sovereign will to overthrow an illegitimate regime that represents only narrow class interests or is backed by a foreign government.

Communal civil wars, in contrast, feature opposing subnational groups divided along ethnic or sectarian lines; they are not about universal class interests or nationalist passions. In such situations, even the government is typically an instrument of one communal group, and its opponents champion the rights of their subgroup over those of others. These conflicts do not revolve around ideas, because no pool of uncommitted citizens is waiting to be swayed by ideology. (Albanian Kosovars, Bosnian Muslims, and Rwandan Tutsis knew whose side they were on.) The fight is about group survival, not about the superiority of one party's ideology or one side's ability to deliver better governance.

The underlying dynamic of many communal wars is a security problem driven by mutual fear. Especially in states lacking strong central governments, communal groups worry that other groups with historical grievances will try to settle scores. The stakes can be existential, and genocide is a real possibility. Ideologues or nationalists can also be brutal toward their enemies—Pol Pot and his Khmer Rouge come to mind—but in communal conflicts the risk of mass slaughter is especially high.

Whereas the Vietnam War was a Maoist people's war, Iraq is a communal civil war. This can be seen in the pattern of violence in Iraq, which is strongly correlated with communal affiliation. The four provinces that make up the country's Sunni heartland account for fully 85 percent of all insurgent attacks; Iraq's other 14 provinces, where almost 60 percent of the Iraqi population lives, account for only 15 percent of the violence. The overwhelming majority of the insurgents in Iraq are indigenous Sunnis, and the small minority who are non-Iraqi members of al Qaeda or its affiliates are able to operate only because Iraqi Sunnis provide them with safe houses, intelligence, and supplies. Much of the violence is aimed at the Iraqi police and military, which recruit disproportionately from among Shiites and Kurds. And most suicide car bombings are directed at Shiite neighborhoods, especially in ethnically mixed areas such as Baghdad, Diyala, or northern Babil, where Sunni bombers have relatively easy access to non-Sunni targets.

If the war in Iraq were chiefly a class-based or nationalist war, the violence would run along national, class, or ideological lines. It does not. Many commentators consider the insurgents to be nationalists opposing the U.S. occupation. Yet there is almost no antioccupation violence in Shiite or Kurdish provinces; only in the Sunni Triangle are some Sunni "nationalists" raising arms against U.S. troops, whom they see as defenders of a Shiite- and Kurdish-dominated government. Defense of sect and ethnic group, not resistance to foreign occupation, accounts for most of the anti-American violence. Class and ideology do not matter much either: little of the violence pits poor Shiites or poor Sunnis against their richer brethren, and there is little evidence that theocrats are killing secularists of their own ethnic group. Nor has the type of ideological battle typical of a nationalist war emerged in Iraq. This should come as no surprise: the insurgents are not competing for Shiite hearts and minds; they are fighting for Sunni self-interest, and hardly need a manifesto to rally supporters.

The uprisings led by Muqtada al-Sadr's Shiite militia in Baghdad and Najaf have been an exception to this general pattern, but it is the exception that confirms the rule. Although Sadr may still have a political future, so far he has failed to spur a broad-based Shiite uprising against either the U.S. occupation or the Shiite-dominated government. Some Iraqi Shiites do resent the U.S. occupation, and nationalism does feed anti-American violence. But nationalism is only a secondary factor in the war, and its main effect is to magnify the virulence of the Sunnis' violence in what is fundamentally a communal civil war.

This is not to claim that there are no Iraqi patriots who place nation above sect, or that a unified state is beyond reach. And this is certainly not to denigrate the courageous efforts of U.S. and Iraqi soldiers who have sacrificed much for a new Iraq. But these efforts may be in vain if the communal civil war in Iraq continues to be misunderstood.

KEEP NIXON OUT OF BAGHDAD

THE PROBLEM with recycling the Vietnam playbook in Iraq is that the strategies devised to win a people's war are either useless or counterproductive in a communal one. Winning hearts and minds, for example, is crucial to defeating a people's rebellion that promises good governance, but in a communal civil war such as that in Iraq, it is a lost cause. Communities in Iraq are increasingly polarized and fear mass violence at one another's hands. Some Sunnis hunger for a return to dominance; many others fear violent Shiite-Kurdish retribution for Saddam's Sunni-dominated tyranny. Some Shiites and Kurds want revenge; others fear they will face mass killings in the event of a Sunni restoration. Economic aid or reconstruction assistance cannot fix the problem: Would Sunnis really get over their fear of Shiite domination if only the sewers were fixed and the electricity kept working? This is not to say that Washington should not provide reconstruction assistance or economic aid; the United States owes Iraq the help on moral grounds, and economic growth could ease communal tensions at the margins and so promote peace in the long term. But in the near term, survival trumps prosperity, and most Iraqis depend on communal solidarity for their survival.

Rapid democratization, meanwhile, could be positively harmful in Iraq. In a Maoist people's war, empowering the population via the ballot box undermines the insurgents' case that the regime is illegitimate and facilitates nonviolent resolution of the inequalities that fuel the conflict. In a communal civil war, however, rapid democratization can further polarize already antagonistic sectarian groups. In an immature polity with little history of compromise, demonizing traditional enemies is an easy—and dangerous—way to mobilize support from frightened voters. And as the political scientists Edward Mansfield and Jack Snyder have shown, although mature democracies rarely go to war with other democracies, emerging democracies are unusually bellicose. Political reform is critical to resolving communal wars, but only if it comes at the right time, after some sort of stable communal compromise has begun to take root.

The biggest problem with treating Iraq like Vietnam is Iraqization—the main component of the current U.S. military strategy. In a people's war, handing the fighting off to local forces makes sense because it undermines the nationalist component of insurgent resistance, improves the quality of local intelligence, and boosts troop strength. But in a communal civil war, it throws gasoline on the fire. Iraq's Sunnis perceive the "national" army and police force as a Shiite-Kurdish militia on steroids. And they have a point: in a communal conflict, the only effective units are the ones that do not intermingle communal enemies. (Because the U.S. military does not keep data on the ethnic makeup of the Iraqi forces, the number of Sunnis in these organizations is unknown and the effectiveness of mixed units cannot be established conclusively. Considerable anecdotal evidence suggests that the troops are dominated by Shiites and Kurds and that the Sunnis' very perception that this is so, accurate or not, helps fuel the conflict. Either way, Iraqization poses serious problems, and the analysis below considers both the possibility that integration might succeed and the possibility that it might fail.) Sunni populations are unlikely to welcome protection provided by their ethnic or sectarian rivals; to them, the defense forces look like agents of a hostile occupation. And the more threatened the Sunnis feel, the more likely they are to fight back even harder. The bigger, stronger, better trained, and better equipped the Iraqi forces become, the worse the communal tensions that underlie the whole conflict will get.

The creation of powerful Shiite-Kurdish security forces will also reduce the chances of reaching the only serious long-term solution to the country's communal conflict: a compromise based on a constitutional deal with ironclad power-sharing arrangements protecting all parties. A national army that effectively excluded Sunnis would make any such constitutional deal irrelevant, because the Shiite-Kurdish alliance would hold the real power regardless of what the constitution said. Increasing evidence that Iraq's military and police have already committed atrocities against Sunnis only confirms the dangers of transferring responsibility for fighting the insurgents to local forces before an acceptable ethnic compromise has been brokered.

On the other hand, the harder the United States works to integrate Sunnis into the security forces, the less effective those forces are likely to become. The inclusion of Sunnis will inevitably entail penetration by insurgents, and it will be difficult to establish trust between members of mixed units whose respective ethnic groups are at one another's throats. Segregating Sunnis in their own battalions is no solution either. Doing so would merely strengthen all sides simultaneously by providing each with direct U.S. assistance and could trigger an unstable, unofficial partition of the country into separate Sunni, Shiite, and Kurdish enclaves, each defended by its own military force.

Unfortunately, the alternatives to the Bush administration's policies currently on the table are no more promising. Shifting from tactical offense to defense, for example, could make things worse. Krepinevich proposes an "oil-spot strategy" that focuses on providing security to civilians rather than on killing insurgents. In principle, such an approach could help by protecting Iraqis against violence perpetrated by ethnic rivals. But finding the appropriate troops to implement it would not be easy. There are too few Americans to protect more than a fraction of Iraq's population, and it is far from clear that Sunnis would accept their help anyway. So the plan would have to rely on Iraqi troops, which will inevitably end up being either integrated and ineffectual or segregated and divisive. Tactical defense by the wrong defenders can be fatal in a communal civil war, and in Iraq it will remain far from clear how to provide appropriate defenders until the communal strife itself has been resolved.

The case for withdrawing U.S. troops is no stronger, largely because the war does not hinge on the United States' winning—or losing—Iraqi hearts and minds. The war is about resolving the communal security problems that divide Iraqis, and it is too early to give up on achieving this goal via constitutional compromise. In fact, the very prospect that today's conflict could degenerate into attempted genocide if compromise fails should be a powerful lever for negotiating a deal. The presence of U.S. troops is essential to

Washington's bargaining position in these negotiations. To withdraw them now, or to start withdrawing them according to a rigid timetable, would undermine the prospect of forging a lasting peace.

THE BEST PLAN

WHAT, THEN, is to be done? Some elements of the current U.S. strategy are worth keeping. The efforts of the U.S. ambassador to Iraq, Zalmay Khalilzad, to broker a constitutional deal between Sunnis, Shiites, and Kurds, for example, are crucial for success; his interventionist approach is a major improvement over the strategy of quiet behind-the-scenes encouragement favored by L. Paul Bremer, the head of the Coalition Provisional Authority from May 2003 to June 2004. Economic assistance is a moral imperative; it should be continued and reinforced whatever its marginal strategic value.

But critical departures from the current strategy are also necessary. First, Washington must slow down the expansion of the Iraqi national military and police. Iraq will eventually need capable indigenous security forces, but their buildup must follow a broad communal compromise, not the other way around. If the development of the army and the police gets ahead of the agreement, the forces will either exclude the Sunnis and be effective but divisive or include the Sunnis but be weak. The latter result would mean lost effort and perhaps lives, but the former would probably be worse, because it would jeopardize any constitutional power-sharing deal that may emerge from Khalilzad's efforts. This dilemma leaves Washington with no choice but to continue providing enough U.S. forces to cap the violence in Iraq.

Second, the United States must bring more pressure to bear on the parties in the constitutional negotiations. And the strongest pressure available is military: the United States must threaten to manipulate the military balance of power among Sunnis, Shiites, and Kurds to coerce them to negotiate. Washington should use the prospect of a U.S.-trained and U.S.-supported Shiite-Kurdish force to compel the Sunnis to come to the negotiating table. At the same time, in order to get the Shiites and the Kurds to negotiate too, it should threaten either to withdraw prematurely, a move that would throw the country into disarray, or to back the Sunnis.

If Washington fails to implement this plan, it will continue to have only limited leverage over the parties, each of which sees compromise as risky. The groups fear that if their rivals gain control of the government, they will face oppression, impoverishment, or mass violence. Compromising means ceding some power to rivals, and a miscalculation that cedes too much power could result in the enemy's seizing the rest later, with catastrophic results. In contrast, an ongoing low-intensity war does not look so bad: as long as U.S. forces patrol Iraq, the country will not break up and the conflict will not descend into all-out chaos. The parties' refusal to compromise may be an obstacle to real peace, but it is also a way to avert mass violence.

The only way to break the logjam is to change the parties' relative comfort with the status quo by drastically raising the costs of their failure to negotiate. The U.S. presence now caps the war's intensity, and U.S. aid could give any side an enormous military advantage. Thus Washington should threaten to use its influence to alter the balance of power depending on the parties' behavior. By doing so, it could make stubbornness look worse than cooperation and compel all sides to compromise.

Today, however, Washington is doing just the opposite. Washington's stated policy is to field an ethnically mixed Iraqi military as quickly as possible in order to replace U.S. troops, with or without a stable constitutional deal in place—an approach that forfeits Washington's primary source of leverage with all three local factions. The Sunnis have little to fear from the plan, for if it succeeds, they will have been saved from a powerful U.S.-trained Shiite-Kurdish army without having had to make any concessions. The prospect that the United States' policy could fail, thus leaving the Sunnis on their own, may frighten them, but since the likelihood of that happening is unrelated to their willingness to make political compromises, they have little reason to negotiate. Iraqization gives Washington no more sway with the Shiites or the Kurds, because it involves keeping U.S. troops in Iraq until these groups can defend themselves, regardless of whether they negotiate seriously in the meantime. So the only way out of this problem is for Washington to postpone Iraqization and make it contingent on the parties' willingness to bargain.

This shift in strategy will require changes in other current policies, too. For example, Washington will have to suspend its campaign against the Sunni insurgent leadership, former senior Baathists, and Sunni tribal leaders. If the key to success is a negotiated communal compromise, Washington needs negotiating partners who can make a deal stick—in other words, leaders with authority among their own people and combatants. But many of the Sunnis with such stature are now fighting in the insurgency, are in hiding, or are banned from politics because of their Baathist pasts; others are excluded by Washington's reluctance to reinforce a tribal loyalty system based on graft and patronage. The result is a weak Sunni political leadership lacking both the legitimacy and the power to negotiate a settlement. Since such weakness could be fatal to the prospects for ethnic compromise, Washington should consider trying to accelerate the emergence of a credible Sunni leadership by endorsing a wider amnesty for former Baathists and insurgents and learning to tolerate nepotistic tribal leaders.

Washington should also avoid setting any more arbitrary deadlines for democratization. Pressure to reach demanding political milestones can further polarize factional politics, and the parliamentary elections in December 2005 may already have hardened communal divides. In a people's war, early electoral deadlines can make sense; in a communal civil war, they are dangerous. Democracy is the long-term goal in Iraq, of course, but getting there will require a near-term constitutional compromise whose key provision must be an agreement to limit the freedom of Iraqi voters to elect governments that concentrate ethnic and sectarian power. Resolving the country's communal security problems must take priority over bringing self-determination to the Iraqi people—or the democracy that many hope for will never emerge.

BACK ON TRACK

PUTTING SUCH a program in place would not be easy. It would deny President Bush the chance to offer restless Americans an early troop withdrawal, replace a Manichaean narrative featuring evil insurgents and a noble government with a complicated story of multiparty interethnic intrigue, and require that Washington be willing to shift its loyalties in the conflict according to the parties' readiness to negotiate. Explaining these changes to U.S. voters would be a challenge. Washington would have to recalibrate its dealings with Sunnis, Shiites, and Kurds with great precision, making sure to neither unduly frighten nor unduly reassure any of the groups. Even the most adroit diplomacy could fail if the Iraqis do not grasp the strategic logic of their situation or if a strong and sensible Sunni political leadership does not emerge. And the failure to reach a stable ethnic compromise soon could strain the U.S. military beyond its breaking point.

Nevertheless, there are good reasons to think such a plan could work. Most important, the underlying interests of all local parties would be far better served by a constitutional compromise than by an all-out war. The losers would have to pay the butcher's bill of combat and bear the oppressor's yoke in the aftermath; even the winners would pay a terrible price. Since no side today can be confident that it would come out on top in a war, the prospect of losing should be a powerful motivation to compromise. The December 2005 round of negotiations in Baghdad suggested that the parties may have started to understand these stakes: the willingness of the Shiite negotiators to yield to the Sunnis' preferences on the procedures for amending the constitution indicates that compromise may be possible. The current U.S. strategy in Iraq makes this compromise less likely by shielding Iraqis from the full consequences of their stubbornness and thereby weakening Washington's potentially formidable leverage over the military balance of power. But if that changes—and it can change—the chances for success will be significantly increased.

At a minimum, Washington should stop making matters worse. Understanding the war in Iraq as a communal civil war cannot guarantee success, but without this understanding failure is far too likely. Whatever the prospects for peace, they would be considerably better if Washington stopped mistaking Iraq for Vietnam and started seeing it for what it really is.

What to Do in Iraq

A Roundtable

HOW TO END IT

Larry Diamond

In his trenchant analysis, Stephen Biddle ("Seeing Baghdad, Thinking Saigon," March/April 2006) argues that the escalating violence in Iraq is not a nationalist insurgency, as was the Vietnam War, but rather a "communal civil war" and that it must therefore be addressed by pursuing a strategy different from "Vietnamization": if the United States were simply to turn over responsibility for counterinsurgency to the new Iraqi army and police forces, it would risk inflaming the communal conflict, either by empowering the Shiites and the Kurds to slaughter the Sunnis or by enabling a Trojan horse full of Sunni insurgents to penetrate the multiethnic security forces and undermine them.

Biddle is right in many respects. First, Iraq is already in the midst of a very violent civil conflict, which claims 500 to 1,000 lives or more every month. Second, this internal conflict has become primarily communal in nature; as Biddle writes, it is a fight "about group survival." It pits Sunnis against Shiites, in particular, but also Kurds

---

LARRY DIAMOND, *a Senior Fellow at the Hoover Institution, is the author of* Squandered Victory: The American Occupation and the Bungled Effort to Bring Democracy to Iraq.

JAMES DOBBINS *directs the International Security and Defense Policy Center at the RAND Corporation and is the lead author of* The RAND History of Nation-Building.

CHAIM KAUFMANN *is Associate Professor of International Relations at Lehigh University.*

LESLIE H. GELB *is President Emeritus of the Council on Foreign Relations.*

---

against Sunnis and, more generally, group against group, with smaller minorities coming under attack on multiple fronts. Third, as Biddle warns, the current moderate-intensity communal war could descend into an all-out conflagration, with a high "risk of mass slaughter." Thus the United States cannot in good conscience withdraw from Iraq abruptly—and doing so would not even be in the United States' national interest—because that would remove the last significant barrier to a total conflagration.

Washington needs a new strategy, and, as Biddle writes, it cannot simply be "Iraqization" of the conflict. Biddle proposes two bold steps: slowing down the buildup of the Iraqi army and police and threatening to "manipulate the military balance of power among Sunnis, Shiites, and Kurds to coerce them to negotiate." But these steps (particularly the latter) are dangerous and unlikely to work, because they follow from an incomplete analysis of the formidably complex, multidimensional nature of the Iraqi conflict.

Although the war in Iraq is mainly a communal conflict, it is not only that. It also contains an important element of nationalist insurgency. One misses an essential piece of the puzzle—and a reason the conflict is so difficult to contain—if one does not grasp that many Iraqis (mostly Sunnis) are fighting in some significant measure because they believe they are waging a war of resistance against American occupiers and the Iraqi "traitors" who cooperate with them. Among the score or more of Sunni insurgent groups, both the radical Islamist forces and the secular resistance (which includes Saddam loyalists and surviving Baath Party members) have as one of their principal aims the expulsion of U.S. forces from Iraq. That this goal coincides with the ambition of some to return the Baath Party to power or with the dream of others to establish a Sunni Islamic caliphate—and with the conviction of all that the Shiite Islamist parties are controlled by Iran or at least stalking-horses for Tehran—should not obscure the insurgents' dedicated, ideological resistance to the U.S. presence. The communal hatred that extreme Sunni Islamists have deliberately provoked (a cynical tactic in a war of destabilization, eviction, and conquest) has overshadowed the resistance's nationalist dimension but has not removed it.

The Sunni resistance believes the United States seeks to establish permanent military bases in Iraq in order to control the country and its oil indefinitely. Some of the most ideologically extreme insurgent forces, such as al Qaeda in Iraq, will fight to the death to expel the Americans and achieve their own goal of domination. But since the autumn of 2003, other insurgent groups (accounting for a significant portion of the Sunni insurgency) have sent signals through international intermediaries that they want to talk directly to the United States. Two of these groups' objectives have been to obtain an unambiguous statement from Washington that it will not seek permanent military bases in Iraq and to set up a timetable for a complete U.S. military withdrawal, even if it stretches over two or three years. For more than two years now, Washington has had the opportunity to open negotiations, with the help of international mediators, with these elements of the insurgency and then draw Iraqi government leaders into those talks. The result could have been—and might still be—an agreement by key elements of the resistance to wind down the insurgency: Sunni political and religious leaders could send clear messages to their constituencies to suspend the war of resistance and pursue their political interests through the emerging game of peaceful politics and governance instead. In exchange, the United States would need to commit at least to a flexible timetable for the withdrawal of its troops, tied not only to dates but also to facts on the ground and confidence-building measures. Now that the conflict has become "communalized," much more will likely be required to curb the violence. But the need and the opportunity for dealing with the Sunni-based resistance remain.

CURSED ARE THE PEACEMAKERS

Biddle misses another crucial element of the conflict in Iraq. His proposed strategy of threatening to manipulate the military balance of power among the factions rests on two reciprocal assumptions, both highly questionable. On the one hand, Biddle assumes that the Sunni resistance would be compelled "to come to the negotiating table" if Washington threatened to throw in its lot with a Shiite-Kurdish force. He implies, and other strategists have explicitly argued, that the United States could solve the insurgency problem by backing a joint

Shiite-Kurdish military campaign to crush the Sunni resistance. But this threat is not likely to move Sunni forces: many of them believe Sunnis actually represent a majority of the country's population, and all of them would expect and probably receive massive assistance from neighboring Sunni Arab states in any all-out conflict with the Shiites and the Kurds.

By the same token, Biddle is on shaky grounds when he assumes that a U.S. threat to back the Sunnis militarily would be credible or that a U.S. threat to withdraw altogether militarily would necessarily panic the Shiites. Many of the Shiite Islamist parties and Shiite militia factions that constitute the ruling United Iraqi Alliance—most of all, Muqtada al-Sadr's political movement and his irregular Mahdi Army (which fought two campaigns against coalition forces in 2004)—are eager to be rid of the Americans and might well call their bluff. At that point, Washington would have to either back down from its threat and surrender its remaining leverage with the Shiites or follow through and watch Iraq descend into just the kind of civil war it has been trying to avert.

Biddle is right to argue that the United States does not have the leverage to achieve needed compromises over the fundamental issues that divide Iraq: the constitutional structure, the distribution of oil revenues, and security. But Washington is not likely to summon that leverage through hollow strategic threats. A better strategy—perhaps the only remaining alternative—would be for the United States to accelerate its mediation efforts and do so with international assistance. Washington needs and, at this critical juncture, can obtain the active partnership of the United Nations and the European Union to help the U.S. ambassador to Iraq, Zalmay Khalilzad, and other senior U.S. officials broker political compromises.

A combined diplomatic effort by the United States, the UN, and the EU, working in close coordination and speaking with one voice, might well engage all the relevant actors and gain the leverage to extract concessions from them on key issues. One crucial actor with whom UN or other mediators could talk—but who will not talk with the U.S. occupiers—is Grand Ayatollah Ali al-Sistani, still the most widely revered Shiite religious leader in Iraq and still a vastly underestimated force for moderation and compromise. But there are many others who might respond better to coordinated international appeals and to the financial and political incentives that the United States and Europe could together provide. A critical element of this approach would be for the U.S.-UN-EU team to bring into the negotiations, at the right moment, the Arab League, which has developed ties with a number of political actors in the Sunni resistance and thus could offer them credible assurances and induce them to compromise.

U.S. and international mediation must being by facilitating the work of the Constitutional Review Commission. This commission, which was conceived just before last year's October 15 constitutional referendum but has yet to be formed, is to be appointed by the Iraqi Parliament and given four months to recommend amendments to the constitution; those amendments will then have to be adopted by a simple parliamentary majority and approved by another referendum. This process was established because the current constitution has not been able to garner a consensus and is thus not viable. The document leaves Iraq with an extremely weak central authority. And it implicitly splits control over future oil and gas fields between a new Shiite superregion containing 80 percent of the country's oil and gas resources and a Kurdish region that, once it incorporates Kirkuk, will contain the other 20 percent.

If a constitutional compromise can be brokered, joint mediation might then address the other imperative concern, security, and with the various militias produce a plan, backed by extensive international financing, for the demobilization and disarmament of the various nonstate militias and the reintegration of their members into civilian economic life. Until the militias' control of territory and state structures (including the police) is substantially diminished, Iraq will lack a state with sufficient authority to hold the country together and restore some measure of order.

While intensified efforts at mediation proceed, the rebuilding of the Iraqi police and armed forces must go forward as well. It is true that the penetration of the police (and the Ministry of the Interior) by sectarian militias has been alarming and must be reversed; a new leadership and perhaps the embedding of U.S. forces in some police units could help. The rebuilding of the Iraqi army is one area in which the United States has achieved at least some incremental success. Such efforts must continue: Iraq simply cannot be held together much longer without a national army that can defend the new political order.

A truly international mediation process in Iraq would need to be carefully planned, designed, and coordinated. And there is relatively little time to do this. But there is no better option for achieving the political compromise necessary to stabilize Iraq and prevent it from descending into all-out civil war.

NO MODEL WAR

James Dobbins

Stephen Biddle has provided a very useful reminder that history teaches a variety of relevant lessons—even if official Washington often has difficulty absorbing more than one at a time. In 2003, the Bush administration based its plans for the reconstruction of Iraq on the U.S. occupations of Germany and Japan. Its critics have increasingly compared the results to Vietnam. Biddle suggests that the better analogy may be post–Cold War Yugoslavia.

Biddle's choice is apt in many respects. The Bush administration invoked Germany and Japan as models for Iraq's transformation because the occupations of those countries were highly successful and because those successes had nothing to do with Bill Clinton, Lyndon Johnson, or, for that matter, Richard Nixon. But if the administration's choice was politically safe, it was not otherwise very instructive. In 1945, when the United States occupied Germany and Japan, those countries were both highly homogenous societies with First World economies. And they had both surrendered following devastating defeats after years of brutal warfare.

None of these conditions existed in Yugoslavia in the 1990s or in Iraq a decade later. Both these countries had been created in the early twentieth century from the remnants of other empires (the Austrian and the Ottoman) and were established within borders that included disparate ethnic and religious groups that would have preferred not to live in the same state. Neither Yugoslavia nor Iraq ever developed a First World economy, nor had either surrendered.

Had the Bush administration used Bosnia or Kosovo as the model for Iraq, it would have realized that the stabilization and reconstruction of that country was going to require a lot more time, money, and manpower than it had planned. It would have anticipated the security vacuum that was likely to emerge immediately after the fall of Saddam Hussein's regime. It would have arrived with plans for the orderly disarmament, demobilization, and reintegration into society of sectarian militias and Republican Guard troops, and with blueprints for expanding the police and reforming the army. It would have moved quickly in the aftermath of the invasion—at a time when U.S. prestige was high, when no significant resistance has emerged, and when the world still assumed that weapons of mass destruction would be found—to expand international participation in the occupation and reconstruction of Iraq.

But it did none of these things. Instead, a faulty historical analogy led to faulty policy choices. When Baghdad fell, the Bush administration initially seemed to view Iraq as a prize won rather than as a burden acquired. It banned French, German, and Russian companies from reconstruction contracts. President George W. Bush rebuffed Prime Minister Tony Blair's efforts to give the United Nations a central role in the mission. The United States chose to designate itself an occupying power, basing its continued military presence on the laws of armed conflict rather than the UN Charter. All these positions were eventually reversed. But by then, an armed resistance movement had emerged, and with it disappeared any opportunity to draw the rest of the international community into Iraq more deeply.

As the possibility of Balkan-style peace enforcement in Iraq receded, that of Vietnam-style counterinsurgency advanced. Some critics of the administration have used the Vietnam analogy to argue for a withdrawal of U.S. troops. For others, it provides a model for how to redirect U.S. efforts. A number of experts (such as the Brookings Institution's Kenneth Pollack) have drawn on the Vietnam experience to make the case for a step-by-step pacification campaign, in which coalition forces would concentrate on securing a gradually expanding swath of territory and on protecting the local population therein, giving it better government and thereby winning its cooperation in marginalizing violent extremists.

DOING MORE WITH LESS

In his article, Biddle argues against a campaign based on such a "hearts and minds" approach, insisting that Iraqis are not fighting for good government, but for a state dominated by their own group (Sunni, Shiite, or Kurd). However, like some of those employing the Vietnam analogy, Biddle identifies the Kurdish and Shiite militias as the greatest long-term threat to Iraqi unity and urges the United States to shift the weight of its operations in Iraq from hunting down insurgents in the Sunni heartland to establishing secure areas, initially in Baghdad and the Shiite south.

There is much to be said for the Vietnamese and Balkan models. Today, U.S. troops in Iraq are having to relearn valuable techniques honed in Vietnam but since forgotten. Ethnic tensions in Iraq are reminiscent of those that led to the breakup of Yugoslavia, and they could produce a similar result. The Shiite and Kurdish militias do present a growing threat, if not to U.S. forces, then certainly to the unity of Iraq. Some repositioning of U.S. and Iraqi troops to ensure greater control over Baghdad—the country's center of gravity and home to 20 percent of its population, where the Shiite, Kurdish, and Sunni communities are thoroughly intermixed—may well be desirable.

It seems unlikely, however, that the United States at this late stage will deploy a force in Iraq large enough to successfully execute either Balkan-style peace enforcement or Vietnam-style pacification. The United States put 500,000 troops into South Vietnam, a country that in 1970 had a population that was little more than half the size of the population of Iraq today. NATO put over 100,000 troops into Bosnia and Kosovo, societies that in combination are around a fifth of the size of Iraq's. Coalition forces are currently not numerous enough even to suppress the Sunni insurgency; they are certainly insufficient to take on the much more powerful Shiite and Kurdish militias as well.

Biddle and those using the Vietnam analogy have made good abstract cases for a deeper, larger, and longer U.S. military role in Iraq. Unfortunately, the political basis for such a commitment is absent in both U.S. and Iraqi societies. U.S. economic assistance to Iraq has already largely dried up. And the U.S. military presence seems likely to diminish over the coming year. If the United States is to avert a wider civil war in Iraq, it must supplement the influence it derives from these two waning assets with a much more deft and active campaign of regional diplomacy.

Holding together ethnically divided societies is hardly a new or unfamiliar task. Similar efforts were required to end the war in Bosnia in the mid-1990s and to install a successor to the Taliban regime in Afghanistan in late 2001. Iraq is not a more divided society than was Bosnia or Afghanistan. Both of those states were in the midst of open, long-running civil wars when the United States stepped in. What makes Iraq different and a particularly difficult case is that for the first time the United States has tried to put a society back together without securing the cooperation, however grudging, of the principal neighbors of the state in question.

In contrast to the administration's earlier approach in Afghanistan, its approach in Iraq—especially the way Washington has characterized its objectives there—has precluded any sort of regional cooperation. The United States did not invade Afghanistan in order to remake that country as a model for Central Asia, nor did Washington announce an intention to subsequently promote the democratization of all of the states neighboring Afghanistan. Had the United States committed itself to such a program, it would never have secured the support of Iran, Pakistan, Russia, Tajikistan, or Uzbekistan for the war, nor would it have had their help in shaping the subsequent peace.

The United States, however, did invade Iraq with the intention of making that state a model for the Middle East, promising that success in Iraq would be followed by efforts to transform the political systems of Iraq's neighbors. This was not a vision any of those regimes was likely to embrace. Nor have they.

When states disintegrate, the competing claimants to power inevitably turn to external sponsors for support. Faced with the prospect of a neighboring state's failure, the governments of adjoining states inevitably develop local clientele in the failing state and back rival aspirants to power. Much as one may regret and deplore such activity, neighbors can be neither safely ignored nor effectively barred from exercising their considerable influence. It has always proved wise, therefore, to find ways to engage them constructively.

Washington's vocal commitment to regional democratization and its concomitant challenge to the legitimacy of neighboring regimes work at cross-purposes to its effort to form, consolidate, and support a government of national unity in Iraq. Iraqi political leaders will work together only if and when they receive convergent signals from their various external sponsors. The administration's drive for democratization in the region, therefore, should be subordinated (at least for the next several years) to its efforts to avert civil war in Iraq. Unless Washington can craft a vision of Iraq and of its neighborhood that all the governments of the region can buy into, it will have no chance of securing those governments' help in holding that country together. The central objective of U.S. diplomacy, therefore, should shift from the transformation of Iraq to its stabilization, with an emphasis on power sharing, sovereignty, and regional cooperation, all concepts that Iraq's neighbors can reasonably be asked to endorse.

Neither the American nor the Iraqi people are likely to support a larger, longer U.S. military role in Iraq. Neither the Balkan model of peace enforcement nor the Vietnamese model of pacification is open to the United States. Insofar as a future U.S. military role in Iraq is concerned, the more apt analogy would be the counterinsurgency campaigns of Central America in the 1980s, where U.S. military involvement was largely limited to advice and training. In Iraq, however, this reduced military engagement will have to be paired with a much more active U.S. campaign of regional diplomacy if the slide toward wider civil war is to be averted.

SEPARATING IRAQIS, SAVING IRAQ

Chaim Kaufmann

Three different civil wars are now raging in Iraq: the first between U.S.-led coalition forces and antigovernment insurgents, the second between the Kurds and other communities in northern Iraq, and the third between Sunni Arabs and Shiite Arabs in the center of the country. The last is the most important because it represents the greatest potential for humanitarian disaster as well as for long-term instability in Iraq and in the region.

Stephen Biddle offers the right diagnosis of the situation but the wrong prescription for treating it. The conflict between Sunnis and Shiites is, as Biddle argues, a communal civil war, not a war based on class or ideology, and the U.S. military's efforts to learn, or relearn, best practices for fighting a counterinsurgency from the Vietnam War are thus beside the point. But his proposal for communal power sharing—which has been the Bush administration's policy since January 2006 and has become conventional wisdom—is impractical. Power sharing rarely works well, and in Iraq its prospects are especially bleak: the Shiites are too strong to want or need to share power, there is too little trust between communal elites, and no institution in Iraq is capable of guaranteeing anything to anyone. Worse, the level of violence has passed the threshold where the communities can safely live together. At an earlier stage, this conflict might have been resolvable by compromise. But at this point, that no longer is possible.

Today, all members of both the Sunni and the Shiite communities face real security threats. The violence has escalated dramatically since the bombing of the Askariya shrine, in Samarra, on February 22, 2006, but it had been intensifying for several years. Sunni insurgents have been killing Shiite civilians since 2003, and since Shiite parties won control of the Iraqi government in early 2005, the Shiite-dominated police forces have often operated as death squads. As of late April 2006, the U.S. press alone had recorded 3,500 deaths over the previous two months, and the total number of actual deaths was probably higher. During that period, according to the Iraqi Red Crescent, more than 89,000 Iraqis became refugees. This estimate is likely low too, as it implies a ratio of deaths to refugees of about 1 to 20, and in ethnic-cleansing campaigns such ratios typically run closer to 1 to 100.

Today, no Iraqi Sunni is safe anywhere within the reach of Shiite militias or Shiite-controlled police forces, and no Shiite whom Sunni suicide bombers or assassination squads can get to is safe either. The danger is greatest and the violence worst where the two communities cohabit, as in Baghdad and in parts of the four surrounding provinces—Anbar, Babil, Diyala, and Salahuddin.

And the situation will get worse, because communal atrocities have hardened sectarian affiliations. Before 2003, virtually all Iraqi Arabs identified themselves as Arabs, in opposition to Kurds and others. Since then, national and ethnic identities have not vanished, but they have been overshadowed by more specific, sectarian identities. Some 92 percent of the votes in the December 2005 elections were cast for sectarian parties, and both communities now use increasingly extreme language, each describing the other in sweeping generalities.

MISSION: IMPOSSIBLE

Biddle recommends that Washington suspend its efforts to strengthen the Iraqi state until it can broker a grand bargain among all the communities, coercing them to compromise by threatening to manipulate their relative military power. In practice, such a policy would mean trying to force the United Iraqi Alliance (UIA), the main bloc of Shiite religious parties, to surrender the victory it won in last December's elections. The idea would be to threaten to remove U.S. support for the Iraqi police and army if the forces remained split along sectarian lines and refused to reorganize based on loyalty to Iraq. The United States' trump card would be the threat to leave Iraq altogether. (Except for the last point, this essentially is current U.S. policy.)

This strategy is likely to fail. Attempts to compel power sharing among sectarian groups in Iraq will not stop the fighting and could even accelerate it. Prime Minister Ibrahim al-Jaafari has stepped down, but the UIA has not split. Despite serious internal rivalries, Shiite leaders have redoubled their commitment to make key decisions among themselves before negotiating with the U.S. government or anyone else. In April, the UIA chose Nouri al-Maliki to replace Jaafari. The main Kurdish and Sunni parties promptly accepted the nomination even though Maliki, whom they see as inflexible and excessively sectarian, was their least favorite candidate (their endorsement may reflect the fact that they have little leverage). Shiite leaders will retain control of the all-important Interior Ministry. In early May, it was still unclear whether the Defense Ministry would remain under

UIA authority or if its control would go to a technocrat not affiliated with the alliance.

A governing coalition has yet to be formed. But it might come to resemble the Kurdish-Shiite accord that underpinned the last government: Baghdad turned a blind eye toward Kurdish activities in the north in return for Kurdish acquiescence on anything the central government did elsewhere. A few Sunni ministers might be appointed, but the Shiites do not want—nor do they need—to offer significant concessions. Even if an all-party unity government could be formed, it would not be able to function; the parties' demands cannot be reconciled, and their mutual distrust is far too great.

Trying to create a genuinely Iraqi security force will not work either, because there is no powerful, legitimate political movement loyal to "Iraq," in or out of government. Nor could most members of the security forces be persuaded to identify with such a force if it did exist. Some Iraqi army units, under tight U.S. control, have been deterred from using violence for purely sectarian goals, but others are openly loyal to Kurdish or Shiite leaders. Reforming the police is a lost cause; any U.S. remark about the force's performance is met with heated retorts from Shiite leaders. In March, UIA spokes-people demanded that U.S. forces stand aside from further involvement in internal security. Most Shiite leaders do not desire an immediate U.S. departure, but only because they hope to collect more U.S. aid before the civil war escalates further. An additional barrier to coercing Shiite leaders is the fact that Shiite militias are already receiving aid from Tehran on a moderate scale.

Any serious attempt to compel the Iraqis to share power would result in either a quick, ignominious reduction in U.S. troops or an actual U.S. withdrawal followed by a massive escalation of hostilities. Control over every mixed settlement and neighborhood in the country would be up for grabs, which would increase incentives for ethnic cleansing throughout the country. The Shiite-dominated Iraqi government might also find itself forced deeper into a clientelistic relationship with Iran.

In any case, it is beyond the power of any Iraqi government to stop the violence between the communities if they are not separated first. Although the main Shiite militias are controlled by factions within the UIA, they do not answer to it or to one another. The most active death squads seem to be those of the Badr Brigades, the armed wing of the Supreme Council for the Islamic Revolution in Iraq, which controls the Interior Ministry. Muqtada al-Sadr's Mahdi Army has also killed many people.

As a result, Iraq is breaking up into communal cantons. As they become unsafe, mixed towns and urban neighborhoods are becoming segregated. No one knows how far this process has gone already; some reports suggest that many towns have already become monoethnic. Shiite and Sunni militias have been inundated by new volunteers, and new independent neighborhood militias are forming, too. Free movement between Sunni and Shiite areas will be increasingly curtailed by checkpoints manned by militias, if not by government forces, as is already happening within and around Baghdad.

Iraq will eventually develop internal communal borders with a few heavily guarded crossing points. Since the ethnic makeup of Baghdad is far too complex for the city to be divided into just two parts, some of its neighborhoods will become isolated enclaves surrounded by barbed wire. This ugly solution has worked before: in Jerusalem, Mount Scopus was a Jewish island from 1948 to 1967. Any such partition of Iraq would likely be de facto, because many Shiite leaders still hope that a unified country can emerge, and no regime in the Middle East would tolerate formal independence for the Kurds.

MISSION: POSSIBLE

In the meantime, the United States will remain the strongest military force in Iraq. As such, it will have one remaining duty: the moral obligation to minimize the damage, human and otherwise, caused by ethnic cleansing. This is also a U.S. national security interest: the U.S. government is—and will continue to be—blamed by most of the world for all of the harm that befalls the people of Iraq. The shorter that bill of indictment, the better.

Satisfying this obligation would mean using U.S. military strength to protect Iraqi refugees who wish to relocate. U.S. forces must defend the most vulnerable mixed towns and urban neighborhoods from both Sunni and Shiite attackers for long enough to organize transport for those who want to move to safer locations. Otherwise, who controls Baghdad and dozens, perhaps even hundreds, of towns in central Iraq will be determined by full-scale sectarian battles that could go on for months or even years.

Which settlements need to be defended and which communities need to be evacuated are questions that would largely determine the location of the de facto line that would separate Sunni and Shiite communities. Protection and relocation would have to be coordinated with the strongest forces in Iraq, the main Shiite factions. These groups would not be enthusiastic: two of the main UIA factions—the Dawa Party and the Sadrists—still want a unitary Iraq. But sober Shiite leaders would also realize that such a policy would save many Shiite lives and bring the Shiite-dominated government greater control over more settlements than it could manage otherwise.

Little active cooperation would be required; all that would be needed is enough forbearance on the part of the Shiite militias to let temporary defensive garrisons and evacuation convoys complete their tasks without having to fight. Washington would have to explain its intentions clearly and establish firm limits to its mission both in aim and in time. The tolerance of the Sunni militias would also be needed in areas under their control. But if U.S. forces were scheduled to depart shortly—leaving the affected settlements in Sunni hands—the Sunni militias would have little reason to oppose the evacuation of those Shiites who wished to go. So far, few groups have displayed such bloody-mindedness as to suggest that they would take the risk of attacking U.S. forces solely to murder refugees in flight. (Afterward the number of minorities living on the wrong side of the separation line would be small, which would limit incentives for "rescue" offensives.)

In the longer run, it will be important to ensure that the Shiites remain the stronger side militarily, as any change in the balance of power could encourage Sunni factions to challenge them again. The outcome of a civil war tends to be more stable when the party that is most satisfied is also the stronger one.

Some might say that this policy will legitimate ethnic cleansing. But they would have to face squarely the costs of not protecting refugees; to the extent than the policy did succeed, Iraqis would experience less suffering that if it failed or was never attempted. Others will object than the current U.S. administration is unlikely to adopt these measures. Perhaps, but saving at least some lives would require getting only a few brigade commanders in a few places to think seriously about refugee protection.

Such protection would not mollify the Iraqi Sunnis, who would still be out of power, or angry Sunni Arab governments. But no policy can prevent such discontent. It is also inevitable that whatever rump Sunni statelet remains will continue to be poor, disorderly, and unable to prevent terrorists from operating on its soil. Three years of counterinsurgency in Iraq has stimulated more terrorism than it has suppressed. But if Iraqi's sectarian wars were ended, ordinary Iraqi Sunnis might come to realize that the greatest threat to their well-being is not Iraqi Shiites or U.S. troops, but foreign jihadists in their midst. Then, perhaps, they would begin to work at restoring order in their country.

LAST TRAIN FROM BAGHDAD

Leslie H. Gelb

The United States' way forward and out of Iraq now comes down to a fatal choice between President George W. Bush's policy of simply staying the course even as security in Iraq slowly deteriorates and his critics' policy of quickly withdrawing U.S. forces even with civil war looming. The Bush approach looks like an attempt on Bush's part simply to avoid defeat and pass the tar baby on to his successor, Democrat or Republican. The alternative looks like a way to have the United States escape from a quagmire, whatever the consequences. Either way, Americans and Iraqis lose.

There is a third way: for the United States to stop its futile resistance to the inevitable sectarian tides now rolling over Iraq and help the Iraqis channel these forces into a viable political settlement—uniting Iraq by decentralizing it. This deal would be driven into place by bringing the Sunnis in with an offer presenting them with prospects far better than any of their present ones and by promising U.S. troop withdrawals and redeployments before 2009, all backed up with regional diplomacy.

There are three parts to the Bush strategy in Iraq. First, the United States is putting its top priority on creating a government of national unity, with the expectation that doing so will help solve other political problems. But Iraq has had national unity governments for the past three years, the latest one inclusive enough to count seven Sunni ministers holding positions as important as the deputy prime ministership and the ministry of defense, and they have accomplished little on critical issues such as maintaining security and reducing corruption. It would be foolhardy to predict that the next such government will do much better. Second, Washington is planning to withdraw U.S. troops as Iraqis are trained to take over—to "stand down as they stand up." But this policy gives Iraqis little incentive to fight their own battles. Third, and most devastating, although Bush persistently proclaims that he is still pursuing victory, his actions suggest that he is, instead, merely trying to avoid defeat.

According to a *New York Times* article in April, despite small signs of progress, a team of U.S. diplomats and military officers in Iraq described the situation early this year as serious or critical in more than a third of Iraq's provinces. Their report also found that sectarian militias still dominated Iraq's security forces and that rampant ethnic cleansing was taking place throughout the country—all of which adds up to the start of de facto partition. Yet the Bush administration has decided to end further U.S. economic reconstruction aid after this year, even though the insurgents, as everyone knows, cannot be defeated without rebuilding Iraq. It also has slashed funds to develop democracy in Iraq. Finally, it has largely pulled U.S. troops off the streets of big cities, leaving the insurgents with greater control.

The result of this deteriorating situation and of Bush's pulling back on key programs will be a draining stalemate. Although the insurgency will grow, the insurgents will never prevail as long as U.S. troops remain in sufficient force, with, say, 30,000 troops. Any insurgent effort to hold large chunks of territory would fail against the United States' dominant firepower. Thus Bush will be able to avoid defeat in Iraq until he hands the problem over to the next president, in 2009. In the meantime, Iraq and the United States will stagger tragically through the next three years—unless a totally frustrated Congress, supported by an increasingly disillusioned American public, decides that it has had enough of the quagmire and mandates an immediate withdrawal. But a quick U.S. exit from Iraq, however explainable by frustration, would only weaken U.S. national security and the war against terrorism.

AN HONORABLE OPTION

It may be that the situation has reached the point where no strategy, no matter how clever on paper, can work. But to believe there is no choice save to follow Bush deeper into the quagmire would be speak moral and strategic bankruptcy. There is, in fact, a way to keep Iraq whole and make it politically stable: rather than continue to tear the country apart with futile efforts at centralization, decentralize it. This strategy flows legally from Iraq's existing constitution and is consistent with both U.S. military thinking about orderly troop withdrawal and the desire of U.S. diplomats for a more active regional diplomacy. The United States, along with its friends and allies, can and should lead the Iraqis in this direction. Vital U.S. interests are involved as well as Iraqi ones. But the final decision must be the Iraqis', and Washington should not impose it on them. Helping decentralize Iraq is also more honorable and realistic than either hanging in there or getting out.

This policy has five elements. The first is to establish, consistent with the current constitution, three strong regions with a limited but effective central government in a federally united Iraq. Doing so would build the post–Saddam Hussein Iraq around Kurdish, Sunni Arab, and Shiite Arab regions, each largely responsible for its own legislation and administration. Each region's government could pass laws superseding those passed by the central government, as stated in the present constitution, except in areas of the central government's exclusive jurisdiction. The central government would have the deciding responsibility for foreign affairs, border defense, oil and gas production and revenues, and other countrywide matters, as agreed to by the regions. Its writ would be limited and restricted to areas of clear common interests, which would allow Baghdad to meet its responsibilities effectively. The oil provision, in particular, would strengthen the central government beyond its present powers. The underlying principle behind this policy would be to hold Iraq together by allowing each group to satisfy its real ethnic and religious aspirations.

Keeping Iraq united in this manner would be in the interest of all parties. Key oil pipelines run through the country, north to south, and Baghdad remains the only possible business hub for the country. Most Iraqis also share a powerful interest in seeing that their regions and their country do not get picked apart by greedy neighbors. Divided, Iraq would be an irresistible target for outside meddling; united, the country would stand a chance of survival. More and more leaders—among the Kurds, the Shiites, and, increasingly, the Sunnis as well—are favoring negotiated regionalism and moving toward a federal system over civil war. (The existing constitution provides for federalism by allowing provinces to unite with each other and form a regional government.) Nonetheless, Washington would have to play a pivotal role in helping the Iraqis secure this agreement.

Big cities with highly mixed sectarian populations, such as Baghdad, Kirkuk, and Mosul, pose a huge problem now and would continue to do so under a federal solution—or any other solution. To fix this, the Iraqis will have to make special security arrangements, such as ensuring that the police forces in these cities are composed of members from all the sectarian groups and backed by international police. The factor that will most determine the fate of these cities, however, will be whether the sectarian groups find the overall political settlement fair and viable. And as painful as it may be, the United States will have to assist those Iraqis who wish to relocate to safer terrain, temporarily or permanently. It is essential to realize that this proposal will not cause ethnic cleansing or the country's breakup. These terrible things are already happening. Regionalism may be the only option left to stop them.

The second element of this policy is to bring the Sunnis on board with regionalism with an offer they cannot reasonably refuse. The carrot will have to be very sweet, namely, control of their own region in the center of the country and a constitutionally guaranteed share of oil revenues. Until recently, most Sunni leaders flatly opposed controlling their own region because they fully expected to be running the whole country again. They still saw themselves as masters of their universe and wanted Iraq to remain intact and ready for them to reassume the power they held for hundreds of years. And they pressed for the strongest possible central government.

Now, however, growing numbers of Sunnis are recalculating. Many see that a centralized structure would leave the Sunnis as a permanent minority in a government run by Shiites and Kurds. And whereas the Sunnis used to be convinced that they were invincible in battle, they now understand that they would be the principal victims of a civil war. Today it is obvious, except to Sunni fanatics, that the Kurds have the best militia in the country and that the Shiites are willing and able to fight. And so the prospect of running their own affairs in a Sunni region now looks more appealing to Sunni leaders.

The Sunnis' remaining nightmare is about money, but this could be taken care of with a second carrot: oil revenues. The present constitution calls for distributing "oil and gas revenues in a fair manner in proportion to population." But it does not define "fair" or provide population percentages. It refers to "extracted" oil, suggesting that the rule applies only to current revenues, not to future revenues, which are expected to be much greater, thanks to increased production. The current constitution also disadvantages the Sunnis by giving the final say on oil revenues to the governments in the regions that have the oil, leaving the Sunnis out in the cold, since almost all of Iraq's oil and gas resources sit either in the Kurdish north (about 20 percent) or in the Shiite south (about 80 percent).

The cure is to satisfy all but the greediest Sunnis by amending the constitution to make oil and gas production and revenues the sole province of the central government and to determine that both present and future revenues will be distributed according to population percentages. Such an arrangement would be far better for the Sunnis than the current deal and infinitely preferable to what they would receive—namely, nothing—if the country split into three separate states. It should be sufficient to co-opt most Sunni leaders into subscribing to the federal approach and provide them with considerable incentives to try to curb the insurgency in the Sunni region. The Sunnis would gain far less from being granted a larger role in the central government, the plan the Bush administration is currently advocating.

The third element of this third way would be protecting the rights of minorities and women by linking U.S. aid to regional governments to their respect for the politically and culturally vulnerable people in their regions. For women, especially in Shiite territory, and for Kurds, Sunnis, and Shiites living in a region other than their ethnic group's own, there will be problems. Washington will not be able to solve these problems, but it must be tough and clear about trying to ameliorate them.

Fourth, the U.S. military should prepare a plan for the orderly and safe withdrawal and redeployment of U.S. forces, to be carried out before the end of 2008. It should also provide for a residual force that would deter and fight any large-scale military disruptions by insurgents or others and continue training Iraqis for the Iraqi military and police forces. Such a measure would recognize the fact that U.S. troops are both part of the solution and part of the problem. They must stay in Iraq—although in declining numbers—to take care of the security problem, and they must leave steadily in order to effectively motivate Iraqis to take over security matters.

Finally, Iraq's territorial integrity should be reinforced through a regional non-aggression pact, which must be achieved through active international diplomacy. As a first step, a regional security conference should be convened, where Iraq's neighbors, including Iran, should be encouraged to pledge respect for Iraq's borders and its federal system and to establish procedures to implement a nonaggression plan. Iraq's neighbors have strong incentives to try to make such a deal work. For Turkey, it would be the best way to avoid Kurdistan's becoming a separate state and a rallying point for separatist Kurds in Turkey. States with majority Sunni populations, such as Saudi Arabia and Kuwait, would find consolation in the fact that Iraqi Shiites and Iran would not be controlling all of Iraq. For Iran, stability in Iraq would help it avoid new and unsettling confrontations with other countries. All parties would also share a strong interest in preventing Iraq's meltdown into a civil war, which could draw them into a wider conflict.

The United Nations, particularly the five permanent members of the Security Council plus the European Union, should precede the conference with appropriate diplomacy and help promote some kind of regional mechanism to ensure that the proposed nonaggression deal, once in place, is respected.

Of course, all parties would bring cynicism to such a diplomatic enterprise. But a similar mechanism has worked for Bosnia and is worth trying in regard to Iraq. It is a long shot, but a necessary venture nonetheless.

A BETTER DESTINY

All wars are messy, and all plans for ending them are flawed. But the messy war in Iraq could metastasize into an out-of-control civil war and a regional conflict. The Bush strategy does almost nothing to reduce these terrible risks and only threatens to drag the United States deeper into the Iraq quagmire. As the flaws in this strategy become ever more evident, it is increasingly possible that the American people will sweep aside Bush's strategy in favor of ill-considered demands for an immediate and total pullout. Even optimists about Iraq would be remiss not to confront these looming dangers. Americans and Iraqis must look at other choices.

Uniting Iraq by decentralizing it is not likely to make most Iraqis happy, but it is a plan that gives each group most of what it considers essential: re-blessed autonomy for the Kurds, some degree of autonomy and money for the Sunnis, and for the Shiites, the historic freedom to rule themselves and enjoy their future riches. For all of these parties, it is perhaps the last chance to escape civil war.

This plan provides reasonable time for Iraqis to tend to their own security, and its incentives are tangible. It is carefully paced to salvage the honor of those Americans who served and sacrificed themselves in Iraq. And it allows the U.S. government both to depart honorably and to leave Iraq to the Iraqis for their own disposition—as it should be.

BIDDLE REPLIES

Biddle

It is a privilege to respond to such an august panel, especially when we agree on so much. Larry Diamond, James Dobbins, Chaim Kaufmann, Leslie Gelb, and I all agree that current U.S. strategy in Iraq is unlikely to succeed. Diamond, Dobbins, Kaufmann, and I further agree that Iraq is already embroiled in a civil war, albeit one waged at low intensity for now, and Kaufmann and I agree that "Iraqization" is likely to make things worse.

Perhaps most important, we all agree that if the United States is ever to succeed in Iraq, Washington must help Iraq's communities reach a compromise on a viable constitution that distributes power among them. Kaufmann thinks this goal is impossible to achieve, meaning failure is inevitable. The rest of us believe the United States' current leverage for obtaining such a compromise is limited but propose ways to increase it.

I have argued that the United States' most powerful source of unexploited leverage is military: a U.S. threat to withdraw U.S. troops from Iraq, realign U.S. support for the parties to the conflict, or reinforce any one of them may be necessary to motivate compromise. Diamond, Dobbins, and Gelb propose a variety of other ways for the United States to increase its leverage. Diamond suggests turning to international mediators, Dobbins seeks regional collaboration among Iraq's neighbors, and Gelb advocates U.S. support for a decentralized Iraqi government and both security and financial guarantees for Iraq's Sunnis. These options are not mutually exclusive, and each merits careful consideration.

But each one also has important drawbacks. International mediation, for example, could be hard to obtain. Intervention by the European Union would certainly be very unpopular with the European public, which overwhelmingly opposes the war. Many Iraqis resent the United Nations for having imposed harsh sanctions on Iraq for a decade. Nor is it clear that either the EU or the UN could offer anything to the parties that would outweigh the grave dangers that Iraqis associate with intercommunal compromise.

As Dobbins notes, for regional diplomacy to be effective, the United States must retreat from its initial aim of turning Iraq into a democracy in the near term, because pursuing this goal threatens the political stability of Iraq's neighbors and makes them unwilling to assist. As I argued in my original essay, deferring this project may be necessary anyway. But it would be a bitter pill to swallow for a president who repeatedly cites democratization as the United States' chief interest in Iraq. And it would sacrifice important U.S. interests, at least temporarily. Moreover, regional concord could be difficult to achieve. Iraq's neighbors are as divided over sect and ethnicity as is Iraq itself, and so satisfying their conflicting desiderata could prove far from easy.

Decentralization, which Gelb advocates, would amount to a form of partition. Various partition proposals have been floated since 2003, ranging from a hard division of the country into three separate mini-states (one for Shiites in the south, another for Kurds in the north, and a third for Sunnis in the center-west) to variations on federal systems, with a weak central government and more or less autonomous regions. The problem with hard partition is that the Sunnis will not accept it: as an independent state, the Sunni heartland would not be economically viable. The Sunnis would rather fight than accept such impoverishment; hard partition would therefore not end the war. But a softer form of federalism might well offer a basis for constitutional compromise. The problem is not a shortage of ideas on how to divide oil revenues or protect the rights of different regions; it is getting the Iraqis to agree on one of them. Anything they accept would surely satisfy U.S. interests. But to date they have been unwilling to make the needed compromises. Breaking the parties' intransigence will require not so much a new proposal for softer or harder partition, but a new source of leverage over the parties.

Of course, military leverage, too, has many shortcomings. As I noted in my article, to use its military leverage effectively, the United States might need to keep its forces in Iraq for longer than the troops could endure or than U.S. voters would tolerate; a realignment of U.S. positions would be hard to sell domestically; and both Sunni political development and clear-eyed rationality on all sides would be needed before a successful compromise could be reached (and yet these are two elements that may be unavailable given the emotions the war has triggered and Iraq's cultural complexity). Because there are no easy options for Iraq—all proposals have important disadvantages, and none can guarantee success—a combination of imperfect initiatives may be needed. And Washington must consider using in such a combination every major source of unexploited leverage at its disposal, including the threat that the United Sates will realign itself militarily.

Is this threat likely to be credible or effective? Neither Diamond nor Kaufmann thinks so. Kaufmann thinks it is too similar to current U.S. policy to succeed; Diamond thinks it is too different to be credible. In fact, it is neither. A threat of military realignment would add a missing military dimension to the current U.S. policy of brokering a compromise by pressuring each side to negotiate. Realignment already is U.S. policy, but today that policy excludes military threats from the realignment tool kit. If anything, current U.S. military policy actively undermines Washington's bargaining leverage: it aims to build an indigenous Iraqi military as quickly as possible, regardless of the parties' behavior in negotiations, and then to withdraw U.S. forces whether the war is over or not. This policy promises to get U.S. troops home as soon as possible, but in the meantime it is undermining the prospects for settlement by discouraging the parties from compromising. The Shiites and the Kurds will be protected until they can fight their own war, whether they bargain or not, and the Sunnis will face a U.S.-armed opponent whether they bargain or not. So why should any of them compromise? Rather than pursue a military policy that undoes its diplomacy, the U.S. government should coordinate its military and political strategies by deliberately using contingent military threats to create bargaining leverage.

Skillfully conveyed, such threats could be powerful levers. So far, the United States has actively restrained Iraq's security forces, which are dominated by Shiites and Kurds, granting them only light weapons of limited firepower. If it were to remove such constraints and provide the security forces with liberal quantities of modern tanks, armored personnel carriers, artillery, body armor, night-vision equipment, armed helicopters, and fixed-wing ground-attack aircraft, the capacity of the Kurds and the Shiites to commit mass violence against the Sunnis would increase dramatically—and very visibly. Threatening such a change could provide an important incentive for the Sunnis to compromise.

Conversely, a U.S. threat to cease backing the Shiites, coupled with a program to arm the Sunnis overtly or in a semi clandestine way, would substantially reduce the Shiites' military prospects. Iran might provide more aid to the Shiites to compensate them for some of their loss, but the United States' military potential so far outstrips that of Iran that rational Shiites could hardly welcome the prospect of being abandoned by Washington and having to confront U.S.-armed Sunnis.

This threat could be made credible to the combatants. The Shiites are very attentive to signs that the United States might abandon them or realign itself against them. Many of them already charge that even Washington's limited tilt toward the Sunnis in the ongoing political negotiations amounts to a "second betrayal" (the first one being the United States' failure to support the Shiite uprising against Saddam Hussein in 1991). An official U.S. threat of military realignment would be hard for the Shiites to ignore. On the other side, some Sunnis already view the United States as a potential protector against Shiite violence, as the fighting in Tal Afar last spring suggests.

Effective leverage need not take the form of clumsy ultimatums, which risk forcing the United States into corners, or the kind of blunt expositions that analysts like me put forward in the interest of clarity. Diplomats enjoy a rich palette of subtler signals with which they can indicate incremental movement in one direction without irrevocably committing to a maximum use of force.

Ideally, Washington would combine any threat with an inducement: the promise to keep U.S. troops in Iraq as long as would be necessary to protect the parties who cooperate. Does the U.S. government have enough political capital at home to accomplish this? Perhaps not. Recent polls of U.S. public opinion are not encouraging. On the other hand, public opinion is not independent of government policy, and voters might have a higher tolerance for casualties if they thought both that the stakes of U.S. involvement in Iraq were high and that Washington's policies there were feasible. The stakes certainly are high. But the American public currently lacks a reason to think that the Bush administration's policies can succeed.

Some analysts, however, believe that the war is already lost, whether or not the Bush administration can get the American people to rally behind it. Kaufmann, for example, argues that communal tensions in Iraq have already passed the point of no return. Calming the situation is now impossible regardless of U.S. policy, and so U.S. forces should withdraw, tarrying only long enough to escort Iraqi refugees to new homes.

He may be right. But he overstates his case by ignoring any contradictory evidence. Although Kaufmann sees no hope of intercommunal accommodation, both the Shiites and the Sunnis, when under sufficient pressure form the United States, have made important concessions to ethnic rivals over the past year. Last fall, the Shiites agreed to the Sunnis' demands for more permissive procedures for amending the constitution; in deference to the Sunnis and the Kurds, the Shiites withdrew Ibrahim al-Jaafari as a nominee for the prime ministership of the permanent government last April; and the Sunnis accepted Nouri al-Maliki, a staunch Shiite, for the prime minister's post even though they clearly preferred other candidates. These concessions were made grudgingly and slowly, and they required heavy U.S. pressure. Much heavier pressure would probably be needed to reach a lasting agreement about issues as important as the constitution. But is there really no chance for a compromise solution, as Kaufmann claims, even if the United States uses all the leverage it has?

Perhaps most important, the pattern of sectarian violence that followed the Samarra mosque bombing in February is inconsistent with Kaufmann's argument that communal tensions cannot be contained. Contrary to many dire predictions, the civilian death toll in Iraq did not spiral out of control in the aftermath of the bombing; on the contrary, it fell sharply. According to Iraq Body Count, a British antiwar group, during the week of the bombing, the violence did spike, causing some 270 Iraqi civilian deaths. But the number of casualties then dropped by 40 percent over the next seven weeks. In fact, the death toll declined every week between March 22 and April 18 (the last day for which date was available when this article was being prepared). If communal violence is spiraling out of control, then why is the number of fatalities decreasing? Is it not possible that the two sides have pulled back from the brink? The data provide no conclusive case either way, and the United States might indeed fail to calm the sectarian violence. But the evidence does not exclude the possibility that the United States might succeed if it somehow increased its leverage over the parties.

What, then, is to be done? Given all the uncertainties, how long should the United States keep trying in Iraq? The longer it persists, the more Americans will die. Yet withdrawal could produce near-genocidal sectarian violence, a regional war, the disruption of international oil supplies, and both a recruiting windfall and new basing possibilities for al Qaeda. If these outcomes are inevitable, then the United States should leave Iraq now. But if they are not, then sacrificing U.S. lives now could save many more later, and staying is an imperative.

How does one know if there remains a reasonable chance of success? There is no formula for determining so. But I would offer three guideposts. First, is the gap between the positions of the Iraqi factions on key constitutional issues narrowing or widening under U.S. pressure? Good-faith negotiating generally causes parties' divergences to narrow; backtracking or reneging on past offers is a dangerous omen. Second, are the Shiites unified? Conducting three-way negotiations among the Shiites, the Sunnis, and the Kurds is complex enough, but if the Shiite alliance splinters, then the bargaining will become impossibly challenging. Third, and perhaps most important, has the United States used all its leverage? If Washington has exhausted all resources for compelling a compromise, then it should go. If not, it should try harder.

By these standards, it is not yet time for the United States to leave Iraq. As of late April, when the Shiites withdrew Jaafari's nomination, the parties were still moving—albeit slowly—toward compromise. Worrisome signs of a split among the Shiites receded when Muqtada al-Sadr accepted Jaafari's withdrawal without bolting. And, as I have argued, and as Diamond, Dobbins, and Gelb have suggested in their own ways, the United States has not exhausted all options for increasing its leverage with the parties.

It is time for the United States to start maximizing its leverage. Flexing military muscle is not the only way of doing so, but it is probably a necessary one. At a minimum, the United States must change its policies regarding the Iraqi security forces, which are only making matters worse. The United States might need to try many different levers. But it must seriously consider invoking its military role as a tool for compelling the parties to reach a settlement rather than as a preface to its disengagement.

Review Essay

COIN of the Realm

Is There a Future for Counterinsurgency?

Colin H. Kahl

The U.S. Army/Marine Corps Counterinsurgency Field Manual. BY THE U.S. ARMY AND THE MARINE CORPS. University of Chicago Press, 2007, 472 pp. $15.00.

Violent Politics: A History of Insurgency, Terrorism, and Guerrilla War, From the American Revolution to Iraq. BY WILLIAM R. POLK. HarperCollins, 2007, 304 pp. $23.95.

The invasion of Iraq began on March 19, 2003, and it took only three weeks for the U.S. military to defeat Saddam Hussein's army. But even during those heady days, there were ominous signs of things to come. "The enemy we're fighting is a bit different from the one we war-gamed against," Lieutenant General William Wallace, the army's V Corps commander, told *The New York Times* a week into the conflict. The first U.S. combat fatality was a marine shot at point-blank range by men driving a civilian pickup truck. The first suicide car bombing of a U.S. checkpoint occurred ten days into the war.

Soon after Saddam's regime fell, the occupation began to falter, and a virulent Sunni insurgency took hold. The U.S. military was caught flatfooted. The army and the Marine Corps had not substantially updated their counterinsurgency doctrine since the 1980s, choosing, in the wake of the Vietnam War, to "forget" counterinsurgency and focus instead on preparing for World War III. The blitzkrieg victory in the 1991 Gulf War reinforced this conventional bias, and deployments in Somalia, Haiti, and the Balkans in the 1990s were denigrated as "military operations other than war."

An interim army counterinsurgency manual was released in October 2004, a year and a half after the start of the war,

COLIN H. KAHL is an Assistant Professor in the Security Studies Program at Georgetown University and a Fellow at the Center for a New American Security.

but it was an intellectually sterile document. Work on a much-needed revision did not begin until a year later, when two of the military's most respected commanders, Lieutenant Generals David Petraeus and James Mattis, took charge of the process. Petraeus, now the four-star commanding general of all U.S. forces in Iraq, was then the commander of the U.S. Army Combined Arms Center at Fort Leavenworth, Kansas, and Mattis held a parallel position at the Marine Corps Combat Development Command in Quantico, Virginia. The writing team they assembled included many of the best and the brightest within the army and the Marine Corps; Conrad Crane, the director of the army's Military History Institute, was charged with supervising the effort. The writing process—which included a February 2006 conference at Fort Leavenworth where outside counterinsurgency experts, human rights groups, and military journalists were brought together to comment on a working draft—was unprecedented in its openness. On December 15, 2006, the new *Counterinsurgency Field Manual* was finally released, co-signed by Petraeus and Lieutenant General James Amos, who was brought on after Mattis took command of the I Marine Expeditionary Force.

The COIN FM, as the manual is known, was so widely cited and downloaded that the University of Chicago Press recently decided to republish it as a book. The new version adds a forward by Lieutenant Colonel John Nagl, a member of the manual's writing team, who provides a useful history of its evolution, and an outstanding introductory essay on the "radical" nature of the document by Sarah Sewall, the director of Harvard's Carr Center for Human Rights Policy. The book has helped make counterinsurgency part of the zeitgeist. It has become a coffee-table staple in Washington, prompted a lengthy essay in *The New York Times Book Review*, and even led to an appearance by Nagl on Comedy Central's *The Daily Show*. In short, this is not your parents' military field manual.

HEARTS AND MINDS

Counterinsurgency refers to military, paramilitary, political, economic, psychological, and civic actions taken by governments or occupying forces to quell a rebellion. It is fundamentally a contest between insurgents and the government for control and the support of the population (with intervening outside powers sometimes attempting to tip the scales one way or the other). The COIN FM is not an academic document, but it is deeply informed by classical counterinsurgency theory, which emerged in response to the wave of wars of "national liberation" that followed World War II. Within that tradition, there are two competing schools of thought about the appropriate way to conduct counterinsurgency warfare: "hearts and minds" and "coercion." The COIN FM sides definitively with the former.

The manual embraces a model commonly referred to as "clear, hold, and build." It directs the military to support the "host nation" government in combating insurgents by "clearing" areas and then to transition to a law enforcement model to "hold" them. This, in turn, enables the implementation of political, social, and economic programs designed to reduce the appeal of the insurgency and "build" the government's legitimacy. The COIN FM argues that most active, passive, and potential supporters of an insurgency—

whether they are ideological, ethnic, or religious in character—can be won over through the provision of security, since "citizens seek to ally with groups that can guarantee their safety." Providing basic services and enacting policies aimed at "address[ing] the legitimate grievances insurgents use to generate popular support" also help flip support from the guerrillas to the government. The population, rather than the insurgent movement, is the "center of gravity," and the military's "primary function in COIN is protecting that populace."

To be sure, some insurgents have to be killed and captured. But as the manual contends, "killing every insurgent is normally impossible." Force must be used with incredible restraint and discrimination and in strict compliance with the laws of war, or it "risks generating popular resentment, creating martyrs that motivate new recruits, and producing cycles of revenge."

Protecting and developing relationships with the population also allows counterinsurgents to derive "actionable" intelligence that is vital to efficiently targeting the rebellion. This requires that they live side by side with the people they are protecting, instead of hunkering down on outlying bases. Strategic success in the long term requires accepting more risk in the short term.

Such military action is only the first step. "While security is essential to setting the stage for overall progress," the manual states, "lasting victory comes from a vibrant economy, political participation, and restored hope." Here, it echoes the French counterinsurgency theorist David Galula's famous tenet that "military action is secondary to the political one, its primary purpose being to afford the political power enough freedom to work safely with the population." This means that the military must be prepared to support the efforts of U.S. civilian agencies, international organizations, nongovernmental organizations, and the host-nation government to rebuild critical infrastructure, provide essential services, promote economic development, and empower local and national political institutions. It also means, however, that when civilian entities are slow to arrive, lack sufficient resources, or are incapable of conducting these activities in dangerous environments, the military must be ready to pick up the slack. The military, in other words, is not only the primary protector of the population but also the nation builder of last resort.

Although the guidelines presented in the COIN FM are derived from research on dozens of twentieth-century counterinsurgency campaigns, it is difficult to know whether its template can work in all cases. Every insurgency has unique properties, and no counterinsurgency campaign has ever been conducted in exactly the way the manual describes. The purest example of the clear, hold, build model is the effective British effort during the Malayan Emergency (1948–60). The United States experimented with elements of this approach during the later stages of Vietnam, with some success, but too late to turn the tide. Still, overall, the COIN FM probably represents the single best distillation of current knowledge about irregular warfare.

GLOVES ON

The most powerful critique of the COIN FM's approach comes from the "coercion" school of thought on counterinsurgency, which sees legitimacy as an unattainable—and wholly unnecessary—goal. In the

1960s, the RAND analysts Nathan Leites and Charles Wolf argued that counterinsurgents should worry less about winning popular allegiance and more about raising the costs of supporting the insurgency. As Edward Luttwak put it in a recent essay, "The easy and reliable way of defeating all insurgencies everywhere" is to "out-terrorize the insurgents, so that fear of reprisals outweighs the desire to help the insurgents." In contrast to the COIN FM, the coercion school sees no need for conventional armies to remake themselves into kinder, gentler nation builders; instead, they can win by doing what they do best: employing overwhelming firepower to destroy the adversary and using armed coercion—including harsh collective punishment—to convince the population to shun the insurgents. "The teething-ring nonsense that insurgencies don't have military solutions defies history," the widely read military analyst Ralph Peters has written. "Historically, the common denominator of successful counterinsurgency operations is that only an uncompromising military approach works—not winning hearts and minds nor a negotiated compromise." Ultimately, the thinking goes, military sticks are much more important than civilian carrots.

This position is alive and well in the debate over Iraq. Hawkish commentators contend that the United States' problems in Iraq are the result of overly restrictive rules of engagement and a hesitancy to "take the gloves off." Some have even derided the COIN FM as "malpractice" for allegedly applying the lessons of Vietnam under the guise of learning from Iraq. In particular, they object to its application of political models of nationalist and ideological struggle to contemporary insurgencies that are, they contend, essentially religious. Bing West, assistant secretary of defense in the Reagan administration, argues, for example, that the approach endorsed by the COIN FM "does not apply to the root cause of the insurgency [in Iraq and elsewhere]—a radical religion whose adherents are not susceptible to having their hearts and minds won over."

The proponents of the coercion school generate extraordinary heat but little light. Certainly, there are historical cases in which coercion has proved brutally effective. During the nineteenth century, for example, the U.S. Army used collective punishment on a genocidal scale to destroy the Native American "insurgents," and the United States combined similar techniques with what we would now call "civic-action programs" to defeat the Filipino insurrection after the Spanish-American War. But as William Polk describes in his new book, *Violent Politics: A History of Insurgency, Terrorism, and Guerrilla War, From the American Revolution to Iraq*, coercion has more often than not been ineffective—or counterproductive. Even extraordinary levels of brutality have sometimes proved inadequate to crush determined insurgencies, as Polk's case study of the Nazi occupation of Yugoslavia during World War II powerfully demonstrates. In other instances, namely, those of the British in Kenya and the French in Algeria, massacres of guerrilla supporters, the widespread use of concentration camps, and the frequent torture and execution of prisoners produced the appearance of victory only to give way to strategic defeat as opposition to colonial occupation grew at home and abroad. And for those who believe that harsher measures are required in campaigns against religiously

driven fanatical insurgents, Polk notes that overwhelming and indiscriminate Soviet firepower in Afghanistan proved insufficient to defeat the Islamist rebels and instead generated global sympathy for their plight and attracted scores of foreign fighters to engage in jihad. Russian brutality in Chechnya and Serbian atrocities against Bosnian Muslims during the 1990s—two conflicts not covered by Polk's study—had similar effects.

The bare-knuckle approach seems singularly unsuited to twenty-first-century counterinsurgencies conducted by Western democracies. The immoral and illegal use of indiscriminate violence would require abandoning the very values Western militaries claim to protect, and it would be strategically disastrous. This is especially true of counterinsurgency campaigns, such as those in Iraq and Afghanistan, embedded within the so-called war on terror—a global clash of ideas in which "victory" hinges on the United States' discrediting the tactics used by violent extremists and in which 24-7 satellite media and the Internet allow insurgents and terrorists to exploit incidents of "collateral damage" to create widespread sympathy for their cause. In this context, the COIN FM strikes exactly the right balance. It admits that some religious zealots "are unlikely to be reconciled" and "will most likely have to be killed or captured" but directs commanders to determine how to "eliminate extremists without alienating the populace."

A RECIPE FOR FAILURE

When faced with a growing Sunni insurgency in Iraq, the immediate response of Pentagon officials and the U.S. military was denial. By the late summer and early fall of

2003, however, the reality signaled by daily attacks and a wave of massive bombings had finally sunk in. The military initially responded with a "search and destroy" approach to counterinsurgency, which fell uncomfortably, and dysfunctionally, between the extremes of hearts-and-minds and pure coercion. Lieutenant General Ricardo Sanchez, who led U.S. forces during the first year of the war, was both inept at and uninterested in counterinsurgency. Efforts to protect the Iraqi population were ad hoc, varied tremendously from unit to unit, and were underresourced; most units defined the requirements of counterinsurgency solely in terms of "the enemy" and deployed overwhelming conventional firepower to kill or capture a growing list of "former regime elements," "anti-Iraqi forces," "bad guys," and "terrorists." Although troops took steps to minimize the risks to Iraqi civilians, many innocent Iraqis were shot at U.S. checkpoints and alongside convoys; many others were caught in the crossfire during daily raids and major offensives in Fallujah, Najaf, Sadr City, and elsewhere. Detention centers swelled as thousands of military-aged men were arrested in indiscriminate sweeps of Sunni towns, and evidence of abusive interrogations—most notably at Abu Ghraib—surfaced with gruesome regularity.

Since insurgents almost immediately reinfiltrated areas left unprotected after U.S. raids and offensives, often murdering those Iraqis who had collaborated during these operations, U.S. efforts accomplished little in the way of security. At the same time, heavy-handed tactics were just harsh enough to trigger a cycle of revenge without being sufficient to rule through brute force alone. The early U.S. approach to counterinsurgency in Iraq was thus Goldilocks in reverse: not hot enough, not cold enough, just wrong.

As the self-defeating nature of U.S. operations became apparent, the mindset of the U.S. military began to change. Starting in 2004 and accelerating in 2005, training and education in counterinsurgency were revamped. In November 2005, the White House released its "National Strategy for Victory in Iraq," proclaiming clear, hold, build to be the road map for success, and soon the effort to rewrite U.S. counterinsurgency doctrine was in full swing. On the ground, U.S. forces had become much better at clearing insurgent strongholds without destroying them and alienating the inhabitants. And in a handful of instances—in Fallujah after the devastating November 2004 offensive, in Qaim and Tal Afar in late 2005, and in Ramadi in 2006—the entire clear, hold, build package was actually employed with positive results.

Yet despite these efforts, two countervailing factors stood in the way of effective counterinsurgency. First, beginning in 2004, there was an attempt to reduce the perception of occupation and enhance force protection by pulling U.S. troops out of smaller bases within Iraqi cities and consolidating them into larger forward operating bases in outlying areas. As a result, throughout 2005 and 2006, most U.S. forces remained hunkered down on large bases rather than nested within communities to provide local security. Second, because of insufficient troop levels, the "hold" portion was difficult to execute. Knowing that the administration was reluctant to send more troops and that pressure was building for withdrawal, General John Abizaid (the head of Central

Command) and General George Casey (who had replaced Sanchez in 2004 as the overall commander in Iraq) crafted a strategy to rapidly give Iraqi army and police units the responsibility of providing local security in areas cleared by U.S. forces. Unfortunately, a combination of inadequate capabilities and sectarian bias meant that Iraq's fledgling security forces were not up to the task. The resulting security vacuum, especially in Baghdad, accelerated the action-reaction spiral between Sunni insurgents and Shiite militias—tipping Iraq into an all-out sectarian war in the spring of 2006.

In January 2007, President George W. Bush reversed his long-standing aversion to sending additional troops to Iraq by announcing the "surge." Petraeus replaced Casey and set about using the 30,000 additional forces in Baghdad and surrounding areas to implement the strategy outlined in the field manual he had helped author. Soon U.S. units dispersed to smaller bases, where they were paired with Iraqi forces to provide security for the local populations.

If the U.S. military had gone into the Iraq war with this doctrine and enough troops, success might have been possible. Now it may simply be too little, too late. The current conflict landscape in Iraq has, in many respects, passed the COIN FM by. Coalition forces in Iraq are not only attempting to defeat a Sunni insurgency but also trying to police a fierce sectarian civil war, limit the spread of the intra-Shiite gangland violence in the south, prevent Kurdish separatist ambitions from creating an ethnic conflict in Kirkuk or prompting Turkish intervention, and contain the regional spillover from all these conflicts. Counterinsurgency is hard enough. Pile on these additional missions (which in many cases have contradictory requirements for success), stir in U.S. force levels that remain inadequate in most of the country, sprinkle on incapable and sectarian Iraqi security forces, and add a U.S. domestic political environment with zero support for a long-term commitment—and you have a recipe for likely failure.

EATING SOUP WITH A KNIFE

Whether or not the directives of the COIN FM succeed in Iraq, the general model it embraces probably represents the best of many bad approaches to counterinsurgency. But one should not confuse "best" with "easy." Even under ideal circumstances, the clear, hold, build paradigm is difficult to pull off. The oft-cited textbook case of the British counterinsurgency in Malaya in the 1950s in fact offers a cautionary lesson. The communist insurgents in Malaya were from a clearly distinguishable and unpopular ethnic Chinese minority and were fighting on a peninsula where it was relatively easy to isolate them. And it still took the British army a dozen years to win.

Future U.S. counterinsurgency campaigns are likely to occur in contexts where the COIN FM will be particularly difficult to implement. First, the evolving nature of insurgency within the broader "war on terror"—in which loose cellular networks of fighters operate transnationally and in dense urban environments, exploiting modern communications technologies and virtual domains to coordinate activities and magnify the symbolic effect of attacks—produces immense challenges for counterinsurgents, challenges the manual only scratches the surface of. Second, the most probable scenarios for large-scale U.S. interventions in the decades ahead are incursions into failed states or postconflict operations in the wake of forcible regime change. The military manpower requirements identified by the COIN FM (20 counterinsurgents per 1,000 civilians) may simply be too large in many of these cases. The humbling experiences of nation building during the 1990s and the postinvasion fiascos in Iraq and Afghanistan also suggest that the degree of civil-military, multinational, and cross-sectoral planning, preparation, and coordination needed to succeed in these environments outstrips the current capacity of the U.S. government. Given the modest increases in U.S. ground forces and the utter failure of the administration and Congress to give adequate resources to civilian agencies, the ability of the State Department, the U.S. Agency for International Development, and other civilian entities to contribute to counterinsurgency efforts will remain limited for the foreseeable future.

Furthermore, in many large-scale interventions, the U.S. military will be seen as a de facto or de jure occupying force, which poses extraordinary challenges for any counterinsurgency model rooted in promoting legitimacy. Polk contends that the common thread running through all insurgencies, "no matter how much they differ in form, duration, and intensity," is "opposition to foreigners." Although the cases from which Polk derives this conclusion are not fully representative, he provides ample proof that occupying armies—foreign bodies that trigger nationalist anti-bodies—find it excruciatingly difficult to use legitimacy to defeat local insurgents and then exit gracefully. In discussing the COIN FM, therefore, Polk concludes, "The single absolutely necessary ingredient in counterinsurgency is extremely unlikely ever to be available to foreigners." History should thus offer a warning to future U.S. administrations: framing an occupation as a "liberation" does not make it so, and counterinsurgency in this context will be very hard regardless of the doctrine employed.

Last but not least, even when the United States avoids large-scale intervention and instead supports the efforts of host-nation governments—as it did in Central America during the 1980s and continues to do in Colombia, the Horn of Africa, and the Philippines today—counterinsurgency still entails risks. A lower level of U.S. involvement typically implies less influence over the behavior of "partners," and so U.S. efforts may inadvertently empower governments that violate human rights and further alienate their people. Beyond compromising American values, such steps risk redirecting some of the insurgents' ire from the "near enemy" (their government) to the "far enemy" (the United States), a very dangerous scenario in a post-9/11 world.

U.S. leaders should therefore be wary of the potential moral hazard represented by the COIN FM: thinking they have figured out the journey, they may be tempted to go down the road more often. Given how difficult and costly counterinsurgency is, this would be a big mistake. But it would be an equally big mistake to embrace an "Iraq syndrome" that avoids preparing for counterinsurgency altogether, as the U.S. military did after Vietnam. As the COIN FM correctly observes, "The recent success of U.S. military forces in major combat operations undoubtedly will lead many future opponents to pursue asymmetric approaches." It is imperative for the United States to build the military and civilian capabilities necessary to conduct counterinsurgency effectively and morally—even as policymakers try not to do it too often.